Slavery Revisited

Blacks and the Southern Convict Lease System, 1865–1933

Slavery Revisited

Blacks and the Southern Convict Lease System, 1865–1933

Milfred C. Fierce

AFRICANA STUDIES RESEARCH CENTER
Brooklyn College, City University of New York

© 1994 by Milfred C. Fierce

Published by the Africana Studies Research Center, Brooklyn College, City University of New York

Printed in the United States of America

ISBN 0-964-32480-6

First edition

Cover design by Raymond P. Hooper

Editing and page design by Alice L. Tufel

Printed by Science Press

CONTENTS

PREFACE

More than anything else, this book is a study of African-American victimization under convict leasing in the United States South during the years 1865 to 1933.* It chronicles the brutal treatment of Black convicts in particular in the almost seven decades that spanned the life of legalized convict leasing.

Black victimization under convict leasing is a subject about which very little is known. It is treated to some extent in broader studies of leasing, sometimes in studies of the chain gangs, and in general analyses of convict and prison history and related issues. Many of them are duly noted in this examination. Even in those works, published material on the ruthless treatment and management of Black convicts under leasing is comparatively thin.

Some readers of this book will doubtless yearn for more information on one aspect or another of convict leasing, or more in-depth analysis of the economics or politics of leasing, or prison reform and history, or something else. These are matters with which I have no quarrel, and have thought about, and I too feel that all of that and more should be done on the subject, by someone else. I hope, further, that some enterprising graduate student or more advanced scholar will soon produce such work. The need clearly exists. If any individual or group of individuals is inspired to undertake such studies by something that appears in these pages, or does not appear, so much the better for the frontiers of our knowledge. My *raison d'etre*, as I saw it and defined it, was different.

---

*The terms "African-American" and "Black" are used interchangeably to identify people of discernible African descent.

The widespread and merciless mistreatment of leased Black convicts was, more than anything else, the element that characterized the convict lease system and made it infamous. That is the story I set out to tell. Some readers may feel that the brutality angle is overdone, excessive to the point of boredom. For this I make no apology. It is more pertinent to ask whether the contents of these pages are accurate. That question will be answered best by those who make the journey through the criminal justice process that brought Blacks into leasing, who witness their treatment, and who observe their exit from the system or their demise. This is not a book that will make readers feel good.

This project has been a "work in progress" for more than ten years, as most of my closest colleagues know. It is a situation in which many academics, artists, and others often find themselves—that is, working on several research or equivalent endeavors simultaneously, on and off, rarely devoting full attention to any single venture. Time passes and, before you know it, ten years have gone by. Sometimes, as many of us know, these "works in progress" never get finished. I am pleased that this is not the case with my convict lease book (although it may turn out to be with one or two others). Along the way, I became deeply involved in learning about a brand new subject, attempting to better understand South and Southern Africa and U.S. foreign policy there. As part of that experience, I participated in exercises that resulted in several seminal publications in the field. The first, a book entitled *South Africa: Time Running Out* (University of California Press, 1981), by the Study Commission on U.S. Policy Toward Southern Africa—for which I served as research director—was produced with funding from the Rockefeller Foundation. In addition, the Ford Foundation supported the publication of the follow-up "South Africa Update Series," for which I served as consulting editor. This series, which comprised five books on South and Southern Africa by multiple authors, was published jointly by the Ford Foundation and the Foreign Policy Association between 1989 and 1992. I also published a few essays of my own on South Africa and U.S. interest and foreign policy in that country.

There were also two terms (six years) as a department chairman concurrent with continuing research on my convict lease manuscript and other matters as time permitted, which was seldom. In 1991 I wrote a short report on the condition of Africana Studies overseas, entitled *Africana Studies Outside the United States: Africa, the Caribbean and Brazil*, which was later slightly revised and published by the Africana Studies and Research Center at Cornell University. The data for that report were collected during visits to universities in the relevant areas in 1989 and 1990, which was a sabbatical year when I might have worked on the convict lease project. Then, in 1993, I published *The Pan-African Idea in the United States, 1900–1919: African-American Interest in Africa and Interaction with West Africa* (New York: Garland Publishing Company). In between there were other essays on subjects of great interest to me and important in my teaching, the most significant of which was "Abraham Lincoln and Blacks: Some Notes on a Continuing Controversy," *Western Journal of Black Studies* (1988).

So it has been a long haul with this book. Perhaps halfway through the research, including visits to half of the state archives in former Confederate states, some of my colleagues began to suggest that I might confine myself to one or maybe two states, and do a more extensive comparative study later, or leave that to someone else. I, too, had some misgivings about describing leasing in twelve states as a first effort. But I had already visited half of the archives. After much reflection, I decided to continue with the broader study. Nevertheless, that question is moot now. The story I most wanted to tell was what was happening to Black convicts under leasing in *all* of the southern states. Anything less would have made it too easy for critics to dismiss the examples I've given as exceptions or special cases.

The book's focus is on felony convicts under state control. However, leasing permeated state administration and management as well as county and local penal control of misdemeanor and lesser convictions for the incarcerated. Here, too, a more rigorous investigation of this important subject awaits the energy of a new researcher.

A persistent underlying theme is the comparison with slavery, with which convict leasing shares important, if imperfect, likenesses. In several instances the reference to slavery is explicit. That is so because the evidence of convict treatment under leasing as presented here—that is, length and conditions of the work regimen, medical and health care, diet, clothing, worker-supervisor relationships, general labor exploitation, and perhaps, most of all, punishment—conjure up an image that is a vivid reminder of slavery. In the final analysis readers must decide whether or not the treatment that Black convicts faced in the system of southern convict leasing is mindful of their definition of slavery.

Much attention is devoted to race relations between Blacks and Whites in the latter years of the nineteenth century and early years of the twentieth. Those were perhaps the worst years in race relations, manifested by increased violence and race riots, disenfranchisement, Jim Crow, forced segregation and isolation, and the failure of the United States government and local law enforcement (the latter too often a co-conspirator in the racial injustice that pervaded these decades) to protect the legal and other rights of its citizens who were Black. The sociopolitical climate of the era is indispensable for understanding the emergence, the character, and the decline of convict leasing. It is the belief of this writer that without some knowledge of the race context during which leasing flourished, it will be impossible to comprehend the reasons why the system lasted as long as it did and, more important, why Blacks were its primary victims.

ACKNOWLEDGMENTS

Those who supported the research for the publication of this book have included the Professional Staff Congress of the City University of New York Research Fund, the National Endowment for the Humanities, and the Ford Foundation. The most important colleagues who read the manuscript in its early stages, turning me in new directions and helping me to reduce my errors, were Robert L. Harris, Jr., of Cornell University, Patricia Kaurouma of Yale University, Charles Hamilton of Columbia University, and Ruth S. Hamilton of Michigan State University.

I've had very good fortune during visits to state archives, manuscript collections, and university libraries throughout the South, where most of the research for this book was done. There was not a single occasion in which the library staffs in all of these locations were anything but helpful and encouraging.

Persistence was the central ingredient in the completion of this project. It survived personal setbacks, new professional priorities, periodic burn-out, and other delays—seemingly subtle and intangible things. Long periods away from the subject required extra energy to relearn much that was forgotten following one hiatus or another. To all those family members, friends, and colleagues who pushed or pulled me over frequent hurdles, who aided me in getting past what appeared to be impassable barriers, who admonished me to keep my eyes on this prize, I express a collective and heartfelt "thank you." My gratitude is eternal.

Most of my instincts make it easy for me to share whatever strengths this book has with helpful colleagues. Another instinct suggests to me that any particularly egregious errors or omissions should have been spotted with my colleagues' help before publication; however, I accept, without qualification, the blame for all glitches.

It may be trite to say, but it is nevertheless true, that this book was a labor of love. I am delighted that the work is over and that I can now move on to a new romance.

MILFRED C. FIERCE
Bushkill, Pa.

Introduction

THE NOXIOUS CHARACTERISTICS OF the era from 1877 to 1920, which Rayford Logan, the former Howard University historian, dubbed the "nadir" in Black life and history, are well known. We know, for example, a good deal about peonage, Jim Crow, disenfranchisement, race theories, lynching, and violence as they affected southern Blacks, from the works of such scholars as Peter Daniel, C. Vann Woodward, Vernon Lane Wharton, I. A. Newby, George Tindall, George Frederickson, and others. However, one reality of this period about which much less is known, and which affected large numbers of Blacks, is the southern convict lease system.

The lease system, which was instituted in the South soon after the Civil War ended, permitted the leasing of convicts to private parties in exchange for payments made to the state for their labor. Renting prisoners to outsiders who had sole responsibility for regulating their hours, determining their working conditions, and maintaining their health quickly became a vicious, self-serving, and corrupt business. Abuses were rampant in the treatment of inmates and in setting quotas and other requirements for their work day. Prison authorities colluded with lessees (who were sometimes the same people), to the detriment of those incarcerated. Individuals were given lengthy sentences on trumped-up charges and for petty crimes to ensure a regular supply of labor. Releases from prison were delayed or canceled arbitrarily in order to retain prisoners as laborers.

The southern convict lease system became one in which Black convicts, primarily, were victimized by unscrupulous lessees, prison officials, and sometimes by politicians, almost all of whom were White and relatively indifferent to the difficult plight of a prison population that was mainly Black. In their view, Blacks were inferior, habitual criminals, and not deserving of much better treatment than they were receiving in mines, on plantations, and in other businesses operated by lessees. In essence, cheap Black convict lease labor was at the disposal of southern White capitalists and planters in a system that, perhaps more than any other aspect of postbellum southern life, was a return to slavery.

ℒ

A discussion of the convict lease system in the U.S. South cannot be separated from the general context in which it flourished. And because the primary victims of the lease system were Black, the primacy of race cannot be overlooked in an attempt to understand the emergence, maintenance, and decline of leasing. Moreover, an understanding of the plight of Black convicts during the years of convict leasing is crucial to comprehending the social, economic, and political climate that encouraged such an arrangement and enabled it to thrive.

For many African-Americans living in the United States between the end of the Civil War and the outbreak of World War II, especially those in the South, the transition from bondage to freedom was more imagined than real. Life was punctuated with reminders that "freedom" was essentially a change in form rather than in substance. Although the Radical Republican interlude (1867–77) during Reconstruction in the former Confederate states provided an opportunity for a few Blacks to gain influence in local political and civic affairs in some places, for most Blacks emancipation brought with it new difficulties, new oppression and exploitation, and little relief from the vagaries of being Black in the South. Throughout the antebellum era, southern society was preoccupied with the issue of race prejudice and the claim of Black inferiority. Of the four million or so slaves freed by the passage of the Thirteenth Amendment in 1865, the overwhelming majority became sharecroppers, tenant farmers, or victims of the crop lien system pervasive in the South after the Civil War. This circumstance inaugurated a post-emancipation cycle of Black dependency. Therefore, the economic exploitation that Blacks suffered as slaves was merely modernized to accommodate the era of the New South.

As slaves, of course, Blacks were often brutalized by the slavemaster and members of his family, by local authorities, and by southern Whites in general. During the postbellum period, Blacks were often intimidated, threatened, beaten, and murdered by self-styled vigilante groups such as the Ku Klux Klan, Knights of the White Camelia, The 76 Association, and others who had their special vision of the appropriate place for Blacks in the South during the Gilded Age and beyond.

In bondage, rural slaves operated in relative isolation from Whites. Those who worked on plantations and farms lived in separate quarters that were visited by Whites only from time to time. Urban slaves might have lived with their owners or on their own. A handful of urban Blacks, slave and free, lived in what might be considered desegregated neighborhoods by twentieth century standards. Even so, it was rare for Blacks and Whites to meet one another in public accommodations, and even rarer in social settings. There was little interaction, therefore, in housing, or in education and employment. Housing patterns were generally set along class and caste lines. Free Blacks and slaves who lived apart from Whites and their owners ordinarily inhabited areas reserved for members of their color caste. Few free Blacks and almost no slaves were formally educated in the pre–Civil War South. There was no system of free public education. Many Blacks who received more than a rudimentary education did so outside the South, and in some instances outside the United States. Employment opportunities were determined and restricted for most Blacks by their status as slaves. That is, as slaves Blacks were rarely without jobs. They were confined, however, to jobs for slaves. Those Blacks who were not slaves in the antebellum South were severely restricted in their vocational, professional, and career choices.

THE SEGREGATION ERA

The Jim Crow system, prevalent throughout the so-called Segregation Era (1890–1920), brought new problems for southern Blacks one generation beyond emancipation. Although racial segregation did not originate in the South, it was carried to its greatest extreme there. By the close of the nineteenth century almost every institution in the United States, in both the North and the South, was strictly segregated or nearly so. This segregation included schools, residential communities, places of employment and labor unions, churches, politics and government service, movies, beaches, and restaurants. This development was significantly influenced, if not inspired, by the infamous Plessy decision (1896) of the United States Supreme Court, which affirmed the doctrine of "separate but equal."

Also during this time, pseudoscientific race theorists asserting the innate inferiority of Blacks, emboldened by a misapplication of social Darwinism, enjoyed a resurgence and gained a measure of respectability in intellectual circles. Blacks, so the theories went, were hereditarily, biologically inferior to Whites. Such schools of thought alleged that Africans and their descendants were so far behind other racial groups, especially Whites, that it would take them centuries to catch up, if they ever could, which remained doubtful to some.

Perhaps more fundamental to the African-American experience during this period, however, was the right to vote. Black disenfranchisement was not a concern in the South prior to 1865 because Blacks could not vote. Disenfranchisement took center stage with the passage and ratification of the Fifteenth Amendment to the Constitution (February 27, 1869 and March 30, 1870, respectively), declaring the "right of the citizen . . . to vote shall not be denied or abridged . . . on account of race, color or previous condition of servitude."

The systematic elimination of Black voters in southern towns, cities, and states, at first achieved informally, reached its zenith between 1890 and World War I, as states in the South legalized a variety of disenfranchisement devices. The methods employed varied from state to state, and sometimes from county to county within the state, but always had the same objective: to remove Blacks, by any means necessary, as voters and officeholders. When literacy tests and poll taxes did not achieve the desired end, polling places were relocated and multiple ballot boxes—that is, some for Blacks (in which votes were not counted) and some for Whites—were used. These artifices sometimes gave way to grandfather clauses, gerrymandering, and White primaries. When all else failed, intimidation and violence were used by extreme bigots to deter Blacks from voting. By the second decade of the twentieth century, Blacks held no meaningful elective office in the South and only a handful were the beneficiaries of the lowest level of political patronage.

Of all the hardships southern Blacks endured in the late nineteenth and early twentieth centuries, probably the most frightening and the most unnerving was lynching. Lynchings were often carried out in public, with widespread shows of White approval. Blacks who resided near the scene of a lynching lived in perpetual fear that the knock would come next at their own door, or the door of an immediate family member, or that a friend would be discovered "missing." Blacks often struck back in self-defense, but more often than not they were no match for Whites with superior arms and organization. A federal government that by the end of the 1870s had accepted the return of "White supremacy" in southern affairs provided little help.

Compounding the plight of former slaves during the decades following emancipation was economic destitution for many of them. Most were propertyless at a time when land ownership was increasingly becoming a prerequisite for advancement, and sometimes for survival. Few southern Blacks owned animals or tools or other elements to help position them for a degree of economic independence. Those with skills were being excluded from many trades as the years passed, and formal education was an acquisition they hoped their children or their children's children would realize. At the same time, their major competition for jobs and space in the New South—poor Whites—were themselves losing their economic moorings and becoming share-croppers and tenants. It is not surprising that the most impoverished individuals became victims of the South's expanding appetite for more convicts, fueled by the convict lease system.

Emancipation led to a redefinition of crime in the South as the petty pilferage that was tolerated by slave owners became a criminal offense. Emancipation also brought an increase in the number of Black convicts who quickly outnumbered White ones. Before 1865, even free Blacks were not commonly incarcerated. Their numbers were always small, and as was the case with slaves, actions or behavior judged in violation of existing law resulted most often in a whipping on the bare back by the local sheriff or his designee. The number of additional Black prisoners combined with the growth in the number of White convicts accounts for an unprecedented demand for prison facilities, which strained the meager resources of most southern states.

Former slaves came to freedom with bittersweet prospects for the future; they were exuberant about the burden of bondage being lifted, but distressed about being propertyless and dependent on former masters for their livelihood. They were easy prey for the contrivances of landowners bent on depriving them of their entitled wages. Sometimes they were underpaid or, worse, simply not paid. Often facing starvation and usually illiterate, Blacks frequently found themselves at odds with prevailing laws or the agents and enforcers of law. They also became the objects of vengeance on the part of former Confederates who, upset at having lost their human "property," misrepresented the truth.

For example, a dishonest landowner might report that a Black fieldhand ran off without fulfilling his contract, which was a crime. However, the truth may have been that the landowner had attempted to cheat the fieldhand out of his earnings. In accepting the word of the employer, the local judge or sheriff would impose a fine that the fieldhand could not pay. The fine might be paid by a prospective lessee to whom the laborer was now beholden. The debt would be repaid through the mechanism of the lease system. In retrospect, given the *zeitgeist* of the times, it appears that the social and economic status of Blacks—as what C. Vann Woodward referred to as the "mudsills and bottom rails" of the New South—was inevitable. Therefore, under these circumstances Blacks were certain to be the primary source of supply for the burgeoning convict lease system.

BEGINNINGS

The earliest record of convict leasing in the South comes from Kentucky, a state that was not part of the Old Confederacy. In 1825, Joel Scott was appointed by the legislature as Keeper and Agent of the penitentiary and assumed management of eighty-four prisoners, who were living in unsanitary conditions, were suffering from various diseases, and were practically bare of clothing.[1] The first lessees were three individuals "who . . . in addition to what they could make from the labor of the convicts, were to receive a bonus from the state . . . of $300. . . ."[2] Between 1825 and 1865 most other southern states experimented with one form of leasing or another, ranging from the letting of the entire penitentiary to a single entity, to the leasing of selected convicts to a variety of lessees. The state usually received some fixed, agreed-upon remuneration for the labor of inmates.

There were also instances in which the state paid the lessee to take control of and manage the entire prison population.

Even though examples of convict leasing can be found prior to the Civil War, it was right after the war that the system began to blossom and prosper. Barren treasuries, disorganized state governments, the physical destruction of prisons in many southern states during the war, and the chaos of early Reconstruction prompted southern officials to begin to search for ways to defray expenses connected with running an expanding prison system. The drive for revenue and profits was the irreducible motive for the intensification of convict leasing in the post–Civil War South. States, especially, were hell-bent on relieving their meager treasuries of the financial responsibility for maintaining a new network of penitentiaries and prisons and their growing bureaucracies, and paying for the cost of food, clothing, shelter, medical care, and more, for convicts.[3]

The large-scale leasing of prisoners was a departure from earlier practices in American penal history and at variance with the reform movement that began decades earlier, and the otherwise progressive climate of the late nineteenth and early twentieth centuries. By the mid-1870s almost every former Confederate state was experimenting with some form of convict leasing. It is not surprising, however, that once leasing began, most southern states—under pressure from the escalating cost of maintaining a prison system and encouraged by business interests—rushed to adopt an accommodation that appeared both expedient and profitable.

Georgia, in particular, earned a reputation as possibly the most notorious of the convict leasing states. At the same time, Georgia had no monopoly on all of the corrupt and inhumane practices that characterized convict leasing. In the state of Georgia, convicts were engaged essentially, but not exclusively, in railroad construction, road building, plantation labor, and coal mining. Other states were sometimes more specialized: in Tennessee, convict leasing was concentrated in coal mines, and in Florida, in turpentine camps. Most states simultaneously leased convicts out to large and small farmers.

The state legislature in Georgia first authorized leasing in 1866. It was outlawed in 1908. During this forty-two-year period, much of what characterized convict leasing in other southern states was found in Georgia. Throughout the decades of leasing, approximately 90 percent of the state's convicts were Black males. Black females represented an unknown percentage of the total, but possibly fluctuated between 1 and 5 percent. White males and the few White females, Native Americans, and Asians who were imprisoned made up the balance. (See chapter 4 for the racial composition of the Georgia Penitentiary for selected years, particularly Table 4.1, pages 148–49.)

Georgia used both short-term (one- to five-year) and long-term (ten- to twenty-year) leases. Subleasing was popular, and often convicts were held beyond the expiration of their prison sentences. Prison officials were regularly called on to explain mysterious "suicides" and deaths, calling forth the denials and apologies found regularly in the periodic reports of wardens, principal keepers of the penitentiary, prison commissions, and other supervisors of the state's prisons. Legislative investigations and newspaper exposés revealed that convicts were poorly fed, clothed, and housed; that medical care was neglected; and that punishment was often savage. The suggestion is frequently made that an important part of the explanation for why state officials winked at such abuses or looked the other way in the face of them, and why lessees were so indifferent to treatment and conditions, was because most of the convicts were Black. "Negroes were regarded as unworthy of humane treatment," writes Mark Carleton in a study of the Louisiana prison system.[4] They were also equated with criminals, who were considered undeserving of decent treatment, thereby rendering the predicament of Black criminals one of double jeopardy. The feeling that Blacks and criminals were synonymous in Louisiana and other states made abuses tolerable and perpetuated convict leasing.

Brutal enough when operated honestly, the lease system invited corruption, fraud, and impropriety. Local law enforcement agents—sheriffs, for example—often overcharged the state for the transportation of convicts. Companies bidding for leases bribed public officials, and payments due the state under terms of the lease were late, low, and sometimes not made at all. As a result, lessees often made handsome profits in leasing convicts.

A state usually had its share of individuals and companies that "got rich quick" off the lease system. At one point, the entire prison population in Georgia was leased to a single company. At other times, convicts were parceled out to different lessees who might send them on to second, even third parties for a fee. Attempting to keep accurate records of convicts, their comings and goings, diet, escapes, punishment, and work day often became an exercise in futility. There are examples of prisoners being sent directly from conviction to lessee, bypassing altogether the prison bureaucracy—when and where it existed.[5]

DECLINE

Convict leasing—and, more broadly, prison reform—became a political football in several states because some legislators saw it as an opportunity to advance their political ambitions. Hence, legislative investigations took place, frequently with great fanfare and publicity. Governor Hoke Smith of Georgia, for example, at the turn of the twentieth century, as well as some of his predecessors and successors, campaigned on a platform to end the lease system. The governor claimed to be repulsed by the system's corruption and immorality. The leadership role of such politicians in ultimately removing convict leasing, however, was minimal.

When the decline and abolition of convict leasing came in the South it was most often the result of a combination of ongoing opposition from the labor movement, falling profits, public criticism, and general condemnation of the system. State legislation usually required the termination of convict leasing at the expiration of all existing leases. In Georgia, this occurred in 1908. In Arkansas, leasing was outlawed in 1893 but the legislation was not enforced; therefore, it was banned a second and final time in 1913. Leasing the penitentiary was banned in Texas in 1883, and convict contract labor was outlawed in 1914. Tennessee effectively ended leasing in 1896, and Florida did so in 1919. In 1890 Mississippi adopted a constitutional amendment that became effective at the end of 1894. South Carolina and Louisiana acted through legislative abolition in 1901. Leasing fell in Alabama in 1928. North Carolina was the last southern state to outlaw the leasing of convicts, in 1933, sixteen years after its first attempt failed in 1917. In Virginia it appears that convicts remained under the supervision of state officials; therefore, technically, the state never adopted a lease system comparable with all other ex-slave southern states.

But convict leasing did not necessarily end when it became illegal. In some cases the legislation was not enforced; in others, lessees were driven "underground." Most often, however, leasing was "modernized"—that is, it became more subtle, more sophisticated, and more difficult to detect and prove. It was frequently replaced by some variation of the "contract" system, under which convicts remained under the control of the state but labored for private companies with which contracts had been negotiated. Despite the fact that most twentieth century legislation required that convicts be confined to labor on "public works," outsiders continued to lease convicts for years after it became illegal. Leasing was eventually replaced by the well-known chain gangs of the South. It will never be accurately known when the practice of convict leasing finally stopped as opposed to being outlawed. It is highly unlikely that any type of convict leasing of the kind described in these pages is still in existence in the southern states, or anywhere else in the United States.

NOTES

1. William C. Sneed, *A Report on the History and Mode of Management of the Kentucky Penitentiary* (Frankfort, Ky., 1860), 164.

2. Lucien V. Rule, *The City of Dead Souls* (Louisville, Ky., 1920), 45.

3. The most important discussion emphasizing economics in connection with convict leasing, and one that appears to have limited regard for analyses that do not highlight economics, is Mathew Mancini, "Race, Economics, and the Abandonment of Convict Leasing," *Journal of Negro History* (Fall 1978), 339–52.

4. Mark T. Carleton, *Politics and Punishment: The History of the Louisiana State Penal System* (Baton Rouge: Louisiana State University Press, 1971), 46.

5. A. Elizabeth Taylor, "The Convict Lease System in Georgia, 1866–1908," Master's thesis (University of North Carolina, Chapel Hill, 1940), 10–11.

CHAPTER ONE

CONTEXT: BLACK–WHITE RELATIONS IN THE SOUTHERN UNITED STATES, 1865–1933

WHEN THE CIVIL WAR ENDED in the early spring of 1865, General Lee's surrender on behalf of the Confederate states served notice that an end to chattel slavery was imminent. It set the stage for the release of some four million Black slaves from a form of physical bondage and psychic duress that is perhaps without parallel in modern history. Southern slavery, especially, thoroughly stifled the ambitions of many Blacks for decades after 1865 and consigned them to a future as America's foremost underclass.

14

The legacy of slavery continued to haunt the African-American population right through the twentieth century. After three hundred years of enforced labor, this group of Americans of African descent came to legal freedom largely illiterate, unskilled, landless, and generally ill-equipped and unprepared to cope with the complex economic, social, and political life of an evolving United States in general and a New South in particular. To compound their predicament, Blacks found themselves in the midst of a White population that was angry over losing their war, their slaves, and their privilege. Many Whites believed in the innate inferiority of Blacks. Arguments supporting such beliefs had been promulgated by apologists for slavery generations earlier. The doctrine of Black inferiority had insidiously been perpetuated and reinforced for so long that, by the mid-nineteenth century, it was the all-pervasive ideological benchmark for Black proscription, and would remain so for one hundred years to come.

The main currents in southern race relations from the end of the Civil War to the outbreak of World War II provide the backdrop for the years that also spanned the career and ubiquity of the southern convict lease system. This system operated on and off in former Confederate states for some seventy years after the end of the Civil War. It was one in which state and county officials leased convicts to private parties, who assumed total control over the convicts' labor and lives. Payments were made to states and counties for convict labor, but they were also made to individual state officers, who frequently kept the money. The race-relations climate in the South that aided the durability of convict leasing was an important part of leasing's existence, with Black victimization as its centerpiece.

THE EMERGENCE OF CONVICT LEASING

The postbellum period during which the convict lease system was developed and refined was an era initially pregnant with great expectations, which quickly turned to uncertainty and despair among Blacks. Race relations during the years of Confederate Reconstruction (1865–67) were characterized by a generous amnesty program for the former rebels, by pernicious southern White hostility toward the Freedmen's Bureau, by the establishment of Black Codes, by peripatetic violence against Blacks, and by a rapid return to the domination of southern affairs by forces that had fought against the Union and lost, "pursuing most of their prewar policies as though there had never been a war."[1] Furthermore, the South had an ally in Lincoln's successor, Andrew Johnson—an apostate Tennessee Democrat and converted southern sympathizer.

There was cause for optimism, however, when Congress, led by a small but effective band of "radicals," emerged victorious in the power struggle with Johnson over the management of Reconstruction. Representative Thaddeus Stevens (Pennsylvania Republican) and Senator Charles Sumner (Massachusetts Republican) were the principal architects of Radical or Congressional Reconstruction, as it was called, engineering the passage of the Congressional Reconstruction Acts—establishing martial law and Republican hegemony in the former Confederate states. The Radicals also secured the passage of the Fourteenth and Fifteenth Amendments, which granted citizenship to Blacks and provided that persons (men) should not be denied the right to vote on account of race, color, or previous condition, respectively. In addition, they successfully led the fight that extended the life of the Freedmen's Bureau, overriding the veto of Andrew Johnson.

At the same time, a signal failure of Radical Reconstruction was its inability to obtain land for ex-slaves, thereby relegating them to peonage status as sharecroppers, tenant farmers, crop lieners, and agricultural day laborers.

Farm Workers

Simply defined, peonage is debt slavery, which imposes restrictions on freedom and movement from place to place based on debt to an employer. The perceptible differences among sharecropping, the lien system, tenant farming, and day laboring were insignificant; now and then the lines separating them were blurred. Under the first arrangement—sharecropping—the Black farmer might work the land with the owner or under the owner's instruction or direction. When the crop was harvested, and sold, the sharecropper would receive a previously agreed-upon share of the profits from the sale. Alternatively, sharecroppers could work a designated share of the land, market the harvest on their own, and then pay off the landlord. A crop liener might obtain everything or much of what was needed for crop cultivation from an outside source, from the landowner, or otherwise. A lien would be attached to the sale of any crops when outstanding debts were to be satisfied. Similarly, tenant farmers would rent what was needed to grow their crops—for example, land, tools, animals, house, food, clothing, seed, supplies, and other materials. Debts would be paid at the end of the season. Cash was rarely available to pay rent and other costs in advance. Money, when it was available, might be advanced by a bank or landowner. It was not uncommon for landlords to have a plantation full of tenants, lieners, and/or sharecroppers. In addition, depending on need, season, and other factors, the landlord would hire laborers and pay them in cash or kind by the day, week, or month. All these situations were susceptible to every kind of fraud and corruption and a host of other illegalities.[2] They were steeped in controversy and disputes between landowner and farmer. Compounding the predicament for small farmers was their illiteracy. Where peonage existed, grew, and spread, the explanation was found in the lien system, cropping, or tenant farming.[3] Stated another way, "the seeds of peonage grew well in the social and economic soil so fecund with oppression."[4]

Thus, despite the Radicals' success with the "radical" measures already mentioned, Congress was unable or unwilling (or both) to enact a meaningful land reform and redistribution program in the South. Consequently, according to one Reconstruction scholar, this failure to establish an economic foundation for freedmen not only handicapped the entire Radical program but also meant that "the Negroes' civil and political rights would be in a precarious state for many years to come."[5] When Rutherford B. Hayes became president in the controversial election of 1876, he agreed to withdraw Federal troops from the three southern states in which they remained. This event, which was of greater symbolic significance than real importance, sent a clear message to Blacks that Federal protection for their political and legal rights would be honored more in the breach than the observance.[6]

THE REDEEMER INTERLUDE AND BEYOND

The years that followed the overthrow of the so-called carpetbagger regimes and lasted less than a decade after 1877, known as the Redeemer Interlude, have been described as a period of

relative stability in southern history. Race relations were purportedly "fluid" and devoid of the explicit and pronounced
tensions of the immediate post–Civil War era and the twenty-five
years from 1890 to the outbreak of World War I.[7] The Redeemers—conservative middle- and upper-class White Democrats who
did not feel as threatened by Blacks as did other Whites—were
for the most part representatives of the southern business class
and were primarily interested in developing industry, transportation, and commerce in the region. Led by Wade Hampton of
South Carolina, Lucius Lamar of Mississippi, and Alexander
Stephens of Georgia, these conservative Democrats appealed to
Black voters and promised protection for their recently acquired
civil and political rights. They did not believe in social equality
but did, according to their principal spokesperson, Wade
Hampton, "want to conserve the Negro."[8] The Redeemer philosophy of paternalism and *noblesse oblige* was presented by
Senator and later Governor Hampton as a belief that "every
properly regulated society had superiors and subordinates. . . .
The conservatives acknowledged that the Negroes belonged in a
subordinate role, but denied that subordinates had to be ostra-
cized; they believed that the Negro was inferior, but denied that
it followed that inferiors must be segregated or publicly humiliat-
ed."[9] Eventually the Redeemers succumbed to racist fears and
accepted the philosophy of White supremacy. Within a decade
they abandoned their commitment to preserve the legal and
political rights of Blacks; embraced the idea of segregation, Jim
Crow, and Black proscription; and closed ranks with the race
extremists and demagogues of the 1890s.

It is not possible to pinpoint precisely when things began to
go from bad to worse for southern Blacks during the era historians have labeled Redemption. In 1881, Tennessee enacted the

post–Civil War South's first statewide Jim Crow law, segregating railroad coaches. During this transition period, too—from the collapse of Radical Reconstruction in the late 1870s to the emergence of White supremacy ten years later—self-styled vigilantes such as the Knights of the White Camelia, the White Brotherhood, the Pale Faces, the Ku Klux Klan, and others resurrected their orgy of terror and violence against Blacks. And when, in 1883, the United States Supreme Court declared the Civil Rights Act of 1875 unconstitutional, southern Whites gained the legal ammunition they needed to upset the "racial tranquillity" that is supposed to have characterized the period.

Whatever event or events worsened the plight of Blacks in the South, it is clear that by the last decade of the nineteenth century their situation was as desperate as any ten-year period in American history. Even the Populist revolt, which began as a coalition of Black and poor White farmers, was unable to resist racist proclivities, and its failure illustrates, in part, how the 1890s exemplified Black political impotence.

The southern wing of the Populist party was formed at the beginning of the 1890s primarily to represent the interests of poor farmers, Black and White alike. The rise of southern populism triggered the elevation of poor Whites in the South as a potential political force after 1890. It seemed natural and inevitable that, since populism was inspired largely by class interests, Black farmers would be drawn into the net of this radical movement. The chance for poor farmers, both Black and White, to improve their lot by joining forces against a common adversary (the wealthy and powerful landlords), under the banner of populism, seemed appealing and was initially effective. One White Texas Populist expressed his sentiment about Blacks this way: "They are in the ditch just like we are."[10]

Thus, in several states, cooperation took place between Black and White Populists because of the common economic, social, and political problems they faced. Southern Populists in Georgia, for example, repudiated the lynch law. Other Populist party platforms denounced the convict lease system and advocated protection for Black civil and political rights. Populists ran Black and White candidates for local political office, and both races were represented on campaign committees and also served as delegates to the national conventions. The Populist party began to capture the Black and White vote and wield some political influence. Populist officials sought Blacks for jury service and they organized interracial picnics and barbecues. And the achievements of Blacks were prominently displayed by Populist newspaper editors in their columns.

There were, of course, exceptions to all of this, and a plentiful supply of anti-Black sentiment existed among Populists, as elsewhere in the South. Decades of racial prejudice and discrimination against Blacks as slaves and as free persons proved to be a formidable, even insurmountable obstacle to equal treatment within the Populist movement. It was, moreover, the poor White class that felt most threatened by Blacks, leaving them susceptible to the claims of Black domination hysterically asserted by race demagogues. Poor Whites also manifested the strongest phobias about and race prejudices against Blacks because they were in direct competition with them for employment, housing, and community services. Ultimately, race interests triumphed over class interests, and race bigotry appeared to expand in direct proportion to the increase in political democracy among White yeoman farmers.[11] In the end, White farmers capitulated to racist dogma under the slogan "White Solidarity Again" and broke ranks with Blacks, suggesting the strength of race interests versus class. In the metamorphosized view of Georgia's Tom Watson, Populist candidate for president in 1904, "white men would have to unite [against Blacks] before they could divide."[12] Ironically, one result of the failure of populism was that poor Whites went on being exploited almost as much as Blacks.

In retrospect, it appears that racism even among Populists may have been unavoidable, and that the days of this Populist "honeymoon" were numbered from the start. So it was that a potentially significant third-party movement unraveled in the South. Despite its collapse, however, this brief period of coalition between Black and White farmers, under the banner of populism, represented one of the best examples in U.S. history of the potential for class concerns to successfully supersede and transcend racism. That the noble experiment collapsed could suggest that race, fear, prejudice, and ignorance are stronger forces in keeping people apart than are economic and class interests in bringing them together for a common cause.

1890–1930

After White supremacists observed the early successes of populism, they played their trump card and courted the White farmers' insecurities with the claim of "Black domination" and "Black rule." As was the case with Reconstruction, Blacks became the scapegoats for the failure of southern populism, giving many southern Whites yet another justification to exorcise them from almost every aspect of southern life in the years that followed.

It is hazardous at best to propose that any single event could have been responsible for intensifying the general hardships already endured by southern Blacks during the decades that straddled the nineteenth and twentieth centuries. Nonetheless, when the United States Supreme Court upheld a series of Louisiana and lower court decisions, finding against Homer Plessy and in favor of racial distinctions in railroad cars, it represented more than the symbolic "Trojan horse" of southern segregation. With this infamous *Plessy vs. Ferguson* decision in 1896 came the entrenchment of the doctrine of "separate but equal," which was not struck down until fifty-eight years later. So devastating and influential was the case and doctrine that in the decades that followed almost every institution in American society—schools, churches, residential communities, politics, business, labor unions, media, athletics, entertainment, beaches, hospitals, restaurants, even cemeteries—became completely segregated, but rarely equal.

To be sure, in many cities, towns, and other localities, the strict separation of Blacks from Whites began before the Plessy decision. But others, perhaps the majority, were inspired, even provoked, to act by the Supreme Court's affirmation of the legality, the acceptability, of racial segregation. If "Jim Crow" was not an ubiquitous practice in the South by 1896, it quickly became so with an assist from the highest court in the land. By the time W. E. B. DuBois proclaimed in 1903, "The problem of the twentieth century is the problem of the color line," very few southern localities remained that had not proposed or adopted a segregation ordinance. The "separate but equal" doctrine helped cultivate a mind-set that made the idea and practices of the already established convict leasing system tolerable. It could also have been indirectly responsible for an increase in the Black prison population. To the extent that the Plessy case further removed the possibility of Blacks serving on southern juries, thereby reducing the probability that an innocent Black person accused of committing a crime would be acquitted, and increasing the chances of subsequent imprisonment, the Court was a friend of leasing. Moreover, because the Plessy decision reinforced the presumption of guilt over innocence where Blacks were concerned, the number of Blacks who were judged guilty and thus became convicts rose.[13]

Race Demagoguery

Racial segregation and pseudoscientific theories of racial inferiority were, of course, embraced by the race demagogues who littered the political landscape in the postbellum South. The bigotry they fomented was driven by more than an objective of gaining power. Many of them believed much of the propaganda and myth, especially that Black people were innately, biologically inferior to non-Blacks and that absolutely no social intercourse between the races should be tolerated. These bigots, in the words of one historian,

> ... believed firmly and completely that Negroes were racially inferior, and they were concerned that racial policies reflect that belief. The fact that their efforts were misdirected and their beliefs rested upon prejudice, emotion and ignorance did not make them any less real. They acted upon the assumption that they were correct, and their policies were justified by their premises.[14]

The more prominent race demagogues were well known and well liked. They drew large, approving crowds at picnics, barbecues, camp meetings, and political rallies, and were inspired to lofty heights in the vilification of Blacks by their supporters.

On the stump they were masters of crowd manipulation, sometimes forcing opponents to endorse extremist positions on race issues. These demagogues did not create the anti-Black climate extant in the South between the Civil War and World War I, but they effectively capitalized on it, intensified it, and assured its longevity. Such people helped make it possible for convict leasing to flourish, and they were instrumental in delaying its demise, with the racial climate they perpetuated. Southern race demagogues benefited politically by supporting the doctrine of White supremacy but they or their associates also profited personally by leasing convicts.

The list of southern race demagogues is a long one. They range from obscure, shadowy figures, essentially unknown outside the backwaters of their southern whistle-stop towns, to colorful state politicians and others with national reputations. They were congressmen, senators, and governors. Their names and nicknames would almost be amusing in other circumstances. "Pitchfork" Ben Tillman was a governor and United States senator from South Carolina. He was among the first of the racebaiters to ride into power castigating Blacks. The "Agrarian Rebel" and sometime Populist Tom Watson, mentioned above, was a Georgian who, despite his early moderate views calling for the defense of Black political rights, eventually came to believe, like many of his southern White Populist associates, that America was a "White man's country and should always be governed by Whites." Watson's colleague of sorts, Governor Hoke Smith, also from Georgia, felt that Blacks were "a kind and hardy race: were intended to manufacture cotton as well as to hoe it." Not willing to stop there, Governor Smith believed that Blacks were "injured" more than they were "helped" by education, that most Blacks were "incapable of anything but manual labor and many taught from books spurn labor and live in idleness." He echoed an analysis sounded by some of his contemporaries when the governor was quoted as stating, "The Negro race was improved by slavery and . . . the majority of the Negroes in the State have ceased to improve since slavery."[15]

Each southern state had its counterpart to the Tillmans, Watsons, Hoke Smiths, Cole Bleases, and "Cotton Ed" Smiths (the latter two being U.S. senators from South Carolina), but Mississippi enjoyed the dubious distinction of having the "dean of demagogues" in James Kimble "White Chief" Vardaman. Lesser known, but authentic White supremacists nevertheless, were two additional Mississippi senators, Lucius Quintus Cincinnatus Lamar and John Sharp Williams.

The "White Chief" was a paradox in that he was vehemently, even savagely, anti-Black and, at the same time, anti-leasing. Indeed, Vardaman was a champion of prison reform and claimed partial responsibility for the abolition of leasing in Mississippi. "[T]he abolition of convict leasing, and the reorganization of the penitentiary system . . . constituted the major achievements of his administration," states his biographer, William Holmes.[16] Vardaman's principal motive seems to have been to fulfill a commitment to small farmers in Mississippi, who considered convict leasing a system that served the interests of wealthy planters by using cheap labor to dominate agriculture in the state.[17] When the legislature acted to declare leasing illegal in the Mississippi constitution of 1890, the practice did not end; it merely retreated underground, where, as was the case in other states, it continued.

Vardaman's life and professional career as a politician, governor, U.S. senator, and newspaper editor are replete with unquotable anti-Black harangues. His biographer indicates that his views were not atypical among southern Whites in the United States or the Western world, and for that reason they are presented here in some detail. And because the Vardamans of the South were so instrumental in shaping the thinking of all southern Whites, and in creating a regional mind-set that tolerated a racial climate in which Black victimization in convict leasing could be accommodated, their views warrant expanded attention. Vardaman's later opposition to leasing per se does not minimize the virulent racial climate he promoted for most of his life, one that helped Black exploitation in convict leasing endure.

Vardaman's biographer writes, for example, that "Vardaman's view of the Negro actually differed little from that of most White southerners; his appeal to White supremacy aroused concern chiefly because of the *blunt and dramatic way* he presented it, not because of what he said" (emphasis added).[18] He continues, "Racism was not confined to Mississippi at the turn of the twentieth century. The whole country, and indeed most of the Western world, then subscribed to racist and nativist phobias."[19] I. A. Newby, an authority on nineteenth century race bigotry, suggests that American racism and southern racism existed together and complemented one another. The difference was "at most a matter of degree and consisted largely of the fact that southerners lived among Negroes, were more immediately concerned with race problems, and were more inclined toward extremism."[20]

Vardaman was incensed and moved almost to psychoneurosis over Booker T. Washington's dinner at the White House at the invitation of President Theodore Roosevelt in 1901. He referred to Roosevelt as a "coon-flavored miscegenationist," and went on to state of Booker T. Washington that "the saddle-colored philosopher of Tuskegee had been disgraced" by accepting the invitation to mingle "on terms of social equality with a white man who had no more decency than to take a d----d nigger into his home." In doing this, Vardaman thought Theodore Roosevelt dishonored White people in America. He "takes this nigger bastard into his home, introduces him to his family and entertains him on terms of absolute social equality," continued Vardaman in disgust.[21]

Likewise, Vardaman scolded Roosevelt for closing the Indianola, Mississippi, post office after local Whites forced the removal of the Black postmaster, Mrs. Minnie Cox. Vardaman was quick to offer his opinion on the incident and on the President. "The White House," he declared, "is said to be so saturated with the odor of the nigger that the rats have taken refuge in the stable."[22] Not satisfied to stop there, Vardaman continued hurling invectives at Roosevelt, calling him a "spectacular lion masquerading ass." He even included Roosevelt's mother in his slurs, proclaiming, "[P]robably old lady Roosevelt during the period of gestation was frightened by a dog and that fact may account for the qualities of the male pup which are so prominent in Teddy. I would not do her an injustice but I am disposed to apologize to the dog for mentioning it."[23]

However outrageous Vardaman's insults of President Roosevelt were, the "White Chief's" most bitter invective and racial epithets were reserved for alleged Black male rapists, who supposedly violated southern White female virtue. Like many of his colleagues, Vardaman could work himself into an emotional frenzy over this highly inflammatory subject. He repeatedly described these Blacks as "brutes" and "beasts." He believed in immediate and swift "justice" and, although opposed to lynch law generally, he advocated it in these cases. One of his 1902 editorials reveals his view on the matter:

[W]hen one of these devils commit [*sic*] such a deed as this nigger did, somebody must kill him and I am in favor of doing it promptly. In this case, I only regret the brute did not have ten thousand lives to pay for this atrocious deed. An eternity in hell will not be adequate punishment for it.[24]

On another occasion he stated matter-of-factly, "If I were a private citizen and a Negro fiend fell into my hands . . . I would head the mob to string the brute up, and I haven't much respect for a White man who wouldn't."[25]

The alleged raping of White women by Black men was a favorite "whipping boy" of all Vardaman's demagogic contemporaries, as well. Governor Cole Blease of South Carolina, defending lynching, shouted to his hysterically approving audiences, "Whenever the Constitution [of the United States] comes between me and the virtue of White women of the South, I say to hell with the Constitution." To Ben Tillman, southern White women were "in a state of siege."[26] They lived in perpetual fear that "lurking in the dark was a Black brute, a 'sooty desecrator,' a monstrous beast crazed with lust."[27]

Vardaman was once described as a "hard-shelled racist." In his political campaigns, in public office, and in the pages of his newspapers, he was obsessed with advancing his views on the "solution" to the race problem in the South and in the country. He felt that education for Blacks was a serious mistake; it should be abolished where it existed or where it was tolerated. Whites should not teach Blacks. In Vardaman's words, "it is almost an unpardonable offense for a White man or woman to teach [in] the ordinary nigger school. . . . It should be prohibited by law." If education for Blacks was unavoidable, "Let niggers teach niggers," asserted Vardaman.[28] In 1899 Vardaman spoke for many southern Whites when he stated,

> There is no getting around the fact that the whole scheme of Negro education in the South is [a] pitable [*sic*] failure. . . . It is time to . . . say what we mean and mean what we say . . . [to] people who talk about elevating the race by education. It is not only folly, but it comes pretty nearly being criminal folly. The Negro isn't permitted to advance and their education only spoils a good field hand and makes a shyster lawyer or a fourth-rate teacher. It is money thrown away.[29]

> Book knowledge for Blacks only frustrates them and has no positive results. On the contrary it [*sic*], education . . . sharpens his cunning, breeds hopes that cannot be fulfilled, inspires aspirations that cannot be gratified, creates an inclination to avoid honest labor, promotes indolence and in turn leads to crime.[30]

Only Blacks' hearts and hands should be trained, according to the "White Chief." Almost as an afterthought, Vardaman sometimes noted that education might also resurrect unrealistic Black ambitions to once again take part in southern politics by voting and holding office.[31]

Another favorite appeal of Vardaman's was that the Fifteenth Amendment to the U.S. Constitution, which provided that the right to vote should not be denied on the basis of race, color, or previous condition, should be repealed.[32] In addition, he wanted to greatly modify the Fourteenth Amendment, the due process amendment, which also makes Blacks citizens. These actions, Vardaman boasted, would "settle the race problem once and for all."[33] Therefore, Mississippi should take the lead. Apparently, the Congress was not persuaded, or perhaps they realized that such drastic action would only amount to overkill, since Vardaman's concerns had effectively been taken care of by the time the Mississippi constitution of 1890 was adopted. It is possible, furthermore, that Congress realized the dangerous precedent that would be set by tampering with the amendments, and that many Whites, too, would be denied the protection of the Fourteenth and Fifteenth Amendments.

The era of the demagogues left scar tissue in southern race relations that is still discernible in the last decade of the twentieth century. No doubt in our own time, latter-day Vardamans were stimulated by the "White Chief" as they grappled with the civil rights movement of the 1950s and 1960s and the reality of changing times. From Orville Faubus to George Wallace to James Eastland, Ross Barnett, and David Duke, they struggled to revivify the ghost of Vardaman. Despite claims of victory, many have now adapted, however grudgingly, to a social and political evolution in the South that, by and large, has relegated race demagoguery to the dustbin of history.

Violence Escalating

Whether the demagogues inspired such groups as the Ku Klux Klan, Knights of the White Camelia, Whitecapping in Mississippi, the White League of Louisiana, and other self-styled vigilantes—or whether these groups inspired demagoguery—is immaterial. To be sure, coercive groups existed before the demagogues gained prominence in the South. The fact is, however, that race violence aimed primarily at Blacks was, at the very least, tacitly or otherwise, encouraged by the Vardamans, Tillmans, and Hoke

Smiths. Race riots, whipping, maiming, lynching, and cold-blooded murder claimed many more Black lives than White. The misery index and fear imposed by these secret societies were undeniable and unquantifiable. In their attempt to reinforce White supremacy and preserve their sense of White civilization, they used nothing less than terrorism to exclude Blacks from political participation and keep them "in their place."

The reign of terror concocted by the Ku Klux Klan and other "protective societies" began just after the Civil War, ebbed and flowed throughout the remainder of the nineteenth century, and found little to discourage it in the racial climate of the early twentieth century. Local and state governments seemed powerless to control these vigilantes, even where individuals in such governments were not participants. Federal intervention, which moved at about the same relative pace as the legendary tortoise, was the best hope for relief. Although comparatively quiet in the first decade of the twentieth century, by the second decade the Klan was gaining popularity in various quarters. Thomas Dixon's romantic novel, *The Clansmen*, inspired the making of D. W. Griffith's controversial motion picture, *The Birth of a Nation*, and its bigoted treatment of the African-American population. By the 1920s the Klan "mushroomed to national proportions, far exceeding the geographical extent of the Reconstruction Klan."[34] Before its second demise, which coincided with the coming of the Great Depression, the Klan was parading boldly down Pennsylvania Avenue past the White House, "with the government's permission."[35] The long-term impact of the Ku Klux Klan and other "paramilitary organizations" backed up by runaway mob violence is hard to measure. Knowledge of its "most fiendish and diabolical outrages" surely threatened—even crippled—many southern Blacks, destroyed their morale, encouraged a belief in White invincibility, and effectively undermined Black confidence in law and order and equal protection. The result was de facto reduction of Blacks in the minds of most Whites, especially White southerners, to a level of subservience lower than any other racial or ethnic group. This was a view of Blacks generally that hardly provoked Whites' ire, and perhaps not even their interest, once atrocities under convict leasing first began to circulate.

The Ku Klux Klan received the most notoriety during the era, but they were certainly not alone. They and other "desperado groups," spinning more and more out of control, enjoyed the sympathy, if not the active support, of a "large element—perhaps a majority—[of southern Whites] who were both repelled and attracted by the Klan."[36] Opponents lived in fear of retaliation from the Klan and accusations of "treason" against "the South and the White race." Nevertheless, because of widespread support or sympathy for Klan-like objectives, if not its methods, "the Klan," it has been concluded, "wrapped itself in the Stars and Bars, recited the racist litanies" and "willingly or unwillingly [southern Whites] entered into a conspiracy to protect the Klan and advance its works."[37]

Lynching and Race Riots

The lynching bee and wave of race riots in the South and elsewhere that characterized the decades immediately before and after the turn of the twentieth century had their own momentum and needed no inducement from the Klan or the demagogues. They got it anyway. The *New York Age*, one of the leading Black newspapers of the day, reporting on the brutal Atlanta race riot of 1906, in which some thirty Blacks and two

Whites were killed, outlined various causes of the riot. One was the hate campaign conducted by gubernatorial aspirant Hoke Smith. Second was a local newspaper campaign exaggerating Black crime and alleged incidents of the rape of White women by Black men. Third was the offer by the *Atlanta News* of a $1,000 reward for lynching Blacks and advocating the revival of the Ku Klux Klan.[38] Lynching, for its part, was an extreme example of White bigotry toward Blacks. The race riots were often unplanned and spontaneous, but no less brutal than lynchings.

The South of the era of the convict lease system was the primary location where the depraved practice of lynching took place. Blacks were lynched for "White men's crimes, for marrying White women, Negro mothers and wives [were] raped and lynched when mobs were unable to locate their sons and husbands, and Negroes [were] lynched for no reason except that they happened to be Negroes." They were also "lynched for offenses as petty as brushing a White man's horse and refusing to dance when ordered to do so by White men."[39] The total number of those Blacks lynched will probably never be known because so many lynchings went unreported. In any event, the devastation is in no way lessened by a "small" total. One particularly gory episode serves to illustrate the numbing effect of such an uncivilized, primitive practice. This is the 1934 case of Claude Neal, a Black man arrested in Marianna, Florida, for the murder of a White woman:

> After an enraged mob kidnapped [Neal] from an Alabama jail (where he had been placed for his "safety"), they traveled toward the Florida state line as fifteen southern newspapers announced the date of the coming lynching and the

route and progress of the mob. The white men tortured Neal for twelve hours. They hung him until he was almost dead, forced him to eat his own penis, burned him with red-hot irons, slashed his side and stomach, and cut off his fingers and toes before they murdered him and hung his body in the Marianna Courthouse Square.[40]

Terrorism was one of the key contributors to the racial climate that provided the context for most of the problems Blacks faced in convict leasing. There were, however, many others that may not be as apparent.

Black Disenfranchisement

The franchise—the right to vote—along with the rights to run for and hold political office are among the most time-honored citizen entitlements in United States history. The right to vote is the quintessential feature of a functioning democracy. It was just this democratic ideal that attracted so many to the shores of the United States of America throughout the very period when convict leasing prospered. Voting is the best opportunity for individuals in a democracy to register their approval of or dissatisfaction with political leadership, to exercise some measure of control over their lives and their future. Voting rights were within the reach of many southern Blacks from 1890 to the 1930s and on, but beyond their grasp. Much evidence exists to demonstrate the political immobility of southern Blacks during this period, the net effect of which was an inability to compete with Whites on an equal footing for the opportunities that American society offered, and to enjoy basic human rights that are generally assumed for citizens in a democracy. Southern Blacks, especially convicts, were not a significant part of the

White Democratic party political constituency. With Blacks increasingly denied the right to vote, to hold office, and to serve on a jury, even the slight protection ordinarily afforded convicts was swept aside. Until leasing began to decline, there was no effective political voice against it because positions of the greatest political influence were occupied by the Vardamans of the day. Although it is quite a leap to propose that Black politicians would have taken up the cause of Black mistreatment under leasing, given their participation in the authorization and maintenance of leasing in some states, it seems natural that in the racial climate of the period they would have been more inclined to rally behind the convict cause than White politicians holding local or national office who subscribed to the ideas of White supremacy. The failure of the governance system to provide for and ensure equal access to political participation through the electoral process, opening up avenues to other centers of power and influence, consigned most Blacks to the perpetual status, in this epoch and the decades that followed, of "hewers of wood and drawers of water."

As suggested earlier, southern White political leaders who debated the feasibility and strategy of disenfranchisement were initially restrained by a concern that some poor Whites might be eliminated as voters in the process. However, a greater fear that the Black vote would shift the balance of power between contending White factions dominated the debate and eventually carried the day. Disenfranchisement was also rationalized as a progressive step in removing the potential for continued fraud and corruption associated with Blacks selling their vote to the highest bidder. The *Atlanta Journal*, in a pro-disenfranchisement editorial, expressed this view best when it suggested that Black character and manhood would be protected by a denial of the right to the suffrage, removing the chance for a Black man to "barter his ballot." Asserting, editorially, that "this is a White man's government and White men must and shall rule it," the newspaper's opinion closed with an extraordinary demonstration of convoluted logic by proposing that elimination of the franchise would advance Black liberation, improve citizenship, and even be morally advantageous for Blacks. It stated: "[T]he definite settlement of this question of the Negro franchise only hastens the day of real emancipation of the Negro into the higher and better atmosphere of self-respecting citizenship, or moral manhood and material independence."[41]

The state of Mississippi set the pace in disenfranchisement through constitutional change. Blacks were in the majority in the state in 1890 but could not prevent the call for a constitutional convention in which only one Black participated and at which the primary objective was to disenfranchise Blacks. The suffrage amendment included the imposition of a poll tax and an "understanding clause," which required potential voters to be able to read and understand the state constitution "or give a reasonable interpretation of it" to the "satisfaction" of the registrar. Obviously the registrar could refuse to be satisfied by *any* interpretation by Blacks.[42] Consider, for example, the "general opinion" of the Jackson, Mississippi *Clarion-Ledger*: "If every Negro was a graduate of Harvard, and had been elected as class orator . . . he would not be as well fitted to exercise the right of suffrage as the Anglo-Saxon farm laborer, *adscriptus glebae*, of the South and West."[43]

Southern legend and lore contain the story of a Black teacher, a Harvard graduate who appeared before a Mississippi registrar to vote. He read several books, the Constitution, and passages in Latin, Greek, French, German, and Spanish. During the examination, the registrar turned to a collection of Chinese characters and asked the Black teacher, "What does this mean?" The teacher replied, "It means you don't want me to vote."[44]

James Vardaman, on the other hand, was not given to ploys or subterfuge; he was as explicit and unpretentious on Black voting as he was on Blacks in general. According to John Hope Franklin, Vardaman "summed up the Southern White view" when he stated, "I am just as opposed to Booker T. Washington as a voter, with all his Anglo-Saxon reinforcements, as I am to the coconut-headed, chocolate-colored, typical little coon, Andy Dotson, who blacks my shoes every morning. Neither is fit to perform the supreme function of citizenship."[45]

The 1890 Disenfranchisement Amendment in the Mississippi constitution defied both the Fifteenth Amendment to the U.S. Constitution and congressional legislation of February 23, 1870, which readmitted Mississippi to the Union during Reconstruction. Nevertheless, the legality of this disenfranchisement was upheld by the Mississippi Supreme Court in 1892 and by the U.S. Supreme Court in 1898. Following Mississippi, the other southern states established restrictive measures for Black voting, and "like a row of bricks, the first tumbling down precipitated the entire lot."[46] South Carolina achieved disenfranchisement by constitutional convention in 1895. Louisiana and North Carolina adopted exclusionary amendments in 1900. Alabama in 1901, Virginia in the same year, and Georgia in 1908 passed constitutional amendments to eliminate Black suffrage. The remaining states of the Old Confederacy—Arkansas, Florida, Tennessee, and Texas—all succeeded with disenfranchisement by one means or another by 1910.[47]

Southern Blacks living through the disenfranchisement experience were frequently incredulous about what was happening around them. They searched desperately to counter efforts to restrict the Black vote, always in vain. They believed, they hoped, that moral suasion, logic, reason, and right would prevail. Black leaders were quite eloquent in citing the injustice of disenfranchisement. In the final analysis, they said, the situation boiled down to nothing more than an accident of birth. This view was expressed by Thomas Ezekiel Miller, one of six Black delegates to the 1895 South Carolina constitutional convention as he addressed the gathering, asking rhetorically,

> Why do they say the Negro must be disenfranchised? Is it because he is lawless? No! Is it because he is riotous in the discharge of the right of suffrage? . . . No! They answer, "Because his skin is black, he should not vote. Because his skin is black, he is inferior. Because he did not fight for the ballot, he should not have it!"[48]

Despite and over the voice of Black protest, the right to vote gradually slipped away. One of the factors that is so striking about the movement for disenfranchisement is the extraordinary lengths to which the White South went in order to curtail Black voting. It was, it seems, excessive—many of the machinations superfluous, cases of overkill. Popular among the methods used was the poll tax, which was not eliminated as a requirement for voting in federal elections until 1964, by the Twenty-fourth Amendment to the U.S. Constitution. In many states this voting fee was required in advance, sometimes eighteen months beforehand, and collected in the spring when ready cash was most scarce among sharecroppers. It was not unusual for a residency requirement of two years in the state to be linked to the poll tax, which was also sometimes cumulative, requiring all back poll taxes to be paid before voting was allowed.[49] Enterprising Blacks who managed to slip through the poll tax net might be confronted with a new obstacle, the literacy test. This test generally involved some "understanding" and/or recitation of constitutions or other historical documents to the satisfaction of election officials, as discussed above. The use of multiple ballot boxes was also a device for limiting the Black vote. In South Carolina, this stratagem took the form of an "Eight Box Law," which could be construed as a literacy test because voters had to choose the properly labeled box in order for their votes to be counted. "Assistance" might or might not be given to selected voters.[50] Polling places were sometimes relocated without notice. When a handful of diligent Blacks discovered the new polling site, to the chagrin of local Whites, roads might then be blocked or conveniently "out of repair." The grandfather clause was intended to provide an escape hatch for Whites who otherwise might be prevented from voting because of poll taxes, property taxes, literacy tests, and the like, by exempting them from these requirements if their parents or grandparents voted, say, in the presidential election of 1860, when no Blacks were voting in the South. Moreover, a grandfather clause might have required voters in 1900 or 1910 to have voted themselves or been eligible to vote in 1860.[51]

The White primary, not struck down by the U.S. Supreme Court until 1944, along with racial gerrymandering, which may still be practiced in parts of the South and elsewhere, must be added to the list of schemes designed to stop Blacks from exercising their right to vote. The White primary was a Democratic party preferential election and was defended on the grounds that Blacks were not prevented from voting in the general election, and that the party was a private entity that could make its own rules. However, in Texas and many other parts of the South, the primary *was* the election because the area was solidly Democratic. Candidates who won the Democratic party primary often ran unopposed in general elections and were victorious. In the South between 1890 and World War II, election winners rarely included non-Democrats. Therefore, to vote in the general election after being excluded from the primary was the equivalent of being on the proverbial fool's errand.[52]

Gerrymandering—the redrawing of voting districts in order to neutralize the Black vote and reduce Black political representation—was available when needed. When all else failed, and sometimes before anything else was attempted, intimidation and violence were used. Jobs, property, families, and individual lives were jeopardized if Blacks sought to defy instructions not to register and vote. With the consequences ranging from "friendly persuasion" to murder, it is no surprise that Blacks got the message. What is surprising is that some Blacks persisted in demanding and exercising their constitutional right to the franchise in the face of equally insistent White efforts to end Black voting. When the irresistible force met the immovable object, bloodshed was the result. Blacks, more often than not, suffered most.

Peonage

By 1900, the African-American population in the United States was approximately nine million. Nine out of ten lived in the South, where they represented one-third of the population. Of the roughly eight million Blacks that inhabited the southern states at that time, it is estimated that 90 percent were engaged in agriculture.[53] A handful of Blacks were landowners and independent farmers—mainly in the Sea Island area of Georgia and South Carolina and the Black Belt section of Alabama and Mississippi. Between six and seven million Black southerners were sharecroppers, crop lieners, tenant farmers, day laborers, or some modification of one or all of these arrangements. Although numbers are hard to come by, it is certain that a large number of southern Blacks were peons. Indeed, most southern peons were Black. Around the turn of the twentieth century, writes Peter Daniel, "southern Blacks . . . lived in the vortex of peonage."[54] In the state of Alabama, notorious for peonage, contract labor law (a euphemism for peonage) was struck down in the case of Alonzo Bailey.

Alonzo Bailey was jailed early in 1908 on the ground that he violated his contract to work for the Riverside Company in Montgomery, Alabama, as a farm laborer for one year.[55] Bailey obtained a $15 advance on a $12-per-month salary, to be repaid in twelve $1.25 monthly installments.[56] After working for one month and a few days, Bailey quit. The laws of Alabama and other southern states at the time declared that persons who took cash advances and then left their jobs without repaying or working them off should be punished as if the money was stolen. Under the so-called false pretenses law, receiving the money and not making good amounted to intent to defraud, and virtually guaranteed conviction. In Alabama, in such cases, the accused or indicted person was not allowed to testify. Bailey sued, arguing that the contract labor law was unconstitutional. In 1911 the case was returned to the U.S. Supreme Court for a second time. It spanned the terms of Presidents Theodore Roosevelt and William H. Taft, both of whose administrations were involved in the case (especially the Office of the Attorney General) through the influence of Booker T. Washington, who was characteristically engaged in an important support role behind the scene and in secret. Finally, the Bailey case was overturned by the Court, which concluded that contract labor laws were unconstitutional because they were in violation of the Thirteenth Amendment and anti-peonage statutes.

The Bailey case illustrates how peonage fed the convict lease system throughout the years of its existence in the American South. Most of the peons were Black, as were most victims of the lease system. For them, the distinction between antebellum de jure slavery and postbellum de facto slavery was close to being much ado about nothing.[57] And in fact, peonage did not end with Bailey's favorable court ruling; Black farm laborers and others continued to be jailed for contract labor law violations, ending up on chain gangs and, most pertinent for this study, trapped in the convict lease system.[58]

Pseudoscientific Theories Of Racial Inferiority

The *coup de grace* for southern Blacks struggling for equal access to the wealth of opportunities available to Whites, and for dignity throughout the life of the southern convict lease system, was to have to face the reemergence of "scientific" support for theories of Black racial inferiority. This pseudoscientific racism began rearing its ugly head toward the end of the nineteenth century. By the second decade of the twentieth century it was close to orthodoxy, manifesting itself in ways and forms too numerous to count, and substantially influencing public policy toward Blacks, effectively reversing the natural symmetry of cause and effect.[59] These reconstituted ideas were the "scientific" rationale and justification for the pernicious segregation and Jim Crow practices pervasive in the South, although not discernibly absent from the rest of American society. The difference between "American" bigotry and "southern" bigotry was more than anything else a difference in degree.[60] Almost every single institution was infected with this intellectual–philosophical poison: the media, education, politics, the church, industry, labor unions, the arts, civil service, public accommodations, and so on. During these years, "Negrophobia" reached its zenith, witnessing a massive proliferation of anti-Black thought and literature, and becoming immutable, undergirded by the strength of "science." The reality that the ideological superstructure of bigotry obscured the factual base was irrelevant.

The post–Civil War pseudoscientific assault began with European theorists and was imported to the United States, where it was "refined" and expanded, and was formulated with great intensity and with extraordinary detail. Building on the work of Count Arthur de Gobineau (France), Houston Stewart Chamberlain (England and Germany), Ludwig Woltmann (Germany), Carl Penka (Germany), and Theodor Poesche (Germany), American race theorists Lothrop Stoddard and Madison Grant, among the most influential ideologues of the era, spread the doctrine of Black inferiority far and wide. Another wave of Europeans influencing racist thought included Sir Francis Galton (England), Gustave Le Bon (France), August Weismann (Germany), Vasher de la Pouge (France), and Otto Ammon (Germany). These men were all learned scientists—including anthropologists, psychologists, hereditarians, biologists, and geneticists—which for many placed their work and their conclusions beyond reproach.[61]

Another body of work, the research of the inimitable Charles Darwin, was so significant and so influential that a whole new school of thought grew up around it and came to be known as social Darwinism, because of its application to society and people and its public policy impact. Despite the fact that Darwin was uninterested in issues of superiority and inferiority, his theories of "survival of the fittest" in *Origin of the Species* and "natural selection" in *The Descent of Man*, and his general preoccupation with "physical differences"—hair, lungs, brain, formation of the skull, and body proportions—unwittingly gave scientific license to racists clothed in the mantle of scholarship. Darwin's work also made it possible for intellectual bigots to claim respectability and to conclude brazenly that Blacks were unquestionably inferior to Whites, that they were unfit to be more than society's millstones, and that the two racial groups should not mix. Long before 1900 the findings of Darwin were being popularized and disseminated by social Darwinists such as Herbert Spencer and John Fiske, who cared less about truth and accuracy than they did about rationalizing Black inferiority and racial inequality.

One example of the practical application and influence of social Darwinism is found in the insurance industry. A book entitled *Race Traits and Tendencies of the American Negro* was published in 1896 by a German-born insurance specialist who analyzed Black mortality. The book was endorsed by the celebrated American Economic Association and became a handbook for "Negrophobes" and insurance companies who asserted that Blacks were "unacceptable actuarial risks" and therefore should be denied insurance coverage—because they were Black.

George Frederickson argues that this "new prognosis," born of refurbished European and American racist thought in general, and social Darwinism in particular, "pointed . . . to the need to segregate or quarantine a race liable to be a source of contamination and social danger to the White community, as it sank ever deeper into the slough of disease, vice and criminality."[62]

Collectively, this era of Black oppression and pseudoscientific racist thought, essays Frederickson, amounted to "crimes against humanity," and "by appealing to simplistic Darwinian or hereditarian formula, White Americans could make their crimes . . . appear as contributions to the inevitable unfolding of biological destiny."[63]

THE BLACK RESPONSE

The Black response to the gridlock of southern White racism, White supremacy, White intractability, and White intransigence enlisted the imagination and energy of the national Black community. Tactics varied and styles differed, but the general objectives remained constant: relief from oppression, exploitation, and injustice. Demands for equal treatment and opportunity came later. Between the Federal abandonment of Blacks with the collapse of Reconstruction and the "watershed" of opportunity with the coming of World War II, the first order of business was to minimize losses. Sometimes Black leadership was out of step with the masses, such as when Booker T. Washington counseled, "Cast down your bucket where you are," in the face of the floodtide proportions of the Black exodus out of the rural South. As southern Blacks exemplified the "fits and starts" of tough decision-making, they embraced pieces of several strategies. The circumstances, as much as anything, dictated the particular Black reaction.

Passive Resistance And Violent Protest

In 1899, when Black troopers from the 25th Infantry "took possession of the saloons, shot a barkeeper, and terrorized the town" in Winnemuca, Nevada, or when Black soldiers waiting in Key West, Florida, to depart for Cuba, "armed and in uniform, surrounded the jail, overpowered the sheriff, and liberated their comrades" before "smashing up the jail" and leaving, they might have considered their actions a *quid pro quo* for the persistent violence against Blacks.[64] More often than not, however, Blacks responded to White violence against them with nonviolent protest, petitions, and demands for protective legislation. The efforts to have grievances redressed in an organized fashion during the late nineteenth and early twentieth centuries were mounted respectively by the Afro-American League (1890), the Afro-American Council (1898), the Niagara Movement (1905), and the National Association for the Advancement of Colored People (NAACP) (1910). These were organizations with national reputations, and the latter two included major northern White liberal support, participation, and leadership—especially in the case of the NAACP.

In addition to the national organizations, a spate of state and local groups protested and demonstrated against endemic injustice. Sometimes individual Blacks were so unsatisfied with the pace, style, or substance of Black leadership that they broke ranks and waged their own protest. One example was William Monroe Trotter, fiery editor of the *Boston Guardian*, first Black Phi Beta Kappa graduate of Harvard, and bitter adversary of Booker T. Washington. Trotter was a tenacious critic of White-dominated labor unions' failure to accept Blacks. He advocated the use of Blacks as strikebreakers, stating simply, "Negro workers were and are ever ready to take the place of union strikers."[65] Another example was Chandler Owen, copublisher and editor, with A. Philip Randolph, of *Messenger* magazine, who felt that highly visible national Black leadership was out of step with the realities of race bigotry and the needs of rank-and-file Blacks.

James W. Ford, Communist party candidate for vice president of
the United States in 1932 and detractor of the NAACP and the
National Urban League as betrayers of Black people, and William N. Jones, editor of the Baltimore *Afro-American*, were
among the lesser-known Blacks attracted to communism as a
response to racism in the 1920s and 1930s. Nevertheless, it was
the efforts of national organizations that provided the most
lasting record of Black protest against violence and injustice. The
NAACP, for example, waged a relentless struggle in the 1930s
against lynching, and lobbied hard for federal anti-lynching
legislation. This campaign was carried right into the White
House and dropped squarely in the lap of an uneasy Franklin D.
Roosevelt, who eventually but reluctantly supported it.[66]

The Great Migration

In 1895 Booker T. Washington, representing the Tuskegee school
and philosophy of conservative Black leadership, announced his
hope that Blacks and Whites could reach some accommodation
in the South. He accepted a subordinate role for Blacks and
thought it would be wise to eschew politics for the time being.
In his well-known 1895 "Atlanta Compromise" speech, the view
from Tuskegee was that Blacks should remain in the South
because "it is in the South that the Negro is given a man's
chance. . . ."[67] W. E. B. DuBois, militant editor of the *Chicago
Defender* Robert S. Abbot, other Black leaders, and much of the
southern Black masses, by the second decade of the new century,
would have no part of staying in the South. The lure of the
promised land, with what appeared to be attractive employment
possibilities and a chance to escape southern White terrorism and
intimidation, convinced hundreds of thousands of Blacks to head

for Detroit, Chicago, Washington, D.C., New York, and Boston. An editorial in one of the period's leading Black church periodicals outlined the causes for the exodus (which it endorsed) as "lynching, terrorism, oppression, robbery, deception and fraud in business transactions, meager and inadequate school facilities, unjust application of the laws and lack of protection by the courts [and] the denial of political and civil rights."[68]

The "great migration" saw the relocation of more people from one section of the United States to another, during a similar four- or five-year time period, than on any other occasion in American history.[69]

There were other migrations out of the South, as well, in response to hard times for Blacks. Smaller movements also took place, into Mexico, California and the far West, and Oklahoma. As early as 1879, the colorful Benjamin "Pap" Singleton and Henry Adams led a "minor stampede" to Kansas. So desperate was Singleton that he even considered flight to Cyprus.[70]

For some Blacks, no place in the United States was far enough away from the South. Significant attempts, although not substantial (in terms of numbers), were made to return to Africa. The organized post–Civil War colonization schemes continued to be dominated by the American Colonization Society, which had been founded in 1816–17. At the same time, spontaneous emigration schemes were led by individuals like the dynamic Bishop Henry McNeal Turner in the 1890s,[71] an obscure medical doctor named Albert Thorne, also in the 1890s, and a flamboyant African from the Gold Coast, West Africa, named Alfred Charles (Chief) Sam, who operated in Oklahoma and Texas in 1914–15.[72] Marcus Garvey is frequently but incorrectly described as the leader of the back-to-Africa movement in the 1920s and early 1930s. The "movement" he led was a Black nationalist or Pan-Africanist one with a back-to-Africa component, among several others.[73]

Black Self-Help

Part of the Black response to Jim Crow, segregation, and exclusion was to turn inward and build Black institutions. In the North and in the South around the turn of the century, the number of Black businesses and educational, social, and cultural enterprises increased noticeably. Blacks opened restaurants, catering establishments, drug stores, grocery and general stores, and a host of others with variations in size and type. In addition, they ran shirt factories, lumber and fish businesses, and carpet outlets. They became carpenters and building contractors. Some businesses were cooperative ventures and others were partnerships or had single owners. Always an advocate of self-help and Black entrepreneurship, in 1900 Booker T. Washington established the National Negro Business League. Although there was little comparison between the resources of giant White businesses and their smaller Black counterparts, "necessity was the mother of invention." Black banks, over fifty of them by 1915, insurance companies, and real estate operations enjoyed surprising growth in the early twentieth century. Madame C. Walker's hair and skin products company is an economic legend in Chicago and has been a notable inspiration to subsequent generations of Black businesses.

The Black church blossomed during this era and remains the single most important institution owned and controlled by Blacks. The more desperate the plight of Blacks, the more they turned to the church for comfort. By the 1920s and 1930s, storefront churches in urban Black communities abounded. The establishment of Black institutions of higher education began to slow down by the second decade of the twentieth century, after rapid growth during the final quarter of the previous century, but fraternal and charitable organizations and mutual aid societies were on the rise. Organizations such as the Masons, Odd Fellows, and Eastern Stars, and what became the North Carolina Mutual and Atlanta Life Insurance companies, set the pace. The National Association of Colored Women, which concentrated on volunteer work in hospitals and orphanages, began in 1895. The overriding events and philosophy that drove these inward-thinking developments was the incredible depths to which Whites sank in order to exclude Blacks, and the inspiration of the often-cited Biblical passage, "The Lord helps those who help themselves."

The opportunities for Black farmers to redress their grievances while trapped in sharecropping, tenant farming, and the lien system were limited. White landowners and the White business community, as the backbone of the southern White power structure, were perceived as close to invincible. Nevertheless, the Black farmers sought relief by joining the ranks of southern populism (discussed earlier) and, later, through the biracial though short-lived Southern Tenant Farmers Union (STFU).

The STFU was organized in Tyronza, Arkansas, in July of 1934, insisting that federal government subsidy payments be made directly to sharecroppers and tenant farmers since the landlords were keeping them. In addition, the STFU demanded that displacement from the land be stopped. By 1936 the Union's membership was one-third Black and backed by the NAACP. Southern White farmers again had some reservations about coalescing with Blacks, "gripped by superstition and fear," even for common economic interests.[74] Although segregated local affiliates of the STFU existed in a few southern towns, most were integrated. The demise of the STFU is explained by the difficulty of trying to negotiate improved conditions with a group of landlords beset with economic problems themselves as a result of the depression, and who relied on government hand-outs for survival. Furthermore, the landlords, like the race demagogues, exploited the racial fears of White farmers and split the ranks of the STFU while at the same time ruthlessly opposing and terrorizing the coalition. Before 1936 ended, the STFU had collapsed unceremoniously as the southern Populist movement had caved in before it.[75]

Black Intellectuals

One challenge for Black intellectuals during the late nineteenth and early twentieth centuries was to combat the massive out-pouring of anti-Black literature and propaganda.[76] Consistently handicapped by meager resources, poor organization, and pervasive discrimination, they battled indefatigably to defend the dignity of the Black past. A small but dedicated group of Black scholar-intellectuals, along with the Black press, marshaled an unprecedented amount of literature celebrating the African past and Black achievements in America as a way of countering social Darwinism and pseudoscientific racism.

The early twentieth century "Negro History Movement" is an example of one antidote to racist propaganda. The most noteworthy of the groups in the fray were the American Negro Academy, the Negro Society for Historical Research, and the Association for the Study of Negro Life and History (renamed in 1973 the Association for the Study of Afro-American Life and

History). Prominent among the individuals who led these organizations and the intellectual crusade against the defamation of Blacks were W. E. B. DuBois, Carter G. Woodson, John E. Bruce, Joel Rogers, and Arthur Schomburg. They waxed eloquent in defending the Black past and in gathering a corpus of knowledge and literature intended to offset the harmful effects of "scientific proof" of Black inferiority. Their influence far exceeded their numbers, and twentieth century African nationalism, leading to the decline of colonialism in Africa and the Caribbean, the modern civil rights movement in the United States, and what is now known as Black, African-American, and Africana Studies in colleges, universities, and elsewhere, all celebrate the seeds of scholar-activism planted by these pioneers.[77]

CONCLUSION

It was economic need, and not the turbulent years in race relations in the American South following the Civil War, that brought on the convict lease system. Nevertheless, the racial tension that characterized the life span of convict leasing enabled it and all of its abuses to flourish. Political leaders in the former Confederate states needed a solution for the penitentiary problem during the hard times and chaos and confusion of Reconstruction, and they chose leasing over other options because the times made it socially and politically "acceptable."

They could have attempted to increase state and county revenue through higher taxes in order to manage the penitentiary system, but such an option obviously would not have been popular in a climate of destitution. At any rate, the question of the possible effectiveness of increasing taxes remains moot, since it was not done. Assistance from the federal government might have been an alternative, but national political leaders in Washington, D.C. were in no mood to be "Lady Bountiful" in the South after such a destructive war. In addition, the federal government was hard-pressed for funds itself in the aftermath of such a long and costly ordeal. The convict lease possibility was appealing because it appeared to have few monetary costs and a panoply of benefits for all but the victims. It had also been tested in several states before the Civil War and seemed to work well. It was, many felt, an idea whose time had come—and the acrimonious racial context in which it was conceived, and thrived, made its ascendancy and longevity possible.

Invariably there was corruption, fraud, and impropriety in the lease system. Local law enforcement officials—sheriffs, for example—overcharged the state for the transportation of convicts and made money by quickly enlarging the convict population. Seven months before his agreement to get convict labor for the Putnam Lumber Company, the sheriff in the Martin Tabert case in Florida (discussed in chapter 3) held twenty men as vagrants. Seven months later, 154 men were in his custody. The sheriff admitted "delivering" 163 convicts to Putnam for which he earned $2,500.[78] Companies bidding for leases bribed public officials and their staffs in order to obtain lucrative contracts. Payments due the state under terms of lease contracts were late, low, and sometimes not made at all. Handsome profits were made in leasing convicts. Most victims of the system were Black males, who consistently outnumbered their White counterparts from state to state and throughout the region and who, as convicts, regularly exceeded their percentages in the population in individual states and in the South as a whole. Black females were trapped in convict leasing as well, as was an occasional White female. As the post–Civil War era began in the South, the emergence of leasing set no precedent. As will be seen in chapter 2, leasing had a pre–Civil War beginning that, for our purpose here, is significant mainly as a matter of record.

NOTES

1. John Hope Franklin, *Reconstruction After the Civil War* (Chicago, 1961), 53.

2. Most of what the Black farmer needed was obtained from the landlord's commissary, where prices were generally higher than elsewhere. A 10 percent interest rate was often charged on credit or cash advanced. However, the interest paid turned out to be usurious because credit might be needed three separate times per year at 10 percent each four months, aggregating to 30 percent for the year. One student of sharecropping in the 1930s concluded, "Because of high prices and the high interest charges, the commissary was often the most profitable operation on the plantation." See Raymond Wolters, *Negroes and the Great Depression: The Problem of Economic Recovery* (Westport, 1970), chapter 2 and *passim*.

3. For an introduction to these various agricultural arrangements and the impact on Blacks, see Vernon Lane Wharton, *The Negro in Mississippi, 1865–1890* (New York, 1965), chapter 3 and *passim*.

4. Peter Daniel, *The Shadow of Slavery: Peonage in the South* (Urbana, 1972), 21.

5. Kenneth Stampp, *The Era of Reconstruction, 1865–1877* (New York, 1967), 129. New interest in land reform and redistribution prospects for southern Blacks during Reconstruction should begin with several older works, namely, LaWanda Cox, "The Promise of Land for the Freedmen," *Mississippi Valley Historical Review* 45 (1958); Carol R. Bleser, *The Promised Land: The History of the South Carolina Land Commission, 1869–1890* (Columbia, 1969); Claude F. Oubre, *Forty Acres and a Mule: The Freedmen's Bureau*

and *Black Land Ownership* (Baton Rouge, 1978); and Stampp, *The Era of Reconstruction, 1865–1877*. Many years ago, as a graduate student, my thoughts on this subject were presented in "The Black Struggle for Land During Reconstruction," *The Black Scholar* (February 1974), 13–18.

6. Two indispensable books on the Civil War and the Reconstruction era are Eric Foner, *Reconstruction: America's Unfinished Revolution, 1863–1877* (New York, 1988), and James McPherson, *Battle Cry of Freedom: The Civil War Era* (New York, 1988).

7. A good summary of developments in the South and race relations there from the end of Reconstruction to the outbreak of World War I has been provided by C. Vann Woodward in *Origins of the New South, 1877–1913* (Baton Rouge, 1951). See also his *The Strange Career of Jim Crow* (New York, 1966). In addition, see August Meier, *Negro Thought in America, 1880–1915: Racial Ideologies in the Age of Booker T. Washington* (Ann Arbor, 1969) and August Meier and Elliot Rudwick, *From Plantation to Ghetto: An Interpretive History of American Negroes* (New York, 1966), especially chapters 4, 5, and 6. A slightly different perspective on the era appears in Nell Irvin Painter's *Standing at Armageddon: The United States, 1877–1919* (New York, 1987), a book that is, in the author's words, "mostly a hybrid political labor history" that "pays attention to social changes. . . ."

8. Vann Woodward, *The Strange Career of Jim Crow*, 48.

9. Ibid.

10. *Dallas Morning News*, August 18, 1892, cited in Vann Woodward, *Origins of the New South*, 257.

11. This argument is persuasively made by C. Vann Woodward in *The Strange Career of Jim Crow*.

12. Ibid., 89–90.

13. Such incidents occurred, for example, as Blacks who rode in railroad cars *now* reserved for Whites (i.e., after the Plessy decision was handed down) were presumed guilty in this and similar situations.

14. I. A. Newby, *Jim Crow's Defense: Anti-Negro Thought in America 1900–1930* (Baton Rouge, 1965), viii–ix.

15. *Atlanta Journal*, June 2, 1908, 2ff.

16. William F. Holmes, *The White Chief: James Kimble Vardaman* (Baton Rouge, 1970), 195.

17. For a brief discussion of Vardaman's opposition to convict leasing and his role in its abolition see Holmes, *The White Chief*, chapter 6.

18. Holmes, *The White Chief*, 114.

19. Ibid., 384; also 287.

20. Newby, *Jim Crow's Defense*, xi.

21. Holmes, *The White Chief*, 99.

22. *Greenwood Commonwealth*, January 31, 1903, cited in Willard B. Gatewood, Jr., "A Republican President and Democratic State Politics: Theodore Roosevelt in the Mississippi Primary of 1903," *Presidential Studies Quarterly* (Summer 1984), 424–36. Also on the Minnie Cox affair, see Holmes, *The White Chief*, 100–01.

23. Holmes, *The White Chief*, 101.

24. Holmes, *The White Chief*, 89, quoting *Greenwood Commonwealth*, October 10, 1902.

25. Ibid., 109, quoting *Jackson Daily-Clarion Ledger*, July 24, 1903.

26. Wilbur Cash, *The Mind of the South* (New York, 1969), 253.

27. Newby, *Jim Crow's Defense*, 137.

28. Holmes, *The White Chief*, 89, quoting *Greenwood Commonwealth*, May 25, 1900.

29. Ibid., 79, quoting *Greenwood Commonwealth*, June 30, 1899.

30. *Mississippi House Journal* (1904), 840–44, 867–68; Holmes, *The White Chief*.

31. Holmes, *The White Chief*, 103.

32. Of course, this amendment did not include women. Furthermore, many Blacks and many poor Whites were prevented from voting by the wording of the amendment, which permitted the denial of the right to vote by poll taxes, literacy tests, intricate registration requirements, and similar machinations.

33. Holmes, *The White Chief*, 103.

34. Alan Trelease, *White Terror: The Ku Klux Klan Conspiracy and Southern Reconstruction* (New York, 1971), 422.

35. Benjamin Quarles, *The Negro in the Making of America* (New York, 1964), 192.

36. Trelease, *White Terror*, xi.

37. Ibid., xii.

38. *New York Age*, September 27, 1906, 1.

39. Ralph Ginzburg (ed.), *One Hundred Years of Lynchings: A Shocking Documentary of Race Violations in America* (New York, 1962), back cover.

40. Mary Frances Berry and John W. Blassingame, *Long Memory: The Black Experience in America* (New York, 1982), 124–25.

41. *Atlanta Journal*, June 14, 1908. The *Journal* might have seen this as a modification of ideas presented by Booker T. Washington in his "Atlanta Compromise" speech in 1895, the "stair-step plan to progress and citizenship." Consequently, for some, the logic may not have been so convoluted.

42. See Constitution of the State of Mississippi (1890), article 12, Sections 240–47. See also Wharton, *The Negro in Mississippi 1865–1890*, 215, and Woodward, *The Strange Career of Jim Crow*,

84. Lerone Bennet discusses the inclusion of a "good character" clause and other requirements, in *Before the Mayflower: A History of the Negro in America, 1619–1964* (Baltimore, 1966), 234.

43. August 14, 1890, cited in Wharton, *The Negro in Mississippi, 1865–1890*, 210.

44. Bennet, *Before the Mayflower*, 234.

45. John Hope Franklin, *From Slavery to Freedom* (New York, 1980), 226.

46. John W. Crowell, "The Challenge of the Disenfranchised," American Negro Academy Occasional Paper No. 22 (Washington, D.C.: American Negro Academy, 1924), 5.

47. Vann Woodward, *Origins of the New South, 1877–1913*, chapter 12.

48. Thomas E. Miller, "A Plea Against the Disenfranchisement of the Negro," in *The Voice of Black America: Major Speeches by Negroes in the United States, 1797–1971*, ed. Philip Foner (New York, 1972), 586.

49. Ibid., 582–83.

50. George B. Tindall, *South Carolina Negroes, 1877–1900* (Columbia, 1952), 69. Tindall also reports on intricate registration and election laws popular in the state of South Carolina.

51. It is worth noting that this was sometimes an embarrassment for Whites in areas where there was evidence of miscegenation, because some Blacks had White grandparents and parents, especially fathers.

52. Peter M. Bergman, *The Chronological History of the Negro in America* (New York, 1969), 506.

53. Professors Mary Berry and John Blassingame estimate that 79 percent of all Black farmers in 1930 were tenants. The term "tenant" is used inclusively for sharecroppers, crop lieners, and

tenant farmers. See Berry and Blassingame, *Long Memory*, 198.

54. Daniel, *The Shadow of Slavery*, 19.

55. For details on the Alonzo Bailey case, see Peter Daniel, "Up From Slavery and Down to Peonage: The Alonzo Bailey Case," *Journal of American History* (December 1970), 654–70; Daniel, *The Shadow of Slavery*, chapter 4; Ray Stannard Baker, "A Pawn in the Struggle for Freedom," *American Magazine* (September 1911), 609–12; Louis Harlan, *Booker T. Washington: The Wizard of Tuskegee, 1901–1915* (New York, 1983), 250–51.

56. Louis Harlan, in *The Wizard of Tuskegee* (250–51), states that the advance was $20.

57. For more on the connection between slavery, sharecropping, tenant farming, peonage, and convict leasing, see Berry and Blassingame, *Long Memory*, 39–40, 195, 233–34.

58. As Booker T. Washington realized, the southern contract labor laws meant that "any white man who cares to charge that a colored man has promised to work for him and has not done so, or who has gotten money from him and not paid it back, can have the colored man sent to the chain gang." Daniel, *The Shadow of Slavery*, 67.

59. This discussion of pseudoscientific racism is drawn mainly although not exclusively from two sources: George M. Frederickson, *The Black Image in the White Mind: The Debate on Afro-American Character and Destiny, 1817–1914* (New York, 1971); and Newby, *Jim Crow's Defense*.

60. Newby, *Jim Crow's Defense*, xi.

61. The late-twentieth-century theorists Arthur Jensen (Stanford), William Shockley (Harvard), and Michael Levin (City College of New York) may represent the current incarnation of pseudoscientific race theorists in the United States.

62. Fredrickson, *The Black Image*, 255.

63. Ibid.

64. Berry and Blassingame, *Long Memory*, 308.

65. Berry and Blassingame, *Long Memory*, 210.

66. See Robert L. Zangrando, "The NAACP and a Federal Antilynching Bill, 1934–1940," *The Journal of Negro History* (April 1965), 106–17.

67. Booker T. Washington's "Atlanta Exposition Address" (Atlanta, Georgia, 1895) can be found, among many other places, in Booker T. Washington, *Up From Slavery: An Autobiography* (New York: Doubleday and Company, Inc., 1933), 157–71.

68. *AME Church Review* (January 1917).

69. See Alan H. Spear, *Black Chicago: The Making of a Negro Ghetto, 1890–1920* (Chicago, 1967). Spear, although concentrating on the migration from the cotton South to the Midwest (Chicago), makes some generalizations that are useful for understanding Black migration to the North and far West. More recently, Nicholas Lemann has contributed *The Promised Land: The Great Black Migration and How It Changed America* (New York, 1991).

70. For information on the Kansas migration and "Pap" Singleton, consult Roy Garvin, "Benjamin or 'Pap' Singleton and His Followers," *Journal of Negro History* (January 1948), 7–23, and Walter Fleming, "Pap Singleton, The Moses of the Colored Exodus," *American Journal of Sociology* (July 1909), 61–82. Most important, however, see Nell I. Painter, *Exodusters: Black Migration to Kansas After Reconstruction* (New York, 1979).

71. The reasons why Bishop Turner has still not attracted a full-length scholarly biography remain a mystery. In any event, the place to begin for an introduction to the life, thought, and activism of Bishop Turner is Edwin S. Redkey, *Black Exodus: Black Nationalist and Back-to-Africa Movements, 1890–1910* (New Haven, 1969), and Edwin S. Redkey (ed.), *Respect Black: The Writings and Speeches of Henry McNeal Turner* (New York, 1971). A fine

Master's thesis on Bishop Turner is Carol A. Page, "Henry McNeal Turner and the Ethiopian Movement in South Africa, 1896–1904" (Roosevelt University, 1973).

72. For the details on the Chief Sam movement, consult William E. Bittle and Gilbert Geis, *The Longest Way Home: Chief Albert C. Sam's Back-to-Africa Movement* (Detroit, 1964).

73. The best book on Garvey is Tony Martin, *Race First: The Ideological and Organization Struggles of Marcus Garvey and the Universal Negro Improvement Association* (Westport, 1976).

74. Wolters, *Negroes and the Great Depression*, 47–48.

75. Wolters, *Negroes and the Great Depression, passim.*

76. Most of this is captured in an eleven-volume anthology of racist writings entitled *Anti-Black Thought 1863–1925: The Negro Problem*, edited and introduced by John David Smith (New York, 1993). In volume 2 of his *Black Folk Here and There: An Essay in History and Anthropology* (Los Angeles: Center for Afro-American Studies, University of California, 1990), the late St. Clair Drake elevates our understanding of the theories of color prejudice over time and in different locations and therefore is must reading on the subject of race, racism, and history.

77. See Robert L. Harris, Jr., "The Intellectual and Institutional Development of Africana Studies," in *Three Essays: Black Studies in the United States*, by Robert L. Harris, Jr., Darlene Clark Hine, and Nellie McKay (New York, 1990).

78. N. Gordon Carper, "Martin Tabert, Martyr of an Era," *Florida Historical Quarterly* (October 1973), 122–23.

CHAPTER TWO

ORIGINS: THE BEGINNING OF THE SOUTHERN CONVICT LEASE SYSTEM

I T IS EXTREMELY DIFFICULT to establish conclusively when and where the system of convict leasing began in the United States, or in what became the United States. It is also rather hazardous to deal in absolutes such as the best or worst, never, always, or, as in the case in point, the first. It seems reasonably clear, however, that leasing did not begin in the South, although it was certainly made famous—or infamous—there.

Early penal practices in the United States, like much else during the country's infancy, were substantially influenced by British traditions, customs, practices, and laws. One writer makes the bold statement that the Virginia jail system "is the oldest in America"—that is, British America. The explanation goes on that, since the English settled the Virginia colony and it was "coincident with the establishment of . . . Jamestown," they transported their values and culture from the mother country and "the prisons and the treatment of prisoners in Virginia [too] represent a phase of cultural heritage from England, though modified by adaptation to the new environment."[1] Although "no record" could be found of this first Jamestown jail, "something of the sort existed because imprisonment was mentioned as early as 1608."[2] Authorization appears to have been provided by the "Articles, Instructions and Orders" issued by King James I on November 20, 1606, for the "good order and government of the colonies. . . ."[3]

Throughout the seventeenth and eighteenth centuries, penal policy, such as it was, seems to have been informed by a view that administering corporal punishment was the way to deal with those who broke the law. Flogging was commonplace, the number of lashes varying with the offense. Branding, cropping, the pillory, maiming, and the like were widespread. Capital crimes such as murder and rape frequently resulted in death for the perpetrator.

PRE–CIVIL WAR SOUTHERN PRISON SYSTEMS

The nineteenth century represents a watershed of sorts in southern penal history, as several states established penitentiaries for the confinement of criminals based on a new philosophy of punishment—one that, instead of advocating deterrence through retribution, favored crime prevention through reformation, rehabilitation, and instruction. The development of state-controlled penitentiaries for such a purpose posed problems for southern state legislatures and governments. Among them was figuring out a cost-effective means of maintaining a prison system. For some, economic self-sufficiency was satisfactory; others hoped to turn a profit. None wanted to be strapped with the financial burden of caring for convicts, for whom there was generally disdain and repugnance. It was this concern over expense that drove most southern states to adopt some form of convict leasing soon after the Civil War. A few southern states, however, resorted to leasing before 1865.

As the penitentiary system evolved in the nineteenth century in the United States, the South was influenced by the competing philosophies of the Pennsylvania idea and the Auburn system. The Pennsylvania scheme emphasized solitary confinement and work for prisoners. An inmate might spend all of his prison time in isolation, cut off from other prisoners, family, friends, and the outside world. Repentance and rehabilitation would come through labor and the Bible. The Auburn plan, which was not a substantial departure from that of Pennsylvania, originated in Auburn, New York. Prisoners worked together, worked in silence, and remained in isolation during nonwork time. In addition, religion, as an instrument of reformation, enjoyed a priority in Auburn philosophy.[4]

As noted earlier, convict leasing in the South probably began in Kentucky in 1825, when Joel Scott, a merchant living in Scott County, was appointed "keeper and agent of the penitentiary by the Governor." Terms of the agreement were that Scott would have "whole and sole management" of the eighty-four convicts he described as being in a "most destitute and deplorable condition, filthy and diseased, and all of them so bare of clothing as to be wholly unfit for any mechanical occupation."[5] Scott received a 6 percent, $6,000 loan from Kentucky, to be advanced "out of the first sale or sales of raw materials or manufactured articles in the penitentiary."[6] This, apparently, would be the fruit of convict labor. As compensation for his services, the newly appointed Principal Keeper of the penitentiary was to receive one-half of the year's net profits, after the $6,000 owed the state had been deducted. If the profits of the penitentiary during any year of this seven-year lease fell below $1,000, Scott was to "make up the deficiency, so as to guarantee a clear profit of at least one thousand dollars per annum to the State, after the first year. . . ."[7] With the exception of the "right of reprieve of pardon," which the enabling legislation reserved for the governor, Scott had total control over the lives, labor, and fortunes of this group of the state's lawbreakers.

The Kentucky penitentiary opened in 1800 as a place of confinement at hard labor for criminals. Throughout much of its early history, this penitentiary was operated by a lessee who rented the prison and its convicts from the state. The lessee was given total control by the legislature and was usually selected by the state's lawmakers. Lessees were wholly responsible for the prisoners' work day, diet, health care, safety and security, and virtually everything else.

Prison labor in this case included making household furniture, hemp, rope, bags, and other items. The earnings from the sale of goods made by prison labor paid for convict maintenance and care.

It was fairly easy for a lessee to make a handsome profit by cutting corners on necessities for convicts and by neglecting penitentiary buildings and grounds. Moreover, lessees sometimes overcharged the state for expenses and, in addition to being corrupt themselves, took good advantage of the fraud and corruption practiced by legislators, sheriffs, wardens, and other government and county officials. These were practices that generally characterized the system. Lessee James Keigwin assumed control of Kentucky convicts in 1828, after problems emerged with the Scott lease and with lessees who briefly succeeded Scott. He paid all penitentiary expenses and an annual rental of $500. Keigwin was able to take "advantage of a low rental, a steady increase of convicts, economy in the management of the financial affairs of the prison, and [with] a judicious application of convict labor, he succeeded in the eight years of his administration in amassing a considerable fortune."[8] In 1855 Colonel Zeb Ward, who later became the principal lessee in the state of Arkansas, was said to have leased the Kentucky Penitentiary for four years and "managed the institution profitably to himself and satisfactorily to the State."[9]

The development of penitentiaries in the states of the Old Confederacy during the antebellum decades was far from uniform. Many of them experimented with some form of leasing but really did not perfect the system until after the war. All, with the exception of Florida and the Carolinas, erected state prisons for criminals. In these three states, the punishment of lawbreakers and the administration of justice and correction were reserved for the counties and local officials. Corporal punishment and fines usually prevailed.

In pre–Civil War Florida, convicts were leased to both individuals and corporations for work in phosphate mines and turpentine camps. One investigator of Florida leasing states that "the institution of convict leasing is perhaps as ancient as history itself."[10] Convicts were "hired out" in North Carolina as early as 1831. This practice was permitted by the General Assembly primarily for free Blacks unable to pay fines levied against them for breaking the law in the state. They would be turned over to the sheriff, who in turn would lease their labor to anyone willing to pay their fine and give bond for their safety and custody. If no one stepped forward to pay the fine, the convicted individual might be auctioned to the highest bidder for specified periods or service.[11]

The situation in South Carolina differed slightly. Convicts were held in jails in the county of their conviction. Some of the counties maintained workhouses where long-term prisoners (felons) were utilized mainly at cutting stone. Short-term prisoners or misdemeanants were usually fined and, if they could not pay, were flogged and dismissed, therefore posing no serious problem for penal authorities. When the penitentiary was established in 1866, "before reconstruction had interfered with control by the white people," responsibility for convicts passed from the counties to the state.[12]

The establishment of a state penitentiary in Tennessee in 1829 had been delayed for a decade by limited funds and political squabbling, despite agitation from reformers. The local jails and prisons served merely as holding pens until punishment could be administered by "whipping, branding, stocks or death." Eventually this treatment became outmoded and considered "barbarous," at which time the need for more jail space became apparent, leading to increased demand for a state-controlled institution. Small-scale manufacturing such as carpentry, shoemaking, and blacksmithing within the prison walls accompanied the establishment of the Tennessee penitentiary.[13]

In 1838 the Arkansas legislature committed the state to the erection of a penitentiary, which opened to receive convicts eleven years later. From the outset, this institution was leased or subleased to private parties because of the determination of state officials and legislators to make the penitentiary self-supporting. When sectional differences led to war in the United States, the Arkansas State Prison housed prisoners of war and deserters. When Union troops reached the penitentiary in September of 1863, it was empty. The lessee, one A. J. Ward, had fled, and Federal authorities took control and held it until 1867.[14]

The Alabama penitentiary opened for business in 1841. Like several of its southern sister states, Alabama had huge debts and general financial distress, which left little money for the prison's operation and management. On February 4, 1846, legislation was enacted that permitted the state to experiment with "a type of lease." The entire prison, including all the inmates, buildings, machinery, and materials, "lock, stock and barrel," were turned over to lessee J. G. Graham, who became the warden. The offices of physician and inspector of the penitentiary were retained, and all others abolished. The lease was for six years; the state had no financial obligation and the lessee was to receive all earnings from the labor of convicts. Although an annual rental of the penitentiary of $650 was promised to the state in a subsequent six-year lease (1852–58), no record could be found of the state ever receiving any payment for the first or second lease.[15]

By 1844 the Louisiana legislature ceased being influenced by the idea of prison as a place of reform or rehabilitation for convicts. In addition, the governor's message to the legislature that same year noted that the penitentiary, up to 1844, had cost the state almost half a million dollars. The governor recommended consideration of the "Kentucky Plan," which was the lease system. When the Sixteenth Louisiana Legislature adopted legislation authorizing the governor to "lease the said penitentiary for a term not to exceed five years," control of the state's convicts passed into private hands, where it remained until the twentieth century. During this fifty-seven-year hiatus, the Bayou State was held hostage by the convict lease system, which sought to make money from prison labor if it could, but, in any event, to relieve the state of the financial burden of maintaining a costly prison system. Act Number 79 of 1844 meticulously set forth the limits of the lease, which, as was the case with much of the later lease legislation, was frequently ignored by the lessees. No competition was to be permitted with free labor or "the citizen mechanics of Baton Rouge, . . . carpenters, blacksmiths . . . or other mechanical work which is pursued by the citizens of Baton Rouge. . . ." This competition was a source of concern in other states, too. In addition, lessees were to provide "the same rations, clothing and rest, as are given by the existing regulations; and to change nothing in the present treatment of said prisoners. . . ." The labor of the prisoners was to be confined to the "manufacture of coarse cotton and woolen cloths, and of negro shoes, and of cotton bagging and rope from hemp . . . and such other mechanical business as may be needed for and used by said penitentiary. . . ." A bond of $25,000 was to be posted by the lessee "for the faithful performance of his contract" and the state agreed to advance a loan of $15,000, at a rate of 6 percent, "the interest payable semi-annually and the capital to be repaid in three years."[16]

The leasing practices of other southern states were duly noted in Mississippi and stimulated advocates in 1846 and 1848. Because the penitentiary failed to turn a profit in either year, and since the leasing of runaway slaves to counties and municipalities proved to be a way to save money in antebellum Mississippi, propositions to lease the prison were advanced. In 1846 the proposal "was referred to a Joint Legislative Committee which concluded . . . it was better to continue [the penitentiary's] management by officers of the State." Two years later a similar proposal was again rejected in the legislature by a small margin when many of its would-be supporters were absent from Jackson, the state capitol, at the time of the voting, otherwise preoccupied at home by the annual demands of the planting season. Between 1848 and the Civil War the penitentiary's financial fortunes apparently changed for the better, because no new efforts to lease surfaced in the legislature.[17]

In the early "good old days" in Texas, a state penitentiary was not needed because there were few convicts. It is reported that "white men were honest and law abiding and if a negro committed such an indiscretion as stealing his Master's 'shote,' or burglarizing his smoke house, and was accidentally detected in the act, he was forthwith taken in hand and soundly thrashed and admonished to do so no more, which he invariably promised and that was the end of the matter."[18] But the situation changed in Texas, and by 1856 a penitentiary was established at Huntsville. Before 1865, however, few Blacks were incarcerated there. It was state policy until 1876 to confine and work state convicts within the penitentiary walls. No record of pre–Civil War leasing in Texas could be found.[19]

Georgia occupies a special place in the history of convict leasing in the South. Leasing was at least as bad here—brutal for convicts, rife with corruption—as anywhere in the South, perhaps worse. It was as extensive and as widespread, and, as in other states, its collapse was the result of a highly visible persistent public newspaper and legislative effort, not to mention major behind-the-scenes efforts on the part of Black leaders.

In late eighteenth- and early nineteenth-century Georgia, the use of capital punishment kept the number of criminals in need of state care relatively low. Long-term incarceration as punishment was rarely invoked. A penitentiary was authorized and $10,000 appropriated for construction in 1811; the first convicts were admitted in 1817. The penitentiary was abolished by the legislature on Christmas eve of 1831 following an "accidental" fire the previous May, but was reestablished in 1832. Twenty years later, Lewis Zachary, the Principal Keeper of the penitentiary, proposed to lease it for six years if lawmakers would make $10,000 available for refurbishing the buildings. A minority of the House of Assembly Penitentiary Committee recommended approval of the lease, and lease legislation passed in the House by a vote of sixty-five to thirty. However, the bill was defeated in the State Senate and the penitentiary was kept under state control. During the Civil War, Governor Joseph E. Brown offered to pardon all convicts who volunteered to join the Confederate Army. When General Sherman marched through and razed the state, the penitentiary buildings were destroyed and the remaining prisoners escaped. A full-fledged system of convict leasing in Georgia would await Confederate defeat.[20]

THE INFLUENCE OF SLAVERY

The economic, political, and social life of much of antebellum southern society was anchored in slavery and its anticipated expansion beyond existing borders. The South's ideas on everything regarding Blacks in those days were informed and dominated by the slavocracy. The assumption of White superiority and its impact on public policy and practices in a Black/White context went essentially unchanged (although not unchallenged) for centuries in the South, in the United States generally, and in the world. According to one writer,

> [A] characteristic of plantation economy was slavery—a
> system which resulted in the social, political and economic
> domination of white over black. Until slavery was abolished
> and until the Negro could live with the white on a level of
> social equality, there could be no serious attempts at prison
> reform. By its very nature, the institution of slavery negated
> most efforts toward humanitarian reform in the South.[21]

Another writer, a most thorough investigator of southern
penology and prison reform, declared unabashedly that the
reason the penal system was so backward in the South was
because "the section was dominated by the slave-plantation
system, and there could be no serious efforts toward humanitarian reforms so long as black men were forced to live in slavery.
. . . An acceptance of slavery necessarily destroyed the philosophical basis for a prison reform movement."[22] When the southern
slaveholder's defense of slavery shifted from "positive good to
necessary evil" in the 1830s, most of the South's leading intellectuals, politicians, and businesspeople joined the apology.

Because of slavery and the ironclad hold it had on the
thinking of everything related to African-Americans, the question of what to do about those who broke existing laws was
rhetorical. An occasional Black person may have turned up in
prison but, by and large, Blacks were punished for their crimes
by slavemasters. Free Blacks received some arbitrary corporal
punishment (usually whipping) or might be fined and then run
out of town by the local law enforcement agent or his self-appointed surrogates. The Georgia case was typical, where

> . . . under the slavery regime, punishment for crime[s] com-
> mitted by Negro slaves was administered largely by the
> plantations. Neither free Negroes nor slaves were subjected

to imprisonment in the penitentiary. The most common punishment for the misdeeds of Negroes was whipping on the bare back. The number of lashes for each crime was regulated by law.[23]

All of this changed precipitously with the end of the Civil War and the adoption of the Thirteenth Amendment, declaring slavery illegal. At the same time, the number of Blacks in southern jails and prisons rose sharply. The White prison population also increased at this time. The search was now under way by former Confederate states for a solution to a new economic and penal problem. The answer was the convict lease system, which grew rapidly under postwar conditions.

The most decisive event in the history of southern penology was the Civil War. Before this conflict the penal system had been spared extensive involvement with the servile proletariat because the monetary value of slaves led owners to demand a degree of sovereignty over the management and control of their chattels. This economic consideration had led to the development of a dual system of criminal jurisprudence in which slaves were guaranteed most of the legal rights of free persons, but shielded in most cases from the legal punishments mandated by the criminal code. Under this system, corporal punishment on the plantation had been the rule and not the exception, local magistrates had served as arbitrators whenever crimes by slaves reached beyond the confines of a plantation, and penal sanctions relating to slaves was much more severe in law than in practice.[24]

AFTER EMANCIPATION

Union victory in the Civil War immediately resulted in the emancipation of four million African-Americans in the South. Although the passage of the Fourteenth Amendment entitled ex-slaves to legal equality with Whites, they did not gain economic or social equality. Moreover, since Blacks were stripped of their economic value and the "protection" they "enjoyed" from the law and penal code as slaves, after 1865 they quickly became victims of a criminal justice system that left much to be desired. Local jails and state penitentiaries now had to accommodate former slaves who in short order wound up incarcerated far out of proportion to their numbers in the population. This eventuality was assured despite the new political, economic, and social realities of life in the postbellum South, because Blacks were powerless and had long tenure as the "flotsam and jetsam" of Southern society. "After the Civil War, the disposition of convicts became a perplexing problem," concludes one authority on leasing in Georgia.[25]

The difficulties of control and punishment shifted to individual states, which, disrupted by war, were unable and unwilling to meet the challenge effectively. Blacks, for their part, in the view of some, "had little incentive to work; furthermore [they] had little conception of the obligations, advantages and disadvantages of [their] new status. It is not surprising therefore, that [they] fell into crime and paid the penalty in ever increasing numbers."[26]

Notwithstanding their defeat in war, White southerners remained in control of southern society through the years historians call "Presidential Reconstruction." During these years (1865–67), President Lincoln's intent to heal the nation's wounds

as quickly and as painlessly as possible for the South was illustrated by his "with malice toward none but charity for all"
disposition, which led him to promulgate a lenient set of conditions for the South's readmission to the Union. Andrew Johnson, a southerner and a Democrat, became president after Lincoln was assassinated. As former slaves began "testing" their new
freedom by violating Black Codes (which imposed curfews,
prohibited the possession of firearms, and so forth), vagrancy
laws, and other legislation that circumscribed their actions, their
eventual imprisonment became virtually inevitable.

When the Civil War ended, the South was in ruins. Its
coffers were empty, destruction and impoverishment abounded,
White morale was low, and paranoia was pervasive. The special
way of life that had characterized the White South had ended in
the most humiliating fashion, and an "army of occupation" in
the form of Union troops was on the way. Slaves were freed and
made citizens and Blacks would be voting, holding office, and
having a measure of political influence that was antithetical to
everything most Whites in the South could have imagined only
a few years earlier. Governor William Marvin probably spoke
for much of the South when he declared before the Florida
legislature in 1865: "[T]he people are left by the war greatly
impoverished . . . and . . . the state treasury is empty."[27] In
Mississippi the demand for dollars for the penitentiary "fell on
the Legislature at a time when public schools, hospitals, and
other state-supported institutions were struggling to survive on
meager funds, and legislators were not prepared to make penology a high financial priority. The choice was simple: re-establish
corporal punishment or implement the cost-effective but socially
dubious lease system under state control."[28] The situation was
no better in South Carolina, where ". . . the end of the war

found every county in the State depleted in finances. The maintenance of the convicted persons in the jails was quite an item of
expense to each county."[29] And so it went throughout the
South. The entire region "was economically broken, state treasuries were empty, penitentiaries were in ruins, and crime was
increasing. The convict lease system seemed to fit into the pro-
pensities of the times and to offer the solutions for the penal
problems."[30]

The key ingredient in the adoption of convict leasing in the
South was economic. The increase in the prison population and
the overtaxing of state resources placed enormous economic
demands on individual states. The effort to keep costs down in
maintaining the penitentiary was uppermost as a motive of state
legislators and other officials. It was not a time for humanitarian
concerns for convicts. If the prison could be self-supporting, the
first objective was satisfied.[31] If the penitentiary could turn a
profit for the state, that was a bonus; to use a current cliché, it
was "found money." The lessees, for their part, had profit as
"their sole objective." In Louisiana the profit objective of the
state became identical with that of the lessees, "to make money."[32] Expenses had to be held to a bare minimum if profits
were to be maximized. Costs for reform, rehabilitation, food,
clothing, doctors, and other professionals were all big-ticket
items and cut deeply into earnings. Such a profit-driven preoccupation could only permit the system to be maintained at a
subsistence level. There was little fear of exhausting the labor
supply, which was considered unlimited since southern Blacks
could easily be jailed under one pretext or another. This situation was ensured by their peon status and even by the temporary
establishment of Black Codes restricting the movement and
behavior of Blacks. These new Black Codes were not much more

than unsophisticated, warmed-over versions of the old slave codes. But they got the job done. As the lease system grew and developed, little notice was taken of its ignominy and no outcry was sounded.

Pre–Civil War experiments in leasing convicts laid the foundation for what came later. A mature system mushroomed in the South in the last quarter of the nineteenth century and the early years of the twentieth century. Southern Blacks were trapped in this penal quagmire in excessive numbers and percentages of the total prison population of each southern state. For the victims, many of whom were ex-slaves, this predicament represented nothing short of a revisit to slavery. Those Blacks who were former slaves, and became victims of the convict lease system—especially those convicted and incarcerated on trumped-up charges, or otherwise innocent of crimes for which they were imprisoned—must have imagined themselves in a time warp. They could turn to few quarters or in few directions to find relief from their nightmare or to obtain assistance in being released, because too many state and county prison or other officials from whom they might seek help had a direct or indirect stake in maintaining, and even expanding, convict leasing.

Demands for an end to the system did not come until the trail of horrors left by it became an anachronism, and the opportunities for continued profits began to evaporate. In the meantime, all of those elements that came to characterize convict leasing and certify its reputation for opprobrium, varying in order of magnitude and duration, were found in all states of the Old Confederacy from the Reconstruction era through the beginning of World War II.

NOTES

1. Frank William Hoffer et al., *The Jails of Virginia: A Study of the Local Penal System* (New York: Appleton-Century Company Inc., n.d.), 13.

2. *The Virginia Jail System: Past and Present With A Program For The Future*, Report of the Legislative Jail Commission to the General Assembly of Virginia (Richmond, 1939), 8.

3. Hoffer et al., *The Jails of Virginia*, 13.

4. For a discussion of the origins of the prison system in the United States, see an old but still useful study by Harry E. Barnes entitled *The Evolution of Penology in Pennsylvania* (Indianapolis, 1927).

5. William C. Sneed, *A Report on the History and Mode of Management of the Kentucky Penitentiary From Its Origin, in 1798, to March 1, 1860* (Frankfort, 1860), 161, 164.

6. Ibid., 161.

7. Ibid.

8. Lucien V. Rule, *The City of Dead Souls and How It Was Made Alive Again: A Hundred Years Within the Walls* (Louisville, 1920), 45.

9. *Arkansas Gazette*, December 29, 1884, 2.

10. Gordon Carper, "The Convict Lease System in Florida, 1866–1923," Ph.D. diss. (Florida State University, 1964), 3.

11. Herbert Stacy McKay, "Convict Leasing in North Carolina, 1870–1934," Master's thesis (University of North Carolina, Chapel Hill, 1942), 10.

12. Ibid.

13. Jesse Crawford Crowe, "The Origin and Development of Tennessee's Prison Problem, 1831–1871," *Tennessee Historical Quarterly* (June 1956), 112–14.

14. Jane Zimmerman, "The Convict Lease System in Arkansas and the Fight for Abolition," *Arkansas Historical Quarterly* (Autumn 1949), 172–73.

15. Malcolm Moos, *State Penal Administration in Alabama* (Tuscaloosa: University of Alabama, 1942), 5; Saffold Bernet, *Handbook of Alabama* (Spartanburg, SC: The Reprint Company Publishers, reprinted 1975; originally published 1892), 254–57.

16. Acts passed at the second session at the Sixteenth Legislature, 43 (hereinafter cited as "Acts of Louisiana," 1844); Elizabeth Wisner, *Public Welfare Administration in Louisiana* (Chicago: University of Chicago Press, 1930), 147; Leon Stout, "Origins and Early History of the Louisiana Penitentiary," Master's thesis (Louisiana State University, 1934). See, especially, appendix 2 in Stout for a complete text of the 1844 lease.

17. Ruby E. Cooley, "A History of the Mississippi Penal Farm System, 1890–1935: Punishment, Politics and Profit in Penal Affairs," Master's thesis (University of Southern Mississippi, 1981), 6–7.

18. John N. Henderson, "The Lease System in Texas," in *National Prison Association Proceedings for 1897* (Austin, 1897), 1–2. The meaning of "shote" (a colloquialism of the era) is unclear, but it probably refers to chickens, livestock, or something similar.

19. Ibid.

20. A. Elizabeth Taylor, "The Origin and Development of the Convict Lease System in Georgia," *Georgia Historical Quarterly* 26 (1949), 3–5; A. J. McKelway, "The Convict Lease System in Georgia," *The Outlook* (1908), 6–7.

21. Carper, "The Convict Lease System in Florida," 7.

22. Hilda Jane Zimmerman, "Penal Systems and Penal Reforms in the South Since the Civil War," Ph.D. diss. (University of North Carolina, Chapel Hill, 1947), 48.

23. Taylor, "The Origin and Development of the Convict Lease System in Georgia," 5–6.

24. Cooley, "A History of the Mississippi Penal Farm System," 5.

25. Taylor, "The Origin and Development of the Convict Lease System in Georgia," 5–6.

26. McKay, "Convict Leasing in North Carolina," 4.

27. Carper, "The Convict Lease System in Florida," 23.

28. Cooley, "A History of the Mississippi Penal Farm System," 6.

29. Albert D. Oliphant, *The Evolution of the Penal System of South Carolina from 1866 to 1916* (Columbia: The State Company, 1916), 3.

30. Zimmerman, "The Convict Lease System in Arkansas," 172–73; Carper, "The Convict Lease System in Florida," citing Fletcher M. Green, "Some Aspects of the Convict Lease System in Southern States," in *Essays In Southern History*, ed. Fletcher M. Green (Chapel Hill, 1949), 115.

31. McKay, "Convict Leasing in North Carolina," 1; Albert Burton Moore, *History of Alabama and Her People*, vol. 1 (New York: American Historical Society, 1927), 978–79; Mark T. Carleton, *Politics and Punishment: The History of the Louisiana State Penal System* (Baton Rouge: Louisiana State University Press, 1971), 7.

32. Carleton, *Politics and Punishment*, 11.

CHAPTER THREE

CHARACTERISTICS:
RACE AND THE
DOMINANT FEATURES IN
CONVICT LEASING

T HE AUTUMN OF 1921 BEARS NO particular significance for historians. It was not a season to be remembered, like the spring of 1865 when the Civil War ended or the fall of 1929 when the stock market "crashed" into immortality. It had none of the eerie Armageddon-like fear brought on by the United States' entry into World War II with the bombing of Pearl Harbor. It was a time, however, that produced a martyr for convict leasing. When Martin Tabert set out to see the world, infected like so many others of his time by the spirit of wanderlust and buoyed by excitement over Allied victory in the "war to end all wars," he could not know that he would never again see the quiet farming community of Munich, North Dakota, that had been his home.[1]

Martin was twenty-two years of age when he headed south in 1921 to see the sights and have a good time. No clear record exists of the route he took or the amount of time he spent in specific states. He started out with a little money, but he probably worked as he gravitated southward to a warmer climate. By early December he had made it to Florida, a state then notorious for county convict leasing. Events in Martin Tabert's life moved rather quickly following his arrival in the "sunshine state." On December 15 he was arrested as a vagrant for riding the train without a ticket, and was fined $25, which he could not pay. Therefore, he was sentenced to ninety days in the county jail and turned over to the local sheriff. In Florida in 1921, county convicts were leased to private parties. In the Tabert case, the lessee was the Putnam Lumber Company, which was actually owned by a Wisconsin company that paid the county $20 per convict per month for convict labor. Between mid-December and the end of January 1922, Tabert was "enslaved" to Putnam, where it was later revealed that he, like other convicts, was rigorously worked, poorly fed, and frequently beaten.

On February 2, 1922, the Putnam Lumber Company notified the Tabert family that Martin had died the previous day "of fever and other complications."[2] A subsequent investigation of the Martin Tabert case was conducted, involving the governors of North Dakota and Florida and other state officials, both state legislatures, several newspapers, prominent citizens, ex-convicts, Putnam employees (especially the "whipping boss" who was responsible for Martin's death and tried for murder, and the company physician, who initially gave an inaccurate account of the cause of death), and the county sheriff, J. R. Jones, and his deputies. The investigation revealed the following: (1) Tabert's parents had mailed $75 to Sheriff Jones to pay Martin's fine, but the envelope was returned unopened; (2) Sheriff Jones received a $20 commission from Putnam for every male convict sent to them for ninety days or more; (3) the Sheriff and the lumber company attempted to conceal the cause of Martin's death; and (4) Putnam exhibited a pattern of torture, barbaric punishment (including "dragging the strap through sugar and sand" between lashes in whippings), denial of adequate medical care, and a conspiracy to "railroad" men into the lease system and other iniquitous practices.[3] There were no convictions in the Martin Tabert case. The most important result of the investigation was that it attracted national attention to the horrors of county convict leasing in Florida and triggered a movement that led to the end of county leasing in 1923, four years after the leasing of state convicts had been abolished.[4]

Martin Tabert was not Black. As such, his story lends tremendous conviction to the observation that southern convict leasing—regardless of its victim's race—was a pernicious, immoral, and dastardly business. Tabert's case also lends credence to the fact that many Black victims in similar circumstances just "disappeared," never to be heard from again by friends or family. If a White person could get caught in the grip of the convict lease system, a Black person was even more vulnerable. No lawyers took up the cases of Black convicts. There were few enterprising journalists, convicts' rights groups, or societal crusaders turning over stones and following up on slim leads with a single-minded determination to reveal the truth in the case of Black convicts. Leasing contaminated almost everyone associated with its administration: law officers, legislators, state and local officials, and lessees. It remains a sad and little-known chapter in southern, penal, and African-American history.

THE VICTIMS OF CONVICT LEASING

An example of the typical victims of county convict leasing in Florida is provided by the story of three men who were fined in the Criminal Court of Leon County. They were unable to pay their fines and court costs. Instead of allowing the sheriff to "feed and house them in jail at the county's expense," it was thought to be more expedient to lease them to William K. Beard and Robert G. Shepard, for whom they would pick cotton. The value of the prisoners' labor was calculated based on picking one hundred pounds of cotton. When the amount of their fine equaled the amount of cotton picked, the convicts were "to be released."[5] They seem to have disappeared in the system, however, and their release remains in doubt. There is no way to ever know how many convicts were held beyond their sentences in order to satisfy a labor need (especially if some skill had been acquired), while the local prison officials, often friends or relatives of lessees, looked the other way or paid no attention at all.

Vagrancy, the charge for which Martin Tabert was jailed, was a most convenient "offense" during the New South era and one for which southern Blacks were often convicted, fined, and then jailed. Vagrancy became a pretext for incarcerating Blacks and a most convenient mechanism for creating a cheap, fast supply of labor to meet some special demand or sudden need, from harvesting seasonal crops to building a road or filling a large order for coal. The Mississippi Black Code, adopted soon after the end of the Civil War, declared a vagrant "as anyone who was guilty of theft, had run away [from a job, apparently], was drunk, was wanton in conduct or speech, had neglected job or family, handled money carelessly, and . . . all other idle and disorderly persons."[6] It is entirely possible that these "vagrants" were held as long as the labor need lasted and beyond, whether it was three months, six months, nine months, or more. In Florida and elsewhere, men were "railroaded" into leasing for money. According to one authority, "Men charged with vagrancy were brought before the county judge and instructed by the sheriff and his deputy to plead guilty." On several occasions, "trials took place late at night and were carried out by inebriated court officers."[7]

Whether arrested for "vagrancy" or for some other reason, the victims of convict leasing all met with a similar fate. Southern convict leasing was characterized, more than anything else, by widespread and excessively brutal treatment of its victims. Convicts were poorly fed, clothed, and housed. Minimum standards in health and medical care were neglected and physical punishment was often severe and sometimes savage. Consistent throughout convict leasing was the level of brutality through punishment, neglect, indifference, and cruelty that prisoners experienced at the hands of lessees. What was not consistent was the *source* of the brutality. Sometimes it was working conditions; at other times it was punishment. On other occasions, or in other states, or with different lessees, it was poor diet, health, and medical care, or the arbitrary extension of prison sentences. One observer of the situation in Alabama wrote: "County officials and contractors kept such poor records, sometimes none at all, that prisoners were known to have been worked for months or even years after the expiration of their sentences."[8] Convicts were said to be "manufactured" in Florida and then "leased as slaves to the highest bidder." These "manufactured" convicts were "often quite innocent men" and usually Black.[9] They were, according to a retired prison official interviewed in 1963, "pulled off trains and sentenced to as much as six months for vagrancy." Their sentences were arbitrarily extended "for nothing at all." Whites were seldom sent to prison unless they were "pretty bad." Most of the convicts were "niggers . . . a nigger was sent up for anything and sometimes for nothing at all."[10] The prevailing view was that the desire for revenue or profits from convict labor was so great that if innocent people had to be unjustly imprisoned in order to get more convicts, more labor, and more money, "that was tough."[11]

Proportion of Black to White Prisoners

It is most difficult to piece together a concrete record from state to state and year to year of the Black-to-White ratio among convicts during the life of leasing in the post–Civil War South. Such records could not be found in a state like Virginia, for example. Other states maintained such records in some years but not in others. Consistent listings of race ratios could not be found for a single ex-Confederate state for every year during which the lease system operated. The reasons why states did not keep better records on the racial composition of convicts under leasing appear to be a combination of indifference and incompetence—as was the case with much else under leasing.

Despite the absence of reliable statistical data on the number of Black convicts versus the number of White convicts victimized by leasing, sufficient statistics are available to provide an impression through sampling of the ratios. What seems to be very clear is that convicts under the leasing system in the South for the sixty or so years of its legal existence were overwhelmingly Black.

In a study of the Mississippi penal system and convict leasing, two attorneys from the state report that there were 904 Black convicts and 92 Whites in 1878. In 1887 there were 900 Blacks and 112 Whites.[12] The estimate for Florida is that Black convicts exceeded 90 percent of the total inmate population. There, in 1869, 117 convicts were in prison, of whom 102 were Black. The 1908 estimate for Georgia is 91 percent, and for Alabama in 1877, the percentage of Black convicts was also 91. Alabama was a state in which the convict population tripled between 1874 and 1877, and the increase consisted almost entirely of Blacks. The Penitentiary Investigating Committee of the Alabama General Assembly of 1888–89, sampling one of the state's coal mines, indicated that 144 of 147 convicts were Black and 46 were women.[13] A state penitentiary report in Tennessee in 1879 shows a total of 1,153 convicts, of whom 757 were Black males, 366 were White males, 24 were Black females, and 6 were White females. Ten years later in Tennessee, all convicts in the state were held under lease by legislation of 1889 with the Tennessee Coal, Iron and Railroad Company and its sublessees. A penitentiary report from 1893 provides a racial breakdown of convicts at five of the state's six prisons, as follows:

PRISON	BLACKS	WHITES
Coal Creek	135	4
Big Mountain	101	24
Inman	274	27
Tracey City	378	145
Morrow Farm	49	0

There is no explanation of why reports on the main prison at Nashville, with a total of 414 convicts, include no breakdown by race. Two years later, a penitentiary report that did not give race ratios at most of the other prisons in the state gave one for the main prison of 497 prisoners, of whom 444 were Black males, 41 were Black females, and 12 were White (males and females).[14]

The Tennessee State Penitentiary Report covering the years 1892–94, which included a report from the warden, listed 1,587 male convicts in the Tennessee penitentiary, "over 1,200 [of whom] are negroes." The warden further reported that many of the convicts were in prison for "petit larcenies, especially . . . negroes[,] some for stealing a chicken." The warden believed that the 1,200 Black convicts felt a sense of "elevation" from being in jail with 300 Whites.[15] In the mid-1880s a southerner cautioned a Congress of the National Prison Association against imprisoning Whites with Blacks, comparing such a practice to the "ancient torture" of tying up murderers with "decaying corpses," resulting in death to the living murderer. And in 1875 Governor John Brown of Tennessee felt it was unjust—to the Whites—"to imprison together White murderers and a Black who had stolen a pig."[16]

A snapshot from Louisiana prisons in 1901 shows 1 White female, 39 Black females, 158 White males, and 944 Black males. In the following year (1902), there were 2 White females, 33 Black females, 186 White males, 1,014 Black males, 1 Chinese, and 1 Filipino; in 1903 there were 1 White female, 29 Black females, 203 White males, 1,027 Black males, and 1 Filipino. Ten years later, in 1912/13, the racial breakdown was 8 White females, 57 Black females, 388 White males, and 1,581 Black males. Five of the Black prisoners were under twelve years of age. One

Chinese and one Korean were also listed.[17] A member of the American Prison Association, K. B. Johnson, who was commissioner of public welfare in North Carolina, claimed that 78 percent of all "committed persons" in the "thirteen" states of the South were Black. Johnson also asserted, as was characteristic of the thinking and "scholarship" of the period, that the reasons for the large percentage of Blacks in prison could be traced back to the Civil War and the "orgy of crime" that followed, "in which the negro, unprepared in every way for freedom and responsibility, played the principal part." As time passed, "this condition," Johnson claimed, "has not greatly changed," which, he further explained, was the reason Blacks made up almost four-fifths of all southern convicts.[18]

CONVICTS' LIVING CONDITIONS

Despite the denials of lessees, prison officials, and other apologists, conditions for convicts in the lease system in general fluctuated between miserable and wretched. Convicts worked long hours at demanding tasks ranging from picking cotton in Alabama to extracting coal from the mines of Tennessee to making turpentine in Florida to building roads and railroads throughout the post–Civil War South. Some states tended to specialize in certain kinds of labor; others did not. In the nonspecializing states, the type of labor performed was more or less a mixed bag. Indeed, convicts, like slaves in an earlier era, performed almost every kind of labor needed in the South. Southern convict lease labor was also seriously considered (but never used) for work on the construction of the Panama Canal and for a variety of tasks in the Philippines around the turn of the twentieth century. Moreover, as discussed in detail below, sanitary conditions were

Neanderthal, living and sleeping arrangements were vulgar, health and medical care were hostage to lessee frugality, and food—such as it was—was frequently unfit for human consumption.

Since lessees had a virtual free hand in maintaining standards for their convict labor despite guidelines and rules sometimes found in the contracts, and notwithstanding clearly stated though unenforced policies regarding the working conditions, maintenance, and care of prisoners, life for the victims caught in the lease system was a perpetual nightmare. One description of the Tennessee Coal Company in 1891 calls conditions there "atrocious: defective ventilation, insufficient drainage, horrible sanitation, only one entrance to the mine . . . convicts were inadequately fed and forced to work and sleep in the same clothing."[19] Many Alabama coal-mining convicts, perhaps worse off than those in Tennessee, were reported to have experienced these same conditions, in addition to the fact that they "had not seen the sunshine for months."[20] While it is true that conditions for coal miners all over the world at this time were abominable, one difference between convicts and other miners was that paid coal miners were at least, on the face of it, "free." They could, theoretically, walk away at any time and search for other employment. On the other hand, so many of these convicts were innocent men or had committed minor crimes and could not pay small fines, or were held beyond the expiration of their sentences, that they were really no different from their counterparts who were not incarcerated, because they should not have been in prison in the first instance.[21]

Throughout the era of convict leasing, various idiosyncrasies or nuances frequently distinguished leasing among the eleven southern states of the Old Confederacy. It might have been the kinds of labor performed by convicts. Perhaps it was the number of years leasing lasted. The size, racial composition, and sexual makeup of the convict population created an occasional distinction. In addition, the extent to which the state and lessees profited financially from leasing varied. But conditions and the general treatment of convicts per se were routinely bad in all states. Leading lessees and their employees from state to state, almost without exception, earned reputations for brutality, based for the most part on their penchant for administering vicious beatings and whippings, primarily to Black males but also to males and females of all races, as well as to children. It has been reported that one Black inmate on the Patton Plantation in Brazoria County, Texas, was given 604 lashes on his "naked back." A Governor's Committee appointed to investigate the main penitentiary in Huntsville, Texas, and elsewhere, including the Patton Plantation, where convicts were employed in 1875, doubted the accuracy of the report until they examined the individual and "concluded that the shocking testimony was correct."[22]

In 1901 S. P. Horne, a White ex-convict, testified before a legislative committee investigating abuses he witnessed in Florida that "a Negro named Linch Butler . . . was beaten by a pit boss until the skin came off his hips and back and thighs. . . ." Horne went on with his testimony, indicating that a phosphate mine pit foreman named Thomas Allen "literally slaughtered the convicts." He elaborated further:

> He would beat sick men that died two days later, some so badly beaten that they could not lay on their backs for weeks; this treatment went on under the eyes of Jack Camp and in the knowledge of W. N. Camp and Clarence Camp, who are lessees of convicts.[23]

Horne ended his testimony proclaiming that he had provided only a small sample of "hundreds of acts of brutality" that would take weeks to write up, and poignantly stated that there were victims of leasing "who are as innocent of the charges as a babe—that never knew what crime was."[24]

Sometimes it was argued, as was the case with Superintendent J. W. Kirk in Tennessee in the early 1890s, that convicts needed to be whipped in order to get them to do their work. In such cases, he felt, "the strap has to be used, and in almost every case when it is used on that class of indolent and worthless men, with a firm and relentless . . . hand, they came right up with their work."[25] A prison guard felt that Blacks simply could not be controlled without "the strap," suggesting that they should be treated like a pet dog: "[T]reat him good and he will rear up and put his feet on your clean sheet . . . but when he misbehaves himself [he] has to be whipped."[26]

Turpentine and phosphate camps were a major source of employment for prisoners in the state and county convict lease system in Florida. Conditions were as consistently bad here as in other states. State legislators were "disgusted" by Blacks and Whites living in the same quarters, and, in fact, were more outraged than they were at "minors and hardened criminals" occupying the same space. The brutality was so great at the Colonel H. L. Morris and Sons turpentine camp, the largest in the state, that "enlightened citizens" of Marion County wrote the governor to inform him that if nothing was done to change the barbarous treatment of prisoners at the camp, they would "rise en masse and release every convict in the camp."[27] The citizens complained that young children and adults were expected to work at the same pace, that hours of labor were excessive, that punishment did not conform with rules and regulations, and that convicts had to work on Sundays. These "brutal and sadistic violations of humanity" are what provoked the ire of local citizens.[28]

As bad as the situation was at Morris's camp, it was considered worse at another turpentine site. At a camp supervised by Captain J. D. Johnson and owned by two wealthy operators, convict output was required to be one and one-half times that of free labor and sometimes more. A camp guard remarked "that the stench from convicts' sore backs is so great that the guards can scarcely stand to go in the stockade to examine the convicts."[29] Convicts leased to the St. Johns and Lake Eustis Railroad Company during an earlier period in Florida, while working on a line that went through marshes and swamps, were said to have gone to "certain death in the tropical marshes and palmetto jungles of Lake Eustis." Convicts worked without shelter, frequently without food, and "half submerged in mud and slime."[30]

Medical, Hygienic, and Sanitary Conditions

In addition to enduring excessive punishment, particularly whippings, leased convicts endured numerous other difficult conditions. Sanitation and health care for convicts, their food and work day, subleasing, and unlawfully extended sentences are selected aspects of leasing that attracted the attention of legislative investigating committees, newspaper reporters, state and local government officials, and the general public, all of whom grew opposed to leasing. Evidence of these and other intolerable characteristics of leasing is sometimes uneven but, even where it is weakest, it is sufficient to demonstrate leasing's "antediluvian barbarism."[31]

It was a striking paradox that lessees did not go to greater lengths to maintain the good health and strength of convicts, in order to exact more or better labor from them. On the other hand, some greedy lessees, like avaricious slave owners from an earlier day, believed it was more cost-effective to spend as little money as possible on food or medical care in order to maximize profits. Convicts, unlike slaves, were rented rather than "owned" and as such did not have the "protected status" accorded to "property." In any event, descriptions of the food that convicts received paint an unappetizing picture. Convict accounts speak of filthy kitchen conditions and food often in limited supply or availability, sometimes because prison officials took the food and other supplies for use by their own families. In one case convicts were eating "condemned vegetables . . . dumped in the river by garbage carts and fished out in nets by the prisoners." Whatever was left over was fed to the hogs.[32] An account is also given of gravy served to prisoners "with so many dead flies on top of it that you couldn't see the gravy at all on account of the flies."[33] In Texas, convicts mutineed over bad food, and in one case— probably as punishment or for the purpose of humiliation—a guard made a prisoner "eat his own droppings."[34] Testifying before the Penitentiary Investigating Committee, a Texas convict described the food at one of the lease farms as "corn bread all the time; cold and hard; black-eyed peas, cold and hard . . . and nothing but cold water the balance of the day." Another convict stated that "the grub" resembled what a dog would eat and "the bread is sometimes kinder [*sic*] musty, and corn-boll weevil . . . it don't smell good, don't taste good."[35] Convicts in another state "were compelled to attend to the calls of nature in line as they stood day in and day out, their thirst compelling them to drink the water in which they were compelled to deposit their excrement."[36] In Tennessee, the food at the Rockwood Railroad Camp was called "the coarsest and cheapest obtainable."[37] When the "dark cell" was used to discipline and punish convicts in the leased penitentiary in Louisiana, the diet was bread and water for the duration of the sentence but "never longer than sixty days."[38] Bread and water were sometimes denied altogether in Texas (suggesting by implication that convicts were sometimes not fed at all).[39]

A Tennessee warden acknowledges that "the general sanitary condition of the prison was bad" and that "the hospitals were in poor condition"—a surprising admission, since senior prison officials often went to some lengths to conceal the indignity of leasing because they feared it would reflect on their management or supervisory approach. However, he took some comfort in explaining that the hospital situation was the result of the fact that the facility was managed by "inexperienced negroes."[40]

In another case in Tennessee, the State Board of Prison Inspectors removed all leased convicts from the Tennessee Coal Company mine in the summer of 1891 because the company failed to comply with regulations. It is reported that "mining conditions were atrocious: defective ventilation; insufficient drainage; horrible sanitation; only one entrance to the mine; and no protective inspection of the mine prior to work."[41]

Four years later, in July 1895, leased convicts had to be removed from the Rockwood Railroad Camp because of generally bad conditions and because lessees again failed to comply with regulations. Superintendent John H. Trice described the camp locality as "unhealthy" and the men as "poorly housed and the hospital arrangements abominable." Convicts, he said, were "overworked by the contractors and their foremen; the sanitary conditions were bad and, as a consequence, the sick list and death rate increased to an alarming extent."[42]

Another instance of individual brutality manifested by intolerable medical conditions occurred at a railroad camp in Louisiana. *The Baton Rouge Truth*, a local newspaper, disturbed by stories about convict leasing, decided to undertake its own investigation, and discovered a Black man convicted of larceny by a court in New Orleans who had been sentenced to eighteen months at hard labor. He was eventually placed in a railroad camp and forced to work in the cold without shoes. His feet became frostbitten as a result and had to be amputated. He spent the balance of his sentence within the walls of the penitentiary making boots and toys.[43]

George Campbell's death at a turpentine camp in Florida typifies the "mysterious circumstances" under which many Black convicts lost their lives—especially those who were under the supervision of Captain Harman Douglass, warden/principal keeper of turpentine lease facilities from 1906 to 1907. When Campbell came under Douglass's care in January 1906, he "appeared to have been in reasonably good health." When his feet became diseased, and he was unable to work, Campbell was confined to the stockade. His condition worsened and a physician who was visiting the penitentiary to examine other convicts looked at Campbell's "swollen and diseased" feet and "prescribed a disinfectant." The doctor theorized that Campbell might have had typhoid fever and noted that he had "very much emaciated" feet. As the condition of Campbell's feet grew worse, it "became very offensive [in odor], and he was placed in a small house outside the stockade called the hospital."

On March 28, 1906, a lawyer named Jones and the deputy sheriff, named Kirkwood, both from Orlando, visited the camp.

When they found Campbell, he was "lying on a pallet in one corner of the room . . . about 14 by 18 feet . . . made of a slight layer of hay . . . and Campbell was covered with a blanket." There was one other convict in the room lying on a similar pallet. Next to Campbell on the floor was a small can of water, a plate with a piece of cornbread and "perhaps some other article of food, over which, as over Campbell, the flies were swarming in vast numbers." The room was so "filthy and exceedingly offensive" that Kirkwood had to leave after a few minutes for fresh air. Jones, the lawyer, inspected Campbell's feet, which were "filthy and wrapped in rags." Apparently his feet were in such bad shape that "the pus had oozed out from under the edges of the rags and had soaked through them." Campbell's legs were swollen, his face was ashy, his pulse was feeble, and his "skin was soft and clammy." The "stench" from Campbell's feet was "insufferable." Campbell died on March 29, 1906, and "a fair inference from the testimony of the physician is that his death was accelerated, if not caused, by septicemia, or blood poisoning, resulting from the absorption into the system of the poisonous pus from his diseased foot." A court later found this to be the result of "cruel treatment of this negro convict by Capt. Douglass. . . ."[44] It was more specifically alleged that:

> Harman F. Douglass [the Warden] did then and there, unlawfully, feloniously and culpably fail and neglect to provide the necessary food, care, nursing, medicines and medical care and attention and treatment for the said George Campbell, proper and needful for the said George Campbell, in his said ill and crippled condition by reason whereof the said George Campbell then and there sickened and languished of a mortal sickness so as aforesaid, caused, produced, permitted and procured, feloniously and with culpa-

ble negligence then and there by the said Harman F. Douglass until the 29th day of March 1906 . . . [and] then and there he died."[45]

The *Tampa Tribune*, excerpting the report of a penitentiary investigating committee, declared that Campbells' feet and legs were "putrified" and smelled so bad that investigating committee members were "forced to hold their noses." The account continued that this "suffering man," with "flies swarming around him adding to his indescribable agony . . . lying in an old shack with a dirty plate containing a piece of cornbread . . . died that night and death was kind in relieving him of his misery." No one appears to have been punished for Campbell's death or the circumstances that led to it.[46]

Evidence exists that, in 1909, no sanitary system was in place in at least one leased prison in Texas, and most likely elsewhere in the state and throughout the South: prisoners used buckets to remove their waste, which sometimes remained filled and in the cell with them for twelve hours, "in a double cell [with] two to four men in there."[47] Forced sodomy was not uncommon, and in one case, two Black convicts were whipped for fighting and then forced to kiss each other's rectums.[48] Conditions under leasing in Texas—both medical and otherwise—were so bad that one legislator, in a speech criticizing the system, stated, "[I]f an honest committee was appointed to make the investigation it would discover or unearth things possible that would smell to heaven."[49]

PENAL METHODOLOGY

The debate in penal circles over whether the lash—and penitentiaries in general—served as an instrument of reform and rehabilitation or as a method of punishment ebbed and flowed over the decades of the late nineteenth and early twentieth centuries. Prison labor, like slavery, was coerced labor. To some, convict leasing was a labor system and a punitive system. No clear philosophy or consensus emerged on these issues. There was agreement on the need for whipping, although there were differences in criteria. Most whippings appeared to be arbitrary and capricious. Many states had guidelines for whipping convicts, with regard to the size and nomenclature of the strap and other aspects of the flogging enterprise. The guidelines were rarely followed, however, and they were often inconsistent and confusing. At one point in Texas, where a Judge Gill denied the existence of leasing altogether,[50] the dimensions of the strap were to be 2 feet long and 2½ inches wide, and convicts were not to get more than thirty-nine licks.[51] At another time, one T. J. Driscoll, a sergeant at Ramsey State Farm, a lessee location in Texas, testified before a state legislature investigating committee: "I guess the strap is about two and a half or three inches wide. I suppose four feet long with a handle and all leather."[52]

Rule Number 5 for whipping convicts in Texas was as follows: "In whipping, a leather strap about two and one-half inches wide and two feet long fastened in a wooden handle should be used and care should be taken to not break the skin, and every officer shall be held to strict account that it [sic] is not bruised."[53] A penitentiary investigating committee in Texas found straps longer than 5 feet and more than 4 inches wide, "custom-made for the sergeants at their own expense to their own specifications."[54] Compliance with the rules was seldom observed and often "totally ignored" in Texas and in other states. Men, women, and children convicts were whipped for every reason imaginable: some cut off their own fingers to avoid work and were whipped as a result,[55] while others, as in the case of a group of Black convicts, were whipped for testifying before the investigating committee.[56] Sometimes the reasons were not apparent at all.

The leather strap was described as a "moral persuader" and convicts in Texas were said to be as afraid of a Major Durham as they were of death itself because of his reputation as "king of the leather." One inmate was forced to whip another with a bat; another was beaten with a piece of lumber; others were whipped with "knotted rope with bridle reins and hit over the head with a shotgun."[57] More barbaric whippings were conducted with a wet leather strap dragged through sand. A convict testifying before a legislative investigating committee gave an eye-witness account of this common practice at a lessee camp:

> Mac Williamson whipped a man by the name of Petit at Camp Mewshaw, and when he hit him he put the strap down on the ground and put his foot on it (indicating) and drew it under his foot . . . and this man Williamson, when he whips he don't whip you except only on the kidneys and down on the legs.[58]

Another witness testified, "I have seen them whipped . . . and the skin peel off. I have seen the clothes stick to them for a month afterward. . . ."[59] Still another eyewitness saw a sixteen- or seventeen-year-old boy, "a little fellow" named Keyes, whipped and "cut . . . slit open on both sides . . . and black blood oozing out."[60] When reasons were given for convict whippings, they tended to cluster around "sassing guards," not working or "bucking" (defiantly refusing to work), "noticing things," attempting to escape and helping others escape, making mistakes, and malingering. In the case of females, resisting the sexual advances of male prison officials was the frequent but unstated reason for whippings. All in all, the explanations for convict whippings ranged from the "reasonable" to the bizarre.

The Case of Abe Winn

In Georgia, a teenager named Abe Winn (also Wynn or Wynne) was reported to be whipped to death for "resenting [the] social equality of hogs." The youth had thrown hot coffee out an open window onto a deputy warden's pigs; he was whipped in punishment and subsequently died. The case came to the public's attention when a $50,000 fund was announced to "avenge cruelty to convicts."[61]

The Winn case is one of many in which disagreement exists over the "facts." Winn was sixteen years old when he was imprisoned for larceny, having stolen two cans of potted ham, his first offense. He was sent to the Durham Coal and Coke Company in Walter County, which leased convicts from the State of Georgia. He was a "stout," robust youngster, six feet tall, weighing 160–65 pounds. After his whipping, Winn was kicked several times by the deputy warden, J. D. Goode, because he did not get up when told to do so. He then staggered into the hospital nearby. Eyewitness accounts of the incident provided by ex-convicts Keith and Cochran and former guard F. C. Lewis assert that Winn was given sixty-nine lashes by Goode while being held on the ground by four "burly Black convicts," with a strap that was repeatedly dragged on the ground. They reported that he died a week or so later from that beating. Countering that story were the testimonies of two medical doctors, Goode, and J. W. Gillespie of the firm of L. J. Sharp and Company of

Chattanooga, Tennessee, as well as the undertaker who buried Winn at the request of his brother Will Winn. All of these individuals declared that the cause of death was consumption or tuberculosis. Dr. J. H. Hendricks, the prison physician at the time of Winn's death, indicated that Winn was admitted to the hospital on December 22, 1905, for consumption, and died on February 22, 1906, from the same illness. Moreover, the doctor offered the professional opinion based on "his experience and knowledge as a physician of a quarter of a century" that Abe Winn's death could not have "resulted from physical punishment administered by the warden and no punishment . . . was administered by any one other than the warden."[62]

The Winn episode is further complicated by the testimony of his brother Will Winn, who lived twenty-nine miles from the site of the Durham Coal and Coke Company. Will Winn had been informed of his brother's hospitalization by Dr. Hendricks and friends who were in and out of the prison. He visited his brother and found him in terrible shape: Abe Winn had suffered a dramatic weight loss, was filthy, and was in a malodorous hospital bed. Will was told by the doctor that his brother had consumption aggravated by pneumonia. He never examined his brother for evidence of a whipping when he visited him because he was told he had consumption. Still, he was perplexed about Abe's illness because he had been such a healthy, strapping youth before entering prison, and there was not a single case of consumption or tuberculosis in the family's entire history.[63] In addition, he was distraught over his brother's feeble and mephitic condition and wanted the "rust," the dirt, washed off his face, arms, and entire body. He left money for someone to get his brother some decent clothes (he was in prison stripes) and to get him some underclothes, because he appeared to be wearing none.

Will Winn thought that the coal had stuck to his brother's skin, and he had the impression that Abe had not been washed since he was admitted to the hospital. Will Winn believed his brother was near death. Consequently, he began making arrangements for his burial with the Chattanooga, Tennessee, undertaker. He also journeyed to Atlanta to attempt to obtain a pardon for his brother. In the interim Abe died, and the first Will Winn heard about his brother's death, or about a whipping, was when he read it in the newspaper.[64]

Abuse in Other States

Other examples of abuse abound. An Alabama Black convict who was accused of "goldbricking" (shirking assigned tasks) was whipped to death when he complained of being sick and would not work. In Florida, a female convict named Suzie Johnson was held on the ground nude and whipped. A fifteen-year-old boy was whipped the same way. In still another Florida case, a sick convict named Will Black, who was unable to work, was instructed to "dip pine gum" or face a beating. When Black collapsed from exhaustion, the whipping boss beat him over the head with a club. Eyewitnesses and victims reported that "sadistic guards rubbed burned leather and pine gum into wounds" ripped open by whippings.[65]

The Charles Dudley case in Florida is another of those that epitomized the sequence of events in which ordinary men, women, and even children got ensnared in convict leasing. Dudley was sentenced to four months at a county convict camp for stealing a pair of shoes. (He was inebriated at the time.) At the camp, Dudley was required to be more productive and work at a faster pace than he apparently could, and therefore was given more than one hundred lashes as punishment. After a later, more brutal whipping he was unable to get up from the ground when ordered to rise. He was then nearly pistol-whipped to death, but miraculously survived. He was severely emaciated and reduced to 60 pounds body weight as a result of his ordeal.[66]

The only woman reported to have been whipped in North Carolina was a fifteen-year-old "colored girl," according to one investigator of convict leasing in the state. Apparently, other attempts to "reform" the girl, including several visits to the "dark cell" (solitary confinement), had failed, and a punishment of "twelve strokes by the proper official" was the next option.[67]

At least one case of Black convict retaliation against lessee mistreatment exists in Mississippi. On this occasion, Black convicts were so appalled by the death of one of their fellows that they took their own revenge in what must have set some kind of precedent in convict vigilante justice. A guard named S. T. Wilson, after having trouble with a Black prisoner, had the prisoner taken on board his ship, beaten insensible, and thrown overboard. The guard was tried and confined without bail by the local Justice of the Peace. About 300 Blacks "formed an uprising," took Wilson into the swamp, and hung him.[68]

Sexual Abuse of Female Prisoners

Black women suffered greatly under convict leasing, as they had suffered earlier in slavery. The "female prison" in Louisiana was considered "a disgrace to any civilized community."[69] In Tennessee, guards were known to allow their preferred colleagues into the women's section of one of the branch prisons with "the result . . . that four children were born inside the prison—are there today—disgraceful monuments to the guards' perfidy."[70]

The situation of Black female convicts in Texas illustrates and highlights the special burden that Black women bore. According to one commentator, the 1909 Legislative Investigating Committee in the Lone Star State found "evidence [of the treatment of Black women] so shocking that the Committee would not include it in a public document."[71]

The thousand-page Penitentiary Investigating Committee report in the state of Texas is peppered with descriptions of Black female convicts being sexually abused by White prison officials. The abuse included humiliation (for example, being forced to disrobe for "inspections" and whippings, bathing before an audience, and other forms of degradation), rape, and forced orgies. Women were supervised by men because White women were unwilling to take the job and prison authorities and lessees would not give it to a Black woman.[72] During her stay in the hospital, seventeen-year-old Black convict Jerlene Bonds, who had been incarcerated at age fourteen for burglary, told the Committee that she witnessed orgies between the prison guards and Black female prisoners, and that these women were routinely exploited sexually "back behind the woodpile and so on." Part of the exchange between Jerlene Bonds and a member of the Committee is as follows:

Q. *Who did you see?*
A. I seen Phil Robertson and Mr. Strange and Mr. Miller with Lula Lane and Mr. Strange with Rosa Brewing and Phil Robertson with Rosa Brewing, and Ennis Carlisle with Mr. Thornton.
Q. *You saw them?*
A. Yes, sir.
Q. *All in there at the same time?*

A. Yes, sir; turned them all in there at the same time. Some of them would holloa and try to holloa for the sergeant.

Q. *Did the sergeant know it?*

A. Yes, sir; he tried to stop it, but he can't get a picket man that will stop it. There is one of these women in a family way now, three months gone; Cora, that has got those three little children.[73]

The sixty-something-year-old picket guard, Strange, was described as "pretty old and pretty gray." He had a well-known reputation for pursuing Black female convicts for sexual favors, promising them money ("sometimes a dollar, sometimes two, three dollars sometimes") and help in getting released if they complied. He appeared to have a preference for "bright" women or "yellow" women over "dark" ones and was "sent away in a hurry" when scandal threatened.[74] Strange's "sweethearts" never became pregnant because "he might have been a little too old."[75]

The near-savage circumstances and conditions under which children were born to imprisoned and leased Black females generally were not altogether uncommon. One prison medical doctor described the birth of a child in the fields of a Texas lessee farm:

I went out to the Bible farm and four or five women called me off and told me that the baby was in there and that it was born in the field. And I said, "Where is it?" and walked in and there was the mother in the bed and they said it was born in the sand and the sand was in its face and that they begged the captain not to make her go out [to work], for her water had already broke, but he made her go out and it was born and they brought it in a wagon. I walked in and looked at the child and put my hand on its face and felt the little sand in its little skin and there it was and then [I] turned and went on out.[76]

Frequently, the children born in prison had been fathered by White men—prison guards, their friends and colleagues, or even other prisoners—and sometimes an effort was made to shift the blame to a Black man.[77] Other women may have been pregnant when they arrived for incarceration. What is so damning is the brutality of sexual exploitation compounded by the reality that, in many cases, conception could only have taken place after confinement in prison.

Treatment of Children

Not even children escaped the reach and grasp of southern convict leasing. Their treatment and the general conditions to which they were subjected were often as treacherous as those for adult convicts. In 1889 the president of the Alabama Board of Inspectors revealed that, during a period in which the penitentiary was being leased, seventeen children aged sixteen years old and under were living there. All of them were Black, one was a female, and the youngest was eight.[78]

Florida "stood alone in leasing women, . . . the aged, decrepit and the young."[79] Moreover, youngsters in Florida between 1869 and 1874 were expected to match the labor output of grown men. Perhaps worst of all, the children, most of whom were imprisoned for misdemeanors, were not segregated from other convicts. Nine-year-old Samuel Wilson of Bienville Parish in Louisiana was convicted of murder in 1870 and sentenced to serve life alongside adult prisoners.[80] Cy Williams, a Black child, was convicted of horse stealing but was apparently too small to ride a horse (no age was given). In any event, because the boy was too small for a regular prison job, the warden assigned him the task of carrying bricks back and forth in the yard, during which time he "wore out" four sets of bricks before being given other duties.[81] Twelve-year-old Oscar Anderson was described as docile, obedient, and diligent in carrying out his assigned tasks—the equivalent of those given to an able-bodied man. Every day, Oscar was required to carry fifty-two buckets of turpentine from the trees. The job was too difficult; he never managed to get more than thirty. He was beaten each day "that he failed to meet the quota. They beat him with a piece of leather, a strap, and they beat him until he was raw on the back. This was a daily occurrence. . . ."[82]

More than 25 percent of the convicts pardoned by the governor of Texas during one twelve-year period of the lease's operation (roughly 1871–83) were children between ten and seventeen years of age. The governor felt that these children, one-fourth of whom were hopelessly diseased, blind, crippled, or demented, should never have been given penitentiary time with "hardened criminals" anyway.[83] Prison records from Texas show that the age of convicts ranged from seven to ninety-four years.[84] Any question about which lessees or states incarcerated the youngest children are technically moot because, as already observed, babies were often born during their mother's confinement and remained in prison with them.

LEASING IN SPECIFIC STATES

In Alabama in 1890 it was asserted that a more benevolent system of leasing existed in comparison with systems in other southern states, because most convicts were leased to one party and state supervision was more rigorous.[85] Yet the annual death rate for Alabama convicts in the late nineteenth century was as high as in most other southern states. A 1902 legislative investigation in Texas found that the average life span of a convict under leasing was seven years, because "[convicts] were worked when sick and shot on the slightest provocation."[86] Two Mississippi attorneys described leasing there as the "worst form of human slavery" and a "cesspool of crime and infamy," in part because the 1887 death rate among convicts was over 15 percent and, they believed, was the highest in the United States and perhaps in the world for convicts.[87] Comparative death rates in the state for the six-year period 1880–85 show that the death rate for leased Black convicts was twice as high as that for Whites (see Table 3.1). It is noted further that "death rates among Mississippi convicts were from ten to thirty times as great as among . . . [the prisons of Iowa, Illinois, Ohio and New Hampshire]." (In those states, there was no leasing and most of the convicts were White).[88] The Mississippi equivalent of the Martin Tabert tragedy was sixteen-year-old M. N. Hicks, whose brother went to a leasing camp with Hicks's pardon in hand, only to find out that he was already dead and that no family members had been notified.[89]

In the state of Georgia in 1908, a legislative investigation brought the atrocities committed under leasing into the public eye. The revelations boosted the momentum for the abolition of leasing, led by newspapers, legislators, and an aroused public. The *Atlanta Journal* joined the chorus of condemnation of southern convict leasing already under way. It editorialized,

> Posterity will read with wonder and amazement the long, drawn-out chapters of the convict lease system. The laxness

Table 3.1
DEATH RATES AMONG LEASED MISSISSIPPI CONVICTS,
BY RACE, 1880–1885

	White Convicts			Negro Convicts		
Year	Popu- lation (avg.)	No. of Deaths	Death Rate (%)	Popu- lation (avg.)	No. of Deaths	Death Rate (%)
1880	92	4	4.34	843	52	6.19
1881	92	5	5.43	843	74	8.77
1882	83	2	2.40	735	126	17.14
1883	83	5	6.02	735	84	11.42
1884	88	5	5.69	698	87	12.49
1885	88	7	7.95	698	69	10.97
6-yr. avg.	—	—	5.30	—	—	11.16

Source: Paul B. Foreman and Julien R. Tatum, "The Short History of Mississippi's State Penal System," *Mississippi Law Journal* (April 1938), 265.

of officials, the death-dealing bosses training their muscle to greater dexterity in wielding the murderous strap; the millions snatched from the State by conscienceless greedy grabbers—their frauds, fuges [*sic*], subterfuges will make a book worthy of the darkest spots of Europe, Asia or Africa.[90]

One month earlier a Baptist minister, Dr. Len Broughton, had attacked the lease system and the Georgia prison commissioners, stating that "Georgia's reputation is besmirched beyond the seas and especially in England where public notice has been taken of Georgia's notorious lease system with its blood-curdling ball and chain and its damnable lease customs. . . ." Continuing his frontal assault, Rev. Broughton, "speaking before a large audience which filled the Baptist Tabernacle in Atlanta" on the occasion of a major anti-leasing rally in that "capital of the South," declared that leasing "had become a stench in the nostrils of the people of the world; that the prison commissioners were rimless naughts; that the convict broker was a trader in human misfortune. . . ."[91] One week later, Dr. Broughton again criticized leasing and called for the impeachment of members of the prison commission because "they have played traitor to their trust. They have disgraced their state, they have immersed us with innocent blood." Adding his criticism to that of the minister, a local judge, W. A. Covington, scolded the church for not being more aggressive in fighting convict leasing. The judge felt that leasing would not be destroyed until an active and vigorous church championed the cause of justice by using its great influence the same way it had in the fight against prohibition in Georgia. Judge Covington took special exception to the ease with which those who inflicted "brutalities" on the convicts were able to escape the law, which he forcefully deplored and denounced.[92]

Criticism was leveled, to varying degrees, in every other ex-Confederate state to equal that of the criticism against Georgia. Alabama was not known for its liberal ideas on matters of penology or race, and debates on both of these subjects in the state in the late nineteenth century confirm this conclusion. As denunciation of leasing in Alabama intensified, fueling agitation for abolition, the expected apologists came to leasing's defense. Critics predominated, however. Julia Tutwiler, one of the state's best-known and most respected educators and social reformers during this period, argued that the convict lease system "combined all of the evils of slavery without one of its ameliorating features."[93] An Alabama historian proposed that county leasing was much worse than the state system and safeguards for convicts against "physical injury, moral degeneracy, or even murder" were impossible to obtain.[94]

In 1883 Dr. J. B. Gaston, one of Alabama's prominent citizens and president of the state's medical association, delivered a fusillade of criticism against Alabama prisons in the pages of the *Montgomery Daily Advertiser*, and especially against convict leasing at the Newcastle Prison (farm and coal mine), then under the supervision of John T. Milner.[95] Warden Milner also had a contract with the state for the labor of convicts. Dr. Gaston's allegations provoked a reply from Milner and there followed an exchange of views on leasing and the Alabama prison system between the two men and their supporters. Milner's views on Blacks are instructive. They may be representative of the thinking of most of Alabama's and/or the South's Whites, or they may be indicative of the racial attitudes of only some Whites. In any event, they are strongly suggestive of an anti-Black, anti-convict predilection that influenced the views of prison officials who administered the lease system, and therefore help to explain the brutality that pervaded it.

Responding to Gaston's criticism of the high death/ homicide rate in the Alabama penitentiaries, in which "lawlessness," "evil passions," and "bad men" had destroyed human life and in which the state had failed in its protective responsibility, Milner retorted that serving a prison sentence did not "lower or degrade Blacks one whit." He then launched into a dissertation that, in certain parts, made little sense. What can be understood is shot through with contempt for convicts and for Blacks, equaling or surpassing the racial epithets frequently expressed by the more well-known race baiters of the era. Milner offered his version of the White person's burden, stating "nine millions of White people are carrying today in the South a dead weight of five millions of negroes." He argued that, as slaves under White supervision, Blacks laid the "ground work" for the greatest agricultural system ever developed in any "country or age." However, since emancipation, Blacks had become, simply "cumberers of the earth. . . . They are with us, but not of us, nor never will be." Milner turned to a perennial target for race bigots, noting that "amalgamation will not occur here." Reconstruction had convincingly settled that question for him when a "channel" was cut "so deep that it will never overflow. The negro here is an exotic, a foreign substance, so to speak, that cannot and will not resolve itself into the elements that made up the White man's social and political being."[96] As was the case with others of his ilk, this Alabama prison warden and lessee further explained:

> The negro is the problem that confronts the people that rule Alabama today. Politically we must rule him or he will ruin us. Being indifferent as to the restraints, rules, regulations and punishments imposed, made and inflicted under our laws, and also ignorant, indolent and naturally inclined to the ways of uncivilized people, the negro furnishes a criminal class in Alabama one thousand percent greater than the Whites.[97]

He continued that the 600,000 Whites in Alabama could not allow the 500,000 Blacks to "impede the progress of the Country." For Blacks, according to Milner,

> . . . to transgress the rules[,] regulations and laws for gov-
> erning White people is but natural with a race constituted
> and situated as they are. It requires an army of judges, sher-
> iffs and other officers to arrest and convict the transgressors.
> The hard labor of the criminal is the only thing that will
> maintain and render efficient this machinery and the only
> thing that will affect the criminal himself.[98]

This self-appointed student of Blacks, race relations, criminology, psychology, and much else closed the same way that he opened. He stated that Blacks were an "anomaly," and that even if Blacks in southern prisons died in higher ratios than their White counterparts in New York, Ohio, and Pennsylvania, the argument that southern prisons were necessarily characterized by cruelty simply could not be sustained.[99]

Dr. Gaston's rejoinder cited reports from the legislature, from prison officials themselves, including chaplains and physicians, as well as the governor, all of whom concluded that the treatment of convicts was "cruel and inhuman, almost beyond the possibility of exaggeration." Some of the Alabama convicts were given their food in their hands, without plates or utensils, and some had not washed their faces in a year. Gaston used the following metaphor to emphasize his point: "You may as well expect to instill decent habits into a hog as to reform a criminal whose habits and surroundings are as filthy as a pig's." Gaston then delivered what he considered his knockout blow: "The system is a disgrace to the State, a reproach to the civilization and Christian sentiment of the age and ought to be speedily abandoned."[100]

Before this phase of the debate ended, the governor got into the act. He was opposed to leasing and assailed lessee circumvention of state and county laws, which he made clear by declaring in his special message to the General Assembly of Alabama, "If contractors are deaf to the pleadings of humanity and blind enough to their own interests to expect full work from half-naked and half-starved men, they should be compelled [at least] to obey the law."[101] Having made his position public, the governor did little about leasing in Alabama.

As the heyday in leasing in Tennessee began to pass, newspapers, state legislators, and others were as uncompromising in their criticism and condemnation of the system as were their counterparts in Georgia and Alabama. Convict leasing became a major issue in the gubernatorial campaign of 1892. In 1893 a special joint legislative committee investigating leasing and the penitentiary system found convicts without nightclothes, socks, and pillows, "with little or no medical attention . . . covered with running sores, that they were fed on three or four cents per day per convict and that brutal and degrading vices prevailed among the convicts at most of the branch prisons." The prisons themselves have been characterized as nothing but "hell on earth."[102] The *Knoxville Journal* joined the crescendo of criticism, editorializing:

> The mind fails to imagine any situation more awful than that of the poor wretches, miserable outcasts, confined in prison for reformatory reasons, insufficiently clothed and fed, confined in coal banks by day and pestholes by night, infested with vermin, days of wretchedness and nights devoid of hope, exposed to deadly and contagious venereal diseases, practicing unutterable abominations upon each other, subject to scourgings for failure to do the daily task of infractions of discipline . . . what more awfully deplorable state of affairs can the human mind imagine[?][103]

The story was virtually the same in Louisiana, Texas, Florida, and the remaining southern states. Captain J. C. Powell of Florida, who published an exposé on that state's penitentiary system entitled *An American Siberia*, writes that no attention was given to cleanliness or other conditions "necessary to common decency" on Chaire's plantation. The sick and the well fared equally badly. Three or four women are reported to have been in one of the squads at Chaire's camp and "what they endured," as Captain Powell puts it, "cannot be easily or decorously described in words."[104]

Powell tells of an episode of brutality perpetrated against a Black convict named Torcy Tucker as the most brutal of which he knew. Tucker had to be transported to jail after he was arrested because he was some distance away. He was bound by a chain from his hands to his neck. The loose end of the chain was connected to the guard's buggy, and they drove off "at a brisk trot." Tucker ran alongside the buggy as long as he could, then fell and was dragged. When guard and convict reached their destination, Tucker was "more dead than alive." His neck had gouges in it caused by each link in the chain and it had "abcesses [*sic*] which threatened to cut off his breathing." His neck was lanced in twenty places and he was "mortally hurt and really dying by inches" upon arrival to serve his sentence. Those prison officials responsible for this and similar acts of brutality were later indicted for cruel treatment of convicts.[105] Despite the prevalence of such incidents (and worse) in Florida and elsewhere, the 10 percent death rate reported for Louisiana convicts from 1893 to 1901 led some to conclude that Louisiana had the dubious distinction of being home to one of the most vicious lease systems in the South.[106]

While most southern states had more or less of the distinctive aspects that characterized leasing as a "cesspool of crime and infamy," Texas certainly had its share and then some.[107] The state's punishments for convicts ranged from whippings (with variations in the number of strokes and nomenclature of the strap, as indicated earlier) to the "dark cell," to increased workloads, to limitations on and elimination of food and clothing, (sometimes more part of the routine than punishment), to "hanging in the window," and more.[108] There was also Sunday work, purportedly in order for convicts to earn money to buy food from the commissary, which led to a mutiny over low pay in 1909.[109]

In Texas, bedding for convicts was reported to be filthy. One convict testified during an investigation that the beds had not been washed in two years despite the evidence of lice.[110] There were also bedbugs, cockroaches, and fleas; minimum sanitation standards were lacking; the sick, diseased, and healthy all bathed in the same water, water that "the hogs wallow in" and that was "just as muddy as mud can make it."[111] Five to six convicts were said to have washed in the same water at the same time.[112]

George Waverly Briggs of the *San Antonio Express* felt that, because of the atrocities committed against convicts in Texas penitentiaries, "the Spanish Inquisition paled into insignificance by comparison."[113] In addition, the *Texas Sifting* stated that convicts in Texas were worse off than slaves under Egyptian bondage, and Texas leasing was more cruel than Russian serfdom, "and more atrocious in its physical and mental torture than the treatment of convicts of the galleys of southern Europe."[114]

SUBLEASING

If the leasing system was objectionable, subleasing was doubly or triply so. The sublessee had to pay his middleman—the original lessee—a certain profit. This profit was charged against the labor costs, and against the profit the sublessee had to make. The House Legislative Investigating Committee in the state of Mississippi, where subleasing became the accepted practice in the early 1870s, reported: "Of necessity, then, we look for overwork, and undue economy on the part of sublessees, and the testimony submitted shows that such expectation was realized."[115] Subleasing also became common practice in many other leasing states before the end of the century.

Ordinarily, lessees contracted with the state or county for the labor of convicts, then proceeded to contract with a third party for the labor of a portion of those prisoners. Most often this was done without authorization and without the knowledge of state or county officials. Original lessees negotiated the best deal they could with sublessees and sought better terms than in the original lease. For example, if the original lease called for payments of $20 per convict per week over a period of two years, the sublessee could end up paying $40 or $50 per convict per week for a year or eighteen months or some other portion of the initial contract. It is reported that, in Georgia, a Dr. Hamby, "Chief Convict Broker" at the time, had 175 more convicts than the 500 he was allowed. He proceeded to sublet some of them at $630 per year, which was $409 more than the $221 specified in the original lease with the state—and it was all profit for Dr. Hamby.[116] In Arkansas, an original lessee paid the state $3.75 per convict per month, and a sublessee then paid the original lessee $12.50 per convict per month. The net lease profit for the original lessee was $8.75 per convict per month for the ten-year duration of the sublease contract.[117] In addition, the sublessee might be compelled to pay the original lessee the cost of transporting the convicts, or an amount or portion thereof, for which the original lessee may have billed the state or county, thereby collecting those expenses twice—costs that, in any event, were probably inflated or even fabricated to begin with.

The motives for subleasing were obviously economic—to milk the system for greater profits—although sometimes lessees discovered belatedly that they had contracted for more labor than they needed, and merely wanted to cut their losses (but ended up showing a profit from the enterprise). Needless to say, it was difficult for lessees to resist the temptation to contract for larger numbers of convicts than they needed with a view toward subleasing the surplus. When the original lessee was a sheriff or warden or some other official, or an influential local businessperson or landowner, it was a simple matter to implement the entire scheme and to keep it going for years at a time. Virtually no one monitored or reported these "hidden" abuses until a crusade against leasing began. It is not too far-fetched, moreover, to imagine that there were second and even third leases.

One example of the complexity and resulting confusion of subleasing comes from the Coal Creek branch prison in Anderson County, Tennessee, in 1893. The 139 convicts at this prison were held by the Knoxville Iron Company under a sublease made with the original lessee, the Tennessee Coal, Iron and Railroad Company. Yet, under a contract with Knoxville Iron, the prisoners were housed, clothed, and fed by a Captain Chumbly, in which "he [undertook] to feed and clothe them, and pay three-fourths of the guard hire, except that of Warden and expense of recapture of escaped prisoners, for which he received so much per head—forty cents per head per day."[118]

Arrangements in subleasing could be oral or a mere "understanding" or "agreement" between local people who were friends, associates, or family. Records were not kept, money changed hands, convicts did their labor and served their sentences (sometimes serving more than their required time), and few questions were asked.[119] After all, the victims were criminals and, what may have been as bad in the deep South around the turn of the twentieth century, most of them were Black. The sublessees, needless to add, whether first, second, or third, or even beyond state borders and state control (which was limited even when in force), for the most part cared less than the original lessee about the treatment, workday, diet, health care, general conditions, and maintenance for leased convict labor—which is to say they did not care at all. To the extent that there was any accountability, second- and third-level lessees were least accountable. Subleasing lasted as long as the lease system because, for lessees, the substantial advantages constantly outweighed any "inconveniences," which were few.[120]

CORRUPTION IN CONVICT LEASING

Fraud, bribery, and corruption were prominent features of convict leasing because opportunities for each of them were so plentiful. In Arkansas in 1871, a legislative committee claimed it had "no evidence that any bribes were actually received. We do not hesitate to say [however] that the purchase of . . . machinery, material . . . and the letting of . . . contract[s] . . . occasioned an unnecessary draft upon the Treasury of the State to the extent of thousands of dollars."[121]

As common as bribery and fraud in contract letting or materials procurement were, the corruption associated with prison administration and transportation, although perhaps a little bit more subtle, was just as common. A deputy sheriff in Texas, for example, was empowered to take three prisoners to the state penitentiary. He put the convicts in irons, removing the need for guards, and then obtained an order from a local judge for the transfer. The deputy than presented a bill for the cost of three guards in transporting the prisoners.[122] In such situations, it was also easy to bill the state for more convicts than were actually involved or for two or three times the mileage traveled. At the most elementary level, not at all unusual during leasing, guards borrowed money from convicts and convicts bribed guards for small favors or "goodies," as another Texas case illustrates. A prisoner there "gave a trusty [prison officer] a plug of tobacco to change [the sheets on] his bed."[123] A prison sergeant also used convicts as personal servants for himself and his family, and paid the state nothing for their services.[124] In addition, in Texas, Colonel J. A. Herring, a supervising official at a Texas lease farm, told of guards using goods and materials sent for convict use and "eating from State stuff," and reported that guards were dismissed for such actions.[125]

When a convict farm warden complained in 1903 that he was unhappy with his salary, the financial agent told him to pick out the best pair of mules he could find belonging to the state, sell them, and keep the money.[126] Tennessee legislators, in a 1905 report, chronicle a series of instances of "fraud and corruption" in connection with land sales, the purchase and sale of farms, repairs, contracts for new penitentiary construction, and the advertisement of their plans. In one section, the report stated, "The letting of the contracts to build a new penitentiary was as fraudulent and corrupt a transaction as ever took place in the State."[127]

The report also cites the case of an individual holding "the position of commissary for the Tennessee Coal and Iron Company and captain of the guard [a new position unknown to the law] for the State." He was employed and paid by both the lessee and the state. Despite his reputation for "cruelty to convicts," this individual reported prisoners for punishment and administered it, wearing one hat as "guard for the State." Simultaneously, he wore another as "employee of the lessees," as manager of the lessee-owned commissary, which may have worked administratively, but reflected, at the least, a conflict of interest as well as a violation of the law.[128] The Tennessee situation was topped by that in Georgia, where an individual drew three different salaries.[129]

It is pointed out in the case study of convict leasing in Georgia (chapter 4) that it is difficult to discern where the profits went. In the case of individuals, many of the lessees were powerful, influential, and wealthy people with a variety of sources for their acquired wealth, and it would be nearly impossible to determine how much of their fortune was derived from leasing per se when they had so much revenue from banking, railroad holdings, or real estate.[130] With states, as well, the mission is almost as impossible, primarily because records were often poor or nonexistent. It is hard to imagine, however, that states would have continued to maintain a system such as convict leasing if the major incentive (that is, profits) was removed. Therefore, it may be possible that southern states were at least avoiding the cost of maintaining a penitentiary system for as long as leasing remained legal, which yielded a net gain. Anything beyond meeting expenses was a bonus and frequently a windfall.

A survey of the earnings of penitentiary systems in the United States in 1886, one scholar writes, "shows that Alabama's net earnings were far larger than those of any other state reporting."[131] Monthly fees for leased convict labor during the mid-1870s—which was a period when "revenue from convict labor climbed steadily"—rose from "$5 for better workers ($2.50 for poorer) . . . to $8 . . . to $12 for first class hands."[132] Data for the fifteen-year period 1876 through 1890, when revenue increased each year, show total earnings from leasing of $561,971, with the most lucrative period being the two years ending September 30, 1890. Deposited revenue from those years in the state treasury was $184,471, more than ten times what it was in 1876.[133] State income from leasing in Texas from two penitentiaries, Rusk and Huntsville, for 1905–09, were as follows: 1905—$404,000, 1906—$428,000, 1907—$417,000, 1908—$473,000, 1909—$460,000. Profits from selected farms for the fiscal year ending August 31, 1908, were: Burleson and Johns farm, $45,000; Whatley, $6,000; Eastham, $48,000; and Clemens, $300,000. From the railroad mining force, the take was $118,000.[134]

For the seven years from May 1883 to May 1890, Arkansas shows modest and irregular income from convict leasing. Earnings through 1884 were $24,613.13, followed by $26,649.19, $25,399.35, $24,295.81, $25,708.00, $25,421.62, and $28,894.01, for a grand total of $180,981.11[135] For the ten years before 1883, the Arkansas penitentiary was leased to the state's best-known lessee, Zeb Ward. Colonel Ward was a "union man" who leased convicts in Kentucky and Tennessee before coming to Arkansas, and is said to have made a "fortune" from leasing in each state. Ward was of humble beginnings but rose to be an influential and powerful figure in Arkansas politics, with backing from the press, legislators, jurists, and public officials, including governors. Zeb Ward and his son, who had all of the state's convicts for ten years, are described as "mean men," and the older Ward "seemed to have the power to do anything in Arkansas." Ward, who leased federal as well as state convicts in order to increase profits, had such a frightening reputation among federal convicts that some are reported to have requested longer sentences elsewhere in order to avoid serving time in the Arkansas penitentiary under his supervision. One account of Ward's "theory" of prison management was that the penitentiary could not ". . . be too hard on thieves, murderers, and such scoundrels unless [it] cripples and kills them . . ."[136] Despite flagrant and gross violations of his lease and a reputation for irascibility, Ward was able to easily defeat attempts to get him convicted and to abolish his lease arrangement with the state, through "barbecues for legislators" and other "payoffs."[137]

A conclusion in a Tennessee penitentiary report may sum up how other southern states felt about profits when it stated, "It is probably not out of place to allude to the large revenue received by the State under the present management of this Institution, and I trust the lessees may realize a handsome profit on their large investment [as well]."[138]

CONCLUSION

Unjustified arrests, brutal beatings, unspeakably unsanitary conditions, disproportionate numbers of Black convicts, sexual abuse—all of these features characterized the southern convict lease system. What also stands out in bold relief about convict leasing in the South, setting it apart from the prison system before the Civil War and the chain gangs and penitentiary system that followed, is the extent to which governmental authorities and state and county officials abdicated their supervisory responsibility for convicts. This neglect made it possible for a long train of abuses to become routine against prisoners who were completely under the control of lessees, who had few compunctions about handing out less-than-human treatment.

To report that working conditions for leased convicts in the South during this period comprised a "trail of horrors" is not really surprising. After all, such conditions for wage labor in and out of the U.S. South, in agriculture, in coal mines, and in unregulated industries—especially those with many foreign and female workers—left much to be desired in those days. Nonetheless, the "work context" for prisoners caught in the grip of convict leasing contributes significantly to its indictment as an arrangement that made "cheap Black labor available to White capitalists and planters under a system more brutal than slavery."[139]

NOTES

1. For accounts of Martin Tabert's tragic experience with convict leasing in Florida, see N. Gordon Carper, "The Convict Lease System in Florida, 1866–1923," Ph.D. diss. (Florida State University, 1964); and Carper's "Martin Tabert, Martyr of an Era," *Florida Historical Quarterly* (October 1973), 115–31. The Samuel D. McCoy Papers in the Florida State Library in Tallahassee contain an important collection of correspondence and newspaper articles on the Tabert case compiled by the Martin Tabert Committee (Langdon, North Dakota), which was formed after his death.

2. Putnam Lumber Company to E. D. Tabert, Munich, North Dakota, February 2, 1922, Samuel D. McCoy Papers, Florida

State Library, Tallahassee, Florida.

3. Carper, "The Convict Lease System in Florida," 346.

4. The Martin Tabert case represents one of the confounding ironies in southern convict leasing. The Ku Klux Klan in Florida was outraged over this case. Martin Tabert was White. The Florida Klan opposed leasing generally in the state, possibly because it victimized some Whites in the same way it did many Blacks, an association to which the Klan apparently took exception. The Klan referred to leasing as "hellish" and threatened legislators who did not support its abolition with "10 lashes" and a "cote [*sic*] of tar and feathers." See "Justice Committee" of the Ku Klux Klan to State Senators J. B. Johnson and T. J. Knabb (n.d.), Samuel D. McCoy Papers.

5. Carper, "The Convict Lease System in Florida," 190–91.

6. William J. Cooper, Jr. and Thomas E. Terrill, *The American South: A History*, vol. 2 (New York, 1991), 394.

7. Carper, "Martin Tabert," 122–23. Heretofore it has been assumed that accused vagrants were an important source of labor through convict leasing. A 1991 study by William Cohen appears to propose that vagrancy was relatively insignificant. William Cohen, *At Freedom's Edge: Black Mobility and the Southern White Quest for Racial Control, 1861–1915* (Baton Rouge: Louisiana State University Press, 1991).

8. Allen Johnston Going, *Bourbon Democracy in Alabama, 1874–1890* (Westport: Greenwood Press, 1972), 174. In a general discussion of leased convicts in Alabama and their relationship to the outside world, part of a larger study on the history of convict leasing in Alabama, Mary Ellen Curtin notes that the treatment of male and female prisoners in Alabama coal mines was "brutal if not lethal." Mary Ellen Curtin, "The Daily Struggles of Black Prisoners in Alabama: A Gender Analysis," paper presented at the meeting of the Southern Historical Association, Atlanta,

Georgia, November 7, 1992, p. 4. See also Curtin's Ph.D. dissertation, entitled, "Legacies of Struggle: Black Prisoners in the Making of Post-Bellum Alabama, 1865–1895" (Duke University, 1992).

9. *Tampa Tribune*, June 22, 1910.

10. Carper, "The Convict Lease System in Florida," 291.

11. Ibid., 289.

12. See Paul B. Foreman and Julien R. Tatum, "The Short History of Mississippi's State Penal System," *Mississippi Law Journal* (April 1938), 262, n. 20, which cites other studies.

13. For Florida, see Blake McKelvey, "Penal Slavery and Southern Reconstruction," *Journal of Negro History* 20 (1935), 154, and Carper, "The Convict Lease System in Florida," 24. For Georgia, consult A. J. McKelway, "The Convict Lease System of Georgia," *The Outlook* (September 1908), 67. For Alabama, see A. J. Going, *Bourbon Democracy in Alabama*, 176.

14. *Report of the Joint Committee on Penitentiary* (Tennessee, 1893, 1895).

15. "Report of Warden Felix Buchanan," in *Report of the Joint Committee on Penitentiary* (Tennessee, 1895), 4.

16. Both examples are found in Edward L. Ayers, *Vengeance and Justice: Crime and Punishment in the 19th Century American South* (New York, 1984), 198–99.

    A further example of Blacks being jailed for petty crimes under leasing comes from a book by Vernon Lane Wharton, entitled *The Negro in Mississippi* (New York, 1965), in which the author describes the so-called Pig Law in the state. Legislation passed by the post-Reconstruction Democratic legislature, Wharton writes, "declared the theft of any property valued at more than ten dollars, or of any kind of cattle or swine, regardless of value, to be grand larceny, subjecting the thief to a term up to five years in the State penitentiary. This was the famous 'Pig

Law,' which was largely responsible for an increase in the population of the state prison from 272 in 1874 to 1,072 at the end of 1877. It was this law that made of the convict lease system a big business enterprise. . . ." (237).

17. These data come from the 1912–13 prison report in Louisiana, although the reporting year appears to be 1908.

18. *Proceedings of the Annual Congress of the American Prison Association, September 13–19, Boston, Massachusetts* (New York: American Prison Association, 1923), 232.

19. A. C. Hutson, Jr., "The Overthrow of the Convict Lease System in Tennessee," *East Tennessee Historical Society Publications* 8 (1936), 85.

20. *Report of the Joint Committee to Enquire in the Treatment of Convicts* (Alabama, 1881), 35.

21. The emphasis here is on those who could not pay their small fines and had to work off their time with lessees, and those held beyond their sentences, since the annals of penal history are filled with inmates' claims of being unjustly incarcerated.

22. *Report of the Commission Appointed by the Governor of Texas, April 10, 1875, to Investigate the Alleged Mismanagement and Cruel Treatment of Convicts* (Houston: A. C. Gray, State Printer, 1875), 2.

23. Carper, "The Convict Lease System in Florida," 168–69.

24. Ibid., quoting *House Journal* (1901), 993–95.

25. "Report of the Superintendent," in *Tennessee State Penitentiary Report, 1892–1894*, 4.

26. *Report of the Penitentiary Investigating Committee* (Texas, 1909), 708. (Hereafter referred to as *Texas Report.*)

27. Carper, "The Convict Lease System in Florida," 115–16.

28. Ibid. Marion County citizens were enraged by the George Washington incident, which involved a convict who served one-half of his thirty-day sentence with a good record. Poor health prevented him from undertaking further work, which irritated a guard. Washington was handcuffed and hung over the limb of a tree so that his feet could not touch the ground. After twenty minutes he cried out in pain, at which point another guard beat him severely.

29. Ibid., 118–19.

30. Powell, *An American Siberia*, 7, 12ff.

31. Mary F. Berry and John W. Blassingame, *Long Memory: The Black Experience in America* (New York, 1982), 124.

32. *Atlanta Journal*, July 30, 1908, 5ff.

33. "Georgia Proceedings, 1908," 9–15, 71, *passim*.

34. *Texas Report*, 256.

35. Ibid., 222, 224.

36. Foreman and Tatum, "The Short History," 263, n. 21; *New Mississippian,* December 6, 1887.

37. *Superintendent's Biennial Report, Tennessee, December 1, 1894–December 1, 1896*, 4.

38. *House Journal* (Louisiana, 1873), 121–22.

39. *Texas Report*, 329.

40. "Warden's Report," in *Superintendent's Biennial Report, Tennessee, 1894–1896*.

41. Hutson, "The Overthrow of the Convict Lease System in Tennessee," 85.

42. *Superintendent's Biennial Report, Tennessee, December 1, 1894–December 1, 1896*, 4ff.
    A case of Black defiance of convict treatment under leasing, with dire consequences, is that of Caesar White. Caesar White

was of Herculean strength and a "most desperate" character. He was considered a "bad nigger" among prison officers in Tennessee in the mid-1880s. Seemingly "good order" prevailed in general. Although all convicts were described throughout the state at this time as "largely the ignorant and turbulent elements of society," they remained pretty much under control, with one exception. White was unruly and would not submit to prison discipline, and generated fear among inmates and guards alike. He did not obey orders and "with formidable bludgeon defied every attempt at arrest." When he became incorrigible and refused to be taken in without trouble, threatening to kill anyone who attempted to arrest him, he was shot and died a few days later. At his inquest, Caesar White's death was declared "justifiable" and the cause was listed as "vulnus septicemia." See "Report of the Inspectors, Warden of the Tennessee Penitentiary to the Forty-Fourth General Assembly," December 1884, 8–9.

43. Elizabeth Wisner, *Public Welfare Administration in Louisiana* (Chicago, 1930), 159, n. 18.

44. *Florida Reports* 53 (1907), 27ff.

45. Ibid., 29–30.

46. *Tampa Tribune*, October 23, 1908. Also on the Campbell case, see Carper, "The Convict Lease System in Florida," 237ff.

47. *Texas Report*, 222, 628, 484, *passim*.

48. Ibid., 920, 851.

49. Ibid., 220.

50. Ibid., 335.

51. Ibid., 897.

52. Ibid., 712.

53. Ibid., 761.

54. Ibid., 175.

55. Ibid., 445.

56. Ibid., 820–21. Cornelius Malory told why he did not wish to testify about conditions in convict lease camps in Texas when he stated before the Legislative Investigating Committee, "I am afraid to testify before you. You will be gone and I must stay here. You cannot protect me. The niggers at this camp go flying [are hung] all the time." *Texas Report*, 973.

57. Ibid., 706, 806, 386.

58. Ibid., 292.

59. Ibid., 264.

60. Ibid., 282.

61. *Atlanta Journal*, August 1, 1908; see also August 2, 5, and 6 for more on the Abe Winn story.

62. "Proceedings," in *Georgia Penitentiary Legislative Investigation Report, 1908*, 1343. (Hereafter cited as "Georgia Proceedings, 1908.")

63. It is now well known, as it was not in 1908, that tuberculosis is not hereditary.

64. The best place to turn for all of the details on the Abe Winn case is "Georgia Proceedings, 1908," pages 172–73, 1233–35, 1328–34, 1572–80, 1635–37, *passim*, which has all of the corroborating and conflicting accounts of what actually happened to young Abe Winn. The information for the newspaper stories, which sensationalized this tragic case, came from this transcript. There was no record of any convictions in the case and the newspapers appear to have eventually lost interest.

65. Carper, "The Convict Lease System in Florida," 182.

66. Ibid., 257.

67. Herbert Stacy McKay, "Convict Leasing in North Carolina, 1870–1934," M.A. thesis (University of North Carolina, Chapel Hill, 1942), 129.

68. Foreman and Tatum, "The Short History," 263, n. 21.

69. *Board of Control Report* (Louisiana, 1874), 3.

70. *Report of the Joint Committee on Penitentiary, General Assembly of Tennessee* (1893), 17.

71. Herman Lee Crow, "A Political History of the Texas Penal System, 1829–1951," Ph.D. diss. (University of Texas, 1963), 176.

72. *Texas Report*, 575.

73. Ibid., 560.

74. Ibid., 549–50, 573. See additional testimony throughout *Texas Report* for examples of sexual abuse of Black females by prison officials and male inmates, Black and White. Guadalupe Grimsinger testified that she was abused in prison when she was twenty years old, and apparently years before that, because she had a thirteen-year-old daughter at home. *Texas Report*, 546.

75. Ibid.

76. Ibid., 218, 444–45, 525–26. An additional description of this June 24, 1907, childbirth as provided by a prison guard can be found in the *Texas Report* on pages 453–54.

77. *Texas Report*, 560, 564, 566, 311.

78. *Daily Advertiser*, February 5, 1889.

79. Carper, "The Convict Lease System in Florida," 232.

80. *Senate Journal* (Louisiana, 1873), 147; Mark Carleton, *Politics and Punishment: History of the Louisiana State Penal System* (Baton Rouge, 1971), 15.

81. Carper, "The Convict Lease System in Florida," 87–89.

82. Ibid., 259–60.

83. Crow, "A Political History," 147–48.

84. Ibid., 143.

85. Going, *Bourbon Democracy in Alabama*, 190.

86. Crow, "A Political History," 168.

87. *New Mississippian*, December 6, 1887; *New Mississippian*, October 11, 1887; Foreman and Tatum, "The Short History," 265.

88. Ibid., n. 24.

89. *New Mississippian*, October 11, 1887.

90. *Atlanta Journal*, August 9, 1908.

91. *Atlanta Journal*, July 20, 1908.

92. *Atlanta Journal*, July 27, 1908.

93. Albert B. Moore, *History of Alabama and Her People*, vol. 1 (New York: American Historical Society, 1927), 979.

94. Ibid.

95. *Montgomery Daily Advertiser*, January 28, 1883.

96. Ibid.

97. Ibid.

98. Ibid.

99. Ibid.

100. Ibid.

101. Ibid.

102. Hutson, "The Overthrow of the Convict Lease System in Tennessee," 101.

103. Ibid.

104. J. C. Powell, *An American Siberia*, Patterson Smith Reprint Series, Publication Number 105 (Montclair, N.J., repr. 1970), 46–

47; Carper, "The Convict Lease System in Florida," 53–54. There is some confusion about the name of the owner of this plantation. Powell calls him Green Cheers; Carper refers to him as Mr. G. A. Chaires.

105. Powell, *An American Siberia*, 77–78.

106. Mark Carleton, "The Politics of the Convict Lease System in Louisiana: 1868–1901," *Louisiana History* 8, no. 1 (Winter 1967), 6; also Carleton, *Politics and Punishment*.

107. *New Mississippian,* October 11, 1887.

108. "Hanging in the window" means that the window was closed on the hands and/or fingers, and the convict was left to hang there.

109. *Texas Report*, 367, 225, 996.

110. Ibid., 389.

111. Ibid., 493, 387, 506, 606–07, 877, 906, 230, *passim.*

112. Ibid., 496.

113. Crow, "A Political History," 171.

114. Ibid.

115. "Report of the House Committee to Investigate the State Penitentiary," *House Journal* (Mississippi, 1888), Appendix, 4.

116. McKelway, "The Convict Lease System of Georgia," 69.

117. Harry Williams Gilmore, "The Convict Lease System in Arkansas," M.A. thesis (George Peabody College for Teachers, 1930), 31–33.

118. *Report of the Joint Committee on Penitentiary*, General Assembly of Tennessee, 1893, 4.

119. In Mississippi, for example, Benjamin Lamb and James Troy were unlawfully held beyond their sentences. *Jackson Weekly Clarion*, May 23, 1883. In Georgia, Handy Holmes claimed his sentence had expired and he was being illegally incarcerated. "Georgia

Proceedings, 1908," 368.

120. For further examples of subleasing and for discussions of it outside original states, see Carper, "The Convict Lease System in Florida," 100–01, 127, and Crow, "A Political History," 133–35.

121. *Report of Committee on Penitentiary*, Arkansas (1871), 6.

122. Crow, "A Political History," 94, n. 3.

123. *Texas Report*, 702.

124. Ibid., 528.

125. Ibid., 691.

126. Jane Zimmerman, "The Convict Lease System in Arkansas and the Fight for Abolition," *The Arkansas Historical Quarterly* (Autumn 1949), 179–80.

127. *Report of the Joint Investigating Committee on Penitentiary Affairs*, General Assembly of Tennessee (1895), 10–22. There is a curious statement on page 7 indicating that guards charged "entrance fees to the prison," which is confusing.

128. Ibid., 7, *passim*. See, also, *Texas Report*, 309, for examples of prison officials collecting salaries from the state and from lessees.

129. McKelway, "The Convict Lease System of Georgia," 68. Also discussed below in chapter 4.

130. One Georgia sublessee, W. M. Toomer, admitted clearing $180,000 on a contract. See "Georgia Proceedings, 1908," 976.

131. Going, *Bourbon Democracy in Alabama*, 181.

132. Ibid., 176–77.

133. Ibid., 180. This is a strange table. The years 1878, 1877, and 1876 are listed in reverse order. The table starts with 1868, goes up to 1875, and 1878, 1877, and 1876 then follow. After 1876, the table jumps to 1880 and runs in two-year sequences through 1890. No statistics for revenue are given for 1868–75. Statistics are missing

from other categories and other years, and include such notations as "figures not available" and "not given," but no explanation is provided. The original source cited by Going is "Alabama, Convict Inspectors' Reports," which could not be located by this author in the Alabama Department of Archives in Montgomery.

134. Crow, "A Political History," 170; *Texas Report*, 163.

135. Harry Williams Gilmore, "The Convict Lease System in Arkansas," M.A. thesis (George Peabody College for Teachers, 1930), 48.

136. Ibid., 24.

137. For more on Zeb Ward, see Gilmore, "The Convict Lease System in Arkansas," chapter 2, *passim*. Also see Zimmerman, "The Convict Lease System in Arkansas." For a profile of Ward, see his obituary in the *Arkansas Gazette*, December 29, 1894, where he was described as a person "identified prominently with the best interests" and where the value of his "large estate" was estimated at $600,000.

138. *State Penitentiary Report*, Tennessee (January 6, 1879), 12.

139. George Frederickson, *The Black Image in the White Mind* (New York, 1971), 203.

CHAPTER FOUR

NADIR:
A CASE STUDY OF
CONVICT LEASING
IN GEORGIA

T HE STATE OF GEORGIA SERVES as a useful case study in southern convict leasing because it contained most of the characteristics that obtained in all other ex-Confederate states from the end of the Civil War into the twentieth century. The beginning was similar to that elsewhere, as Georgia fell on hard times soon after the defeat of the Confederacy. To offset the expense of maintaining prisons, the state turned to leasing.

Black convicts overwhelmingly outnumbered Whites in

Georgia leasing, from its start in 1866 to its overthrow in 1908. Changes in prison administration over the years determined the pace and direction in leasing, sometimes for better but more frequently for worse. The process of receiving bids for convict labor mirrored that in other leasing states, particularly the opportunity for widespread fraud and corruption in the selection of lessees. Lessees made money and the state turned a profit from convict labor, although the windfall was not always as great as some of its citizens felt it could or should have been. Ex-governors had prominent roles in some companies that were lessees; principal keepers and wardens were linked directly to lessees; and prison officials served two masters—the state and the lessees—and collected salaries from both. Some of Georgia's leading politicians eventually supported the abolition of convict leasing, even though it never became the dominant issue in campaigns for the state's highest elective office. Ultimately, when the abuses of convict leasing in Georgia, with all of its attendant horrors, became known to more and more people and became an embarrassment for the state, several newspapers and a handful of zealous legislators committed themselves to the final destruction of a system that had been described by a Georgia legislator as:

> . . . more inhuman . . . than the barbarities of the Persians and Medes three thousand years ago. It is the counterpart of Russian massacres of today. It is almost as horrible as the thumb-screws and torture tools of the Spanish Inquisition, and it is an everlasting disgrace to the great Christian state of Georgia today.[1]

During the decades before the Civil War, with the exception of the 1830s, the Georgia prison consistently reported an annual deficit. There was little or no income, and costs included mostly routine items such as salaries, repairs, and the ordinary maintenance of inmates. The 1860 prison population of 245, the largest in Georgia up to that time, contained very few Blacks. During the war years, 1861–65, the penitentiary provided "considerable" income for Georgia, as convicts were used in the production of war-related materials as well as other items, mainly for public consumption. By 1864, with Georgia's collapse imminent, Governor Joseph E. Brown, in desperation, pardoned most of the state's convicts (who, as a condition of their pardons, had to agree to join the militia) in an effort to stall General Sherman's advance. In November, the prison at Milledgeville (the state capitol before Atlanta) was razed.[2] When the Civil War ended five months later, four prisoners remained in the penitentiary. By the Autumn of 1865 it was reported that the penitentiary "was without a single dollar to carry on its functions."[3] However, the prison population had grown to 177, and 75 percent of them were Black.[4] Governor Brown, who was unhappy with the Georgia prison during his tenure, estimated that the cost of rebuilding the prison would be $1 million, which the state did not have and the governor did not favor using in any event. Georgia's dilemma and that of its sister states was to find the most cost-effective means of maintaining its prison system, with its increasing population. Many believed that the situation required a fresh approach.[5]

OVERVIEW

The 1866 legislation authorizing the governor to lease the penitentiary for not more than five years on the best possible terms set no precedent in Georgia or elsewhere, as noted in chapter 2.

However, Brown's successor, Governor Charles Jones Jenkins, chose not to implement the 1866 lease law, electing instead to rehabilitate the prison. It was not until 1868 under Provisional Governor General Thomas H. Ruger, who was the Federal military replacement for Jenkins, that the Georgia convict lease system was inaugurated.

This first lease called for one hundred "able-bodied" convicts to be supplied to William A. Fort of Rome, Georgia, to work on the Georgia and Alabama Railroad. Fort agreed to pay Georgia $2,500 on a yearly installment plan, which was comparable with the financial arrangements for leases elsewhere at the time.[6] In July 1868, another lease was signed with William Fort and Joseph Printup for one hundred convicts to work on the Selma, Rome, and Dalton Railroad. The state would be remunerated at a rate of $1,000 per capita annually for this convict labor. As before, all expenses were to be borne by the lessee, relieving Georgia of any financial burden in connection with the supervision and maintenance of state convicts.[7] A third, more comprehensive lease was executed in November with Grant, Alexander and Co., which was a construction firm whose primary business was building railroads. It was agreed that Grant, Alexander and Co. would be supplied "100 to 500" prisoners at $10 per convict per year. This contract was superseded, however, on June 18, 1869, by one in which the governor and the state of Georgia transferred "into the hands of Grant, Alexander and Co., for the term of two years from this date the [entire] Penitentiary of the State of Georgia, together with all appurtenances, fixtures and property there unto belonging, to be held, used, and controlled by them for their own use and benefit. . . ."[8] (See appendix 4.)

The state received no payment for these convicts but was relieved of all penitentiary expenses except the salary of the principal keeper, which it continued to pay. Grant, Alexander and Co. agreed not to overwork the convicts, to treat them "humanely," and to maintain other conditions in accordance with the rules and regulations governing convicts. These three 1868–69 leases launched the era of convict leasing in Georgia, which continued for four more decades.[9]

Of some significance was legislation adopted in March of 1874 at Governor James M. Smith's recommendation (see appendix 2). The governor, who later became a lessee, felt that in order for leasing to be profitable for lessees, with the big cash outlays they required and the need for a large work force, leasing contracts should be in effect for at least five years. Therefore, the legislature extended the term for leasing from two to a minimum of five years and incorporated the usual formal safeguards for the state and for convicts found in earlier agreements. Lessees were to guarantee "humane" treatment and were not to use "corporeal [sic]" punishment unless "absolutely necessary to secure discipline." The State of Georgia, as before, was responsible only for the salary of the principal keeper and paid no other expenses. Convicts, in addition, were not to be worked excessively, or on Sunday, or outside the state. The principal keeper, as the only significant penitentiary official, took on the additional responsibility of inspector of the penitentiary, and regularly checked on the state's convict camps and investigated any violations. The governor was authorized to void contracts breached by "lessees, their agents or employees, or overseers," all of whom were subject to indictment and conviction under the laws governing such offenses.[10]

Several companies won contracts following public advertisements for bids. J. T. and W. D. Grant, involved in "public works," got 180 prisoners at $10 per convict per year for five years. Smith, Riddle, and Co. contracted for one hundred "farm laborers" at $11 per convict per year. One hundred convicts went to ex-Governor Joseph E. Brown's Dade Coal Company at $11 per convict per year to work as coal miners. To build the North Georgia Railroad, Wallis, Haley and Co. received one hundred convicts for two years, which violated the letter and the spirit of the 1874 legislation requiring leases of five years or more. Apparently there were further violations, since the Northeastern Railroad Co. got fifty convicts for twenty-one months, and Henry Stevens leased fifty prisoners for two years for his pottery works, at $20 per convict per year. An additional $20-per-convict-per-year contract went to George D. Harris of the Bartow Iron Works Company. Three of those contracts were later canceled for contract violations and abusive treatment of prisoners. The contracts were turned over to other lessees on similar terms, as required by the 1874 legislation.[11]

The prison population continued to grow and lessees and others went on agitating for longer-term leases. This process culminated in the adoption of legislation, in February 1876, providing for leases of "not less than twenty years." This "watershed" legislation generated bids for convict labor for hundreds of thousands of dollars, higher than any previous bidding, and led to the creation of Georgia Penitentiary Companies One, Two, and Three, which effectively turned over all state prisoners and convict camps to these three companies or their sublessees for twenty years. The agreement called for the three lessees to pay the state $500,000 in pro-rata shares, in $25,000 annual installments every year for twenty years. Penitentiary Company Number One, the Dade Coal Company, received three hundred prisoners. Companies Number Two (B. G. Lockett, L. A. Jordon, W. B. Lowe, and J. B. Gordon) and

Three (Thomas Alexander, W. D. Grant, W. W. Simpson, John W. Murphey, and William Howell) equally divided the remaining prisoners.[12] In addition, the 1876 legislation carefully covered all pertinent areas of concern in convict leasing, such as the "humane" treatment of convicts (the governor was authorized to sue the lessee for $400 for each case of cruelty to convicts); relieving the state of all penitentiary-related expenses except the salaries of the principal keeper, physician, and chaplain; requiring that lessees "shall be a corporate body" (suggesting that individuals were not eligible to lease); and mandating that members of companies leasing convicts "shall be bona fide citizens of this State." The three penitentiary companies were to "procure, at their own expense," within the state of Georgia, "suitable, convenient, safe, healthy, and commodious prisons, barracks, hospitals, guardhouses, and all other dwellings necessary for the safe-keeping and comfort of the convicts under its care and control, which shall be known as the Penitentiary of this State." Subleasing was prohibited, and if it was discovered, the governor was empowered to "sue and recover of said company the sum of Five Hundred Dollars for each instance of sub-leasing or re-leasing."[13]

With the advent of the twenty-year leases in Georgia, which went into effect beginning April 1, 1879, the period of juggling terms essentially ended and there was "relative quietude" in convict lease reorganization, rules and regulations, and general administration, although, as discussed below, there was less calm elsewhere.[14] This "peaceful hiatus" ended when Governor W. Y. Atkinson, as a candidate for the state's top job, condemned convict leasing in his campaign and called for the inclusion of such a plank at the Georgia State Democratic Convention in 1896. No plank wound up in the party platform, but when

Atkinson was subsequently elected governor, he reorganized key aspects of prison administration and served notice that he was no friend of convict leasing. A three-member Prison Commission eventually replaced the principal keeper as the person officially responsible for supervision of the state's convicts. The office of principal keeper was later abolished and that of state warden created. However, the same person, the notorious Jake Moore, was the state's last principal keeper and first state warden.

Atkinson believed that leases should be limited to five years and that the state should retain the power to "manage, direct, punish, or control" convicts. In Atkinson's view, turning over control of convicts to outside parties was "fundamentally wrong and vicious."[15] With the inauguration of the administration of Governor Atkinson in Georgia, the death knell was sounded for convict leasing, but burial would have to wait. The Governor argued his case against leasing and for overhauling the penitentiary system in a detailed message to the legislature in October of 1897. In proposing a new system, Atkinson addressed issues of a boys' reformatory, work and treatment for men and women convicts, the "character of work to be done by convicts," and—waxing philosophical, even moralistic or pious—"reforming influences" in penology.[16]

For the governor, that meant the enactment of legislation creating "the best possible" social climate for convicts so that they could be "induced" to reform their ways and become productive citizens of Georgia. Correct morality should be "inculcated" through religious teaching in order "to impress" upon convicts the value of right over wrong. Prison officials, therefore, "from the highest to the lowest," should be only men of the best "habits and characters." The morality feature had been neglected in the past, the governor felt, and although he was doubtful about its possibilities, he expressed a commitment to ". . . let us do our duty and for results trust in God." Addressing the rate of recidivism, Governor Atkinson implored the legislature to recognize that convicts were "worse men" when they left confinement and "more dangerous" than when they arrived. Even as criminals, convicts should be treated humanely if the objective was reform and improvement, the governor argued. The "security of society" was hostage to convicts being "rescued" for the errors of their past. Atkinson warned that society would pay a price for its failure to reform convicts in the subsequent commission of "more outrageous crimes." Finally, the governor told the lawmakers: "In obedience to the duty which we owe our fellow man, and in behalf of society to which you owe protection, I invoke you to so legislate upon this question as to subserve this high and noble purpose."[17]

Despite the fact that Atkinson's successors more or less opposed leasing, it lasted for eleven more years. The system succumbed only after a vigorous legislative investigation in 1908, a determined newspaper crusade, and at least one leasing-related murder.

Beginnings

With the adoption of the Thirteenth Amendment to the United States Constitution outlawing slavery, Blacks, it seems, with the benefit of hindsight, were doomed to swell the ranks of the prison population in the South. No longer "protected" from general societal punishment by slavemasters for committing "crimes," their petty theft, vagrancy, and contract violations in sharecropping, tenant farming, and so forth earned them fines they could not pay and certain jail terms. When convicts in the jails and prisons of Georgia and the South began to be leased to private parties, it was Blacks in the main who wound up as leased convict labor. Illiteracy and ignorance of prevailing laws were insufficient excuses for the imbalance. The absence of adequate counsel and other shortcomings in a criminal justice nightmare that left so much to be desired were, in addition, no comfort. The Black understanding and definition of "crime," which sometimes differed from that of Whites' understanding—especially such things as taking chickens or "idling" or walking away from unfair contracts with ex-slave owners—made no difference. The record, such as it is, shows that the convict lease system in Georgia and elsewhere was, as much as anything, a Black convict lease system. That is, it was a system in which 70, 80, and 90-plus percent of the victims—the convicts—were Black.

Table 4.1 (pages 148–49) illustrates the Black:White ratios in the penitentiary throughout much of the era of convict leasing in Georgia, from 1866 to 1908. These ratios compare favorably with those of other post–Civil War southern states, all of which, for more or fewer numbers of years, were engaged in leasing.

Exposure

Although news of appalling conditions for and treatment of leased labor leaked out from time to time, and in spite of periodic reports about occasional serious problems in the state's convict camps, it took legislative investigations of the penitentiary and leasing to lay bare the system's more onerous features. Those were then picked up and publicized by the news media, raising public consciousness. The first major inquiry came in 1870 following an 1869 report in which the principal keeper of the penitentiary complained about the general treatment of convicts,

Table 4.1
BLACK:WHITE RATIOS, GEORGIA PENITENTIARY, 1879–1909

Year	Blacks	Whites	(Total)	Black %
Apr. 1, 1879	1,109	121	(1,230)	90.16
Oct. 1, 1880	1,071	115	(1,186)	90.30
Oct. 1, 1882	1,130	113	(1,243)	90.90
Oct. 1, 1884	1,251	126	(1,377)	90.84
Oct. 1, 1886[a]	1,378	149	(1,527)	90.24
Oct. 1, 1888	1,388	149	(1,537)	90.30
Oct. 1, 1890[a]	1,529	168	(1,697)	90.10
Oct. 1, 1892	1,744	196	(1,940)	89.89
Oct. 1, 1893	1,981	187	(2,168)	91.37
Oct. 1, 1894	2,137	191	(2,328)	91.79
Oct. 1, 1895[a]	2,210	214	(2,424)	91.17
Oct. 1, 1896	2,164	193	(2,357)	91.81
Oct. 1, 1897	2,038	197	(2,235)	91.18
Oct. 1, 1898	1,996	241	(2,237)	89.22
Oct. 1, 1899	1,953	248	(2,201)	88.73

noting that lessees kept poor records, that sometimes prisoners were sent directly to lessees after sentencing without his knowledge, that religious services were ignored, and that the state was not getting enough money for leased convict labor. He recommended an investigation.[18] The Joint Committee Appointed to Investigate the Condition of the Georgia Penitentiary took

Table 4.1 (continued)
BLACK:WHITE RATIOS, GEORGIA PENITENTIARY, 1879–1909

Year	Blacks	Whites	(Total)	Black %
Oct. 1, 1900[a]	1,900	258	(2,158)	88.04
Oct. 1, 1901	1,987	258	(2,245)	88.50
Oct. 1, 1902	2,058	257	(2,315)	88.89
June 1, 1904	2,059	256	(2,315)	88.94
June 1, 1905	1,989	291	(2,280)	87.23
June 1, 1906	2,131	213	(2,344)	90.91
June 1, 1907	2,187	277	(2,464)	88.75
June 1, 1908[a]	2,219	320	(2,539)	87.39
June 1, 1909[a]	2,346	262	(2,608)	89.95

Note: This information was reported biennially until 1893, when it became part of annual reporting, except apparently for 1903. As of June 1, 1904, the reporting year ran from June through May.
[a]The original *Prison Commission Report* contained errors in addition in the total number of convicts counted. (The total number of Black males and females, and White males and females, was incorrect.) The above table presents the corrected totals.
Source: *Sixth Biennial Report of the Prison Commission of Georgia from January 1, 1935 to December 31, 1936*, 25.

testimony from all who wished to give it. The Committee deliberated and issued its report to the Georgia General Assembly in July 1870.[19] The investigation revealed that convicts complained about poor food and deficiencies in diet, especially meat; the existence of subleasing; insufficient medical care; being required to work on Sundays (and sometimes whipped if they refused); and denial of religious services. Convicts were held and worked beyond their sentences and without being paid, and men and women were severely whipped, sometimes resulting in death.

There were several descriptions of the latter, but more examples were given like the case of Hubbard Cureton, who was in prison for "sleeping with a white woman" and "whipped from his neck to his knees . . . stark naked." His skin "blistered and then bursted [sic]; . . . [and his] whole back turned black and blue."[20] Another convict, named Robinson, was

> . . . put down on his hands and knees[,] a stick put through his arms and legs; then [he was] turned over on his face, and they dipped the straps into salty water; then they whipped him on the bare skin until he turned right blue. He was whipped from the head to the knees. About a half-hour afterwards, they rubbed spirits of turpentine over him and whipped him again."[21]

The report included specific guidelines for the improved treatment of convicts, but concluded generally that the treatment and condition of convicts were good. Paradoxically, because of the atrocities uncovered, the Joint Committee offered a resolution to the effect that leasing should be abandoned, but it was not adopted.

Women were not treated very differently from men in some instances in work assignments or punishment, and their routine sexual exploitation was described in chapter 3. Amusing to prison guards and male inmates, but mortifying and worse to the victims, female convicts were seen "whipped with their clothes turned over their heads, and the head pulled down between the legs."[22]

One hundred twenty-eight prisoners at the Cherokee Iron and Railroad Company Camp in Cedartown, where convicts were not issued any underwear, complained about being compelled to work at night and on Sundays, and being forced to sleep in their wet clothing.[23] At this same camp, a Black teenage convict who had escaped was discovered hiding under a pile of logs. The guards simply set fire to the logs in order to smoke him out of his sanctuary, severely burning the youngster in the process.[24]

Over the years between the 1870 investigation and a virtual declaration of war against convict leasing at the State Democratic Convention, as well as an announced crusade against it by the *Atlanta Georgian* newspaper, both in the summer of 1908, the fortunes of convict leasing ebbed and flowed. During this thirty-eight-year period, a litany of barbarities was exposed through additional investigations and other means, but defenders and apologists of leasing countered with pious platitudes to blunt the criticism. Nonetheless, when the final and most thorough investigation began in July 1908, Georgia leasing was experiencing its last breath before being smothered by revelations that muted and then scattered its few remaining supporters.

That convict leasing was an economically viable proposition for Georgia and other states goes almost without saying. The expense that the state was spared over a forty-year period is impossible to know. The human cost in abuse and suffering can also never be known and, in any event, can never be quantified.

ECONOMICS

The state was not efficient in its bookkeeping, so that a consistent record of income from leasing and related expenses over time is hard to come by. Moreover, sometimes lessees did not pay, or they did not pay all they owed the state, or they did not pay on time and no record was made. In addition, it will never be known how much money disappeared illegitimately into the pockets of prison officials and others without a trace. Some selected sample years must serve to illustrate the difficulty of producing a satisfactory picture of "profits" made by the state, and to pose the question of the possible value (or lack thereof) of extrapolating for other years.

When the penitentiary was leased for twenty years, we know that the stated income from lessees was to be $25,000 per year aggregating to $500,000. Since the only significant expense was the salary and expenses of the principal keeper—no more than around $2,500 per year (or perhaps one-half that amount, or less)—the net income for the state should have been at least $450,000.[25] In late nineteenth-century Georgia dollars, that was a fair amount of money and might have encouraged unscrupulous individuals to find ways to expand the prison population and leasing. The ten-year period from 1899 to 1908, after the end of the twenty-year lease, shows eight years of profit for the state, ranging from $100,534.29 in fiscal year 1903 (January 1, 1903 to December 31, 1903) to $4,254.60 in fiscal year 1905 (January 1, 1905 to December 31, 1905). However, in 1906 and 1908, the state reported losses of $10,106.60 and $808.47, respectively—a significant discrepancy (see Table 4.2). The net income shown from leasing for Georgia for the ten years was $375,858.97, almost as much as should have been earned during the life of the twenty-year lease. The reasons why Georgia showed losses in 1906 and 1908 can only be the subject of speculation at this point. Corruption on the part of state officials might have been more widespread in those years. Lessees might have taken larger

Table 4.2
GEORGIA PENITENTIARY, INCOME AND EXPENSES, 1899–1908

Year	Income	Expenses	Net Income	Source:[b] year, page
1899	$201,297.40	$156,315.12	$44,982.28	1900, 514–15
1900	156,194.55	109,052.04	47,142.51	1901, 803–04
1901	202,329.25	120,081.60	82,247.65	1902, 768–69
1902[a]	50,883.46	30,000.00	20,883.46	1904, 800–01
1903	218,345.64	117,811.35	100,534.29	1904, 802–03
1904	269,748.75	192,357.16	77,391.59	1905, 1306–07
1905	327,625.12	323,370.52	4,254.60	1906, 1202–03
1906	340,011.22	350,171.82	(10,160.60)	1907, 1050–51
1907	370,101.08	360,709.42	9,391.66	1908, 1176–77
1908	380,709.44	381,517.91	(808.47)	1909, 1610–11

Note: The fiscal year was October 1 through September 30 for the years 1899–1902, and January 1 through December 31 for the years 1903–1908.

[a]Fiscal year 1902 was three months only, from October 1, 1902, through December 31, 1902, at which time the fiscal year was changed to conform to the calendar year.

[b]Citations are from the "State Treasurer's Report" for the ten-year period from 1899 to 1908. This report was selected because of its completeness. It is found in the *Annual Publication of Georgia Laws*, which is the most consistent record of the state's income and expenses, even though for several years before 1899 there is simply no Treasurer's Report and no explanation for its absence.

shares. The record could be inaccurate. It was discovered in 1901 that original lessees were receiving from subcontractors at least twice as much as the amount for which they had contracted in the original lease, shortchanging the state and giving large profits to original lessees.[26] The way in which the income from convict labor was used was not always clear, but, among other things, it went toward the support of public schools and the construction of public roads. There were also expenses for salaries, advertisements for bids, and the cost of land purchases.

Finding hard evidence of individuals and companies who profited handsomely from convict leasing is as challenging as tracing net income for states, perhaps more so. Individuals who amassed huge fortunes were involved in many other enterprises. Therefore, disaggregating their leasing bonanza from other income is a daunting exercise. There is, however, peripatetic hearsay or circumstantial evidence.

Ex-Governor Brown is a case in point of a public official who derived part of his fortune from lease-system earnings.[27] Brown was born on April 15, 1821, in comparative poverty in a mountain cabin. He rose to power in Georgia, serving as governor during the Civil War, and was elected to the U.S. Senate in 1880. His investments and business interests included iron and coal mines, real estate, and railroads. He served as president of the Dade Coal Company, a major lessee in Georgia, and was said to have "used his political influence to obtain the leases and used the extremely cheap labor to mine a scanty amount of minerals and still make a handsome profit."[28] These leased labor profits were central in the fortune he accumulated, which was conservatively estimated at more than $1 million when he died, one of the richest men in the state.[29] Brown's Dade Coal Company received some severe criticism from a legislative subcommittee that visited his mines in 1895. The coal mine camp was described as being in the "worst condition," with starving convicts who were treated with "great cruelty." The system of corporal punishment appeared to be a step beyond cruel, and in one instance was characterized as being "the most brutal [punishment] ever inflicted by one human being upon another." The subcommittee included the following account of convict torture in its report, as well:

> [A] half[-]starved convict is thrown upon his back, and while in that condition a machine attached to a hose is thrown over his nose and water is thrown into his nostrils until he is almost strangled, and as that victim shows signs of reviving the water is turned on and the strangling process [is] repeated until the victim has barely life enough left in him to rise from the ground.[30]

Other ex-governors, such as James M. Smith and John B. Gordon, were also prominent lessees in Georgia, along with a string of other "statesmen," all of whom jumped on the leasing bandwagon and used their influence to profit from leasing.

CRITICS OF LEASING

The story of Robert Augustus Alston, a member of the Georgia State Legislature from DeKalb County near Atlanta, elected in 1877, and chairman of the Committee of the State Penitentiary, provides an example of the fate that befell one critic of convict leasing. Alston was a colorful, flamboyant figure who spent some early years in Charleston, South Carolina, but was born in Bibb County, Georgia, near Macon, on New Year's eve in 1832. He was trained as a lawyer, was a colonel in the Confederate military, and was a former slave-owner who promulgated a report on convict leasing in 1878 during his first term in the legislature.

The report was kind to many of the state's lessee camps, including ex-Governor Brown's, but not so charitable with others. It drew attention to the horrors of leasing—especially the practice of chaining men and women together and forcing them to occupy the same sleeping quarters, which resulted in the births of dozens of children in prison who remained incarcerated with their mothers. Alston's report prompted a sitting U.S. senator, General John B. Gordon—who later became governor and who held a principal interest in Penitentiary Company Number Two—to try and sell his interest quickly and quietly. Alston, with power of attorney, attempted to dispose of Gordon's interest on his behalf, and clashed with a sublessee and longtime friend, William Cox, who felt he would be ruined by the sale. Cox favored selling to a friend of his, hoping to ensure the continued supply of convict labor for his farm, but the price was too high. Despite an attempt by Governor Alfred H. Colquitt and others to mediate the dispute between Alston and Cox, the matter came down to an old-fashioned, Wild West–style gun duel in the state capitol. Although Alston apparently fired several shots first, he was in turn shot and killed by Cox, who was convicted for murder and sentenced to life in prison. He served only three years of light penitentiary labor, arranged by ex-Governor Brown (an early enemy) at one of Brown's mines, before being pardoned by Governor Alexander Stephens in 1882. The episode had an intimidating effect on would-be reformers and critics of convict leasing in Georgia at the time. Robert A. Alston instigated the attack on Georgia leasing starting with the 1878 Penitentiary Report and, to many observers, he eventually paid the ultimate price.[31] The aphorism "one had to go along to get along" now seemed as apt as ever in Georgia leasing.

A contemporary reformer who was not intimidated by the

Alston–Cox affair, and an observer of southern convict leasing in the 1880s, was George Washington Cable. His article "Convict Lease System in the Southern States," published in 1884, summarizes the status of leasing in each ex-Confederate state and is one of the earliest analyses on the subject. His discussion of Georgia points out the challenge of attempting to obtain reliable information on convict leasing. He identifies inaccuracies in principal keepers' reports, and asserts, in part, that "tabulated statements" are very confusing. Cable wrote that:

> One table, purporting to show . . . 1,186 convicts in confinement classified by the crimes under which they were sentenced, has not a single correct number in it, and is an entire hundred short in its true total. The numbers, moreover, are so far out of the way that they cannot possibly be the true exhibit of some other data substituted in error. They report 184 convicts under sentence for burglary, whereas the roll shows 467, and they entirely omit 25 serving sentence for forgery, and 23 for robbery.[32]

Be that as it may, the preponderance of evidence corroborated by investigations, convicts, prison officials, and others focuses unabashedly on a convict lease system in Georgia that was "purgatorial fire" for many prisoners and far from Langston Hughes's proverbial "crystal stair" for most others.

The savage death of convict John Mathews, who was confined in a camp leased to the Marietta and North Georgia Railroad, temporarily provoked public outrage at convict leasing. Mathews was serving a seven-year term for burglary when he embarked on an unsuccessful escape attempt. When he was returned to camp, a guard threw him to the ground and pinned him there by placing his foot on a pick-ax beside Mathews's neck. The guard then proceeded to whip Mathews "until the flesh parted and the blood oozed from the ugly wounds." For two days, this ritual of whipping was repeated until "death prevented further cruelty."[33]

Probably no single episode propelled Senator Thomas S. Felder, an obscure state legislator of Bibb County in Macon, Georgia, along with the *Atlanta Georgian*, to their rendezvous with history in the destruction of Georgia's convict leasing system. Rather, it was the accumulation of a long train of abuses that, by 1908, weighed so heavily on the consciences of a small group of reformers that they were catapulted into action, despite the sobering thought of losing the lucrative earnings that leasing brought to the public till. Standing before his colleagues in the Senate on June 25, 1908, Senator Felder, known by now as the "lightening rod" in the battle against leasing, threw down the gauntlet against the system and announced that he was working on legislation that would deny convict labor to anyone—corporations and individuals—outside the prison system. Although no action was taken that day, "everyone knows," Felder surmised, "that the question of the convict lease system in Georgia [is] so rotten that it smells to heaven."[34] Felder's lead was picked up by the *Georgian*, and two weeks later it made public its intention to expose the evils of leasing for public consumption and for those legislators "interested in the welfare of the state."[35]

Joining the fray as well was the *Atlanta Journal* and other newspapers, legislators, civic groups, and church leaders mobilized by the prospect of victory in a crusade against convict leasing.[36] It should have come as no surprise to anyone familiar with Georgia leasing that a joint legislative committee to investigate the convict lease system was created on July 17, 1908, based on a motion that began in the Senate three days earlier at the behest of Senator Felder. The Committee's mandate was very broad and inclusive, covering everything from abuses of convicts to fraud and corruption to lessee violation of contracts. It was charged to subpoena all necessary witnesses and gather all documents it desired. Before the Committee officially released its extensive report at an extraordinary session of the legislature on August 25, 1908, it sent deputations to visit and interview convicts and prison officials at every convict camp in the state.[37] It took testimony from dozens of other witnesses and collected a voluminous file of documents that was incorporated into its official record. This investigation virtually ensured the demise of Georgia leasing. When the dust settled and the smoke cleared, convict leasing in Georgia was all but dead.

The 1908 Committee Investigation

The legislature gave the bipartisan Committee of three members from the Senate and five from the House very specific instructions and guidance. In addition to examining leasing in the state, on which the inquiry focused primarily, the Committee was to investigate the Georgia Prison Farm and State Reformatory, which housed those prisoners not leased and most of the state's misdemeanor convicts. They were especially to report:

1. If any officer, chief warden, warden, guard or other employee of the State, whose duty it is or was to manage, control or who is or was otherwise connected with the convicts of the State is receiving or has received any emolument, money, compensation, gift or gratuity from the working, trafficking in or controlling of convicts other than the lawful compensation allowed by the state, and this investigation and report shall cover any officer,

chief warden, warden, guard or other employee whether now in the employment of the State or not.

2. If any member of the Prison Commission knew or had reason to believe that any chief warden, warden, guard or other employee or officer of the state was trafficking in the convicts of the State and deriving a profit from the leasing or subleasing of the same or receiving any compensation from any lessee.

3. If any lessee is violating or has violated his contract or any rule or regulation promulgated for the working of the convicts, and if such violation would authorize the forfeiture of the contract and the collection of the damages provided by law.

4. If there is or has been any mismanagement or misconduct on the part of any employee, guard or other officer charged with the control and conduct of the Prison Farm in Baldwin County.

5. If the Georgia State Reformatory is being conducted in accordance with the provisions of the Act creating the institution.

6. If there is any mismanagement of, or cruelty to, or other violations of the law or rules and regulations of the Prison Commission by any of the lessees, or officer or employees of the State in any of the camps where the convicts are worked by the lessees.

7. If there is any mismanagement, cruelty or violation of the law in any road camp, either misdemeanor or felony, and if any counties are illegally disposing of their misdemeanor convicts, and misdemeanor convicts are being illegally employed or worked.

8. The investigating committee is hereby authorized to investigate any and all charges emanating from any

source, and investigate any and all conditions whether the Prison Commission or convict camp, and particularly to find whether or not any of the irregularities charged as existing were within the consent or knowledge of the Prison Commission.[38]

The Committee was in session for twenty-eight days, meeting at least once and sometimes three times daily. Among those "examined" were members of the legislature who earlier visited the different convict camps in the state; members of the Prison Commission, which had overall responsibility for all prisoners in Georgia; the state warden, Jake Moore, who resigned before the investigation began; and the two state inspectors of convicts, who had 135 facilities to visit between them and one of whom, C. E. Deadwyler, was a 73-year-old former slave-owner who was clearly not up to the task.[39] In their testimony, they admitted that conditions in the coal mines were so bad and so dangerous that they refused to enter. Essentially, they accepted the prison warden's word, without visiting on their own, for the causes of injuries, whippings, and deaths. Also called were guards, ex-guards, Prison Commission staff, lower-level wardens, ex-wardens, physicians, ex-convicts, ordinary citizens, lessees, ex-lessees and their employees, and superintendents of convicts, who ostensibly were primarily responsible for the on-site management of the labor of convicts for lessees.

The warden, as the state's representative, had total supervisory responsibility for the entire prison, farm, or camp, and was there to make sure that the rules and regulations regarding work conditions and convict treatment were followed. Sometimes the warden and superintendent got along well; sometimes they did not. And sometimes they were the same individual, which created the much-criticized conflict between the state's interest and private interest. The problem was compounded by the fact that the individual was always paid more by lessees as superintendent than he was paid by the state as warden, even though, as warden, he was "in charge" of the institution. Inevitably there was the nagging question of "primary" interest.[40] Unlike the comprehensive legislative investigation in Texas, in the Georgia case few extant convicts testified—in part because some members of the committee felt that their testimony would be unreliable, believing they would be inclined to exaggerate and seek revenge on prison officials (for past mistreatment) and in part because they would be intimidated and fearful of reprisals from guards and others whom they might incriminate. (Such fears were borne out by the treatment of convicts who testified before earlier investigating committees in Georgia and elsewhere.)

As part of his reaction to the findings of the investigation, Governor Hoke Smith felt that handling the five thousand convicts in the state posed "serious" and "difficult" problems. "They should be punished but not treated brutally," he said. In his message to the legislature at the extraordinary session for dealing with convict leasing, the governor concluded that, "[w]hile no maudlin sentiment should interpose" between the criminal and the punishment for the crime, everyone would "agree that the leasing plan for dealing with the disposition of state convicts" called for: (1) a constitutional amendment to end leasing; (2) a new law to raise revenue for the penitentiary system; (3) the use of county felony and misdemeanor convicts for work on public roads and other public improvements; (4) the consolidation of convicts and the division of their employment in participating counties, in counties where the number of misdemeanor and felony convicts were too small to be cost-effective;

(5) retaining state control of any remaining or leftover convicts, especially those of "dubious character," to be worked on state farms and iron or coal mines; (6) the state's retention of all money derived from the hire of convicts; and (7) a committee investigation and report to the next legislature on the viability of using convict labor in the extension of the Western and Atlantic Railroad.[41] Governor Smith declared that those who leased misdemeanor convicts without any state supervision could be persecuted and sued for false imprisonment.[42] Smith closed his message with a reminder true to the mind-set of the period and consistent with his own bigoted leadership style and administration, that "ample provision" should be made for the separation of the races throughout the prison system in the state of Georgia.[43] The subject was a constant preoccupation of the Investigating Committee.

Under the first category of its charge, the Committee found evidence of widespread fraud and corruption in convict leasing and in the management of the system. More specifically, it found and charged "that the Chief Warden, whose duty it was to represent the interests of the State, was, while acting for the State and drawing the salary allowed him, trafficking in the convicts and making a profit out of the sub-leasing of the same . . ." and that "deputy wardens . . . were, while receiving pay from the State, also receiving money from the lessees. . . ."[44] Jake Moore, the state warden, while on the state payroll, illegally negotiated deals that resulted in the transfer of lease contracts from one lessee to another. Moore was also paid by one or another of the lessees for his services, and sometimes he was paid by both parties—in effect receiving triple compensation.[45] In addition, for several years Moore received his salary as state warden and an additional, separate salary as "inspector of misdemeanor camps," which the Investigating Committee opined "was improper, illegal, and without authority of law."[46] There were other "irregularities" as well, such as the fact that Moore "never took an oath of office" and that he never gave bond for the "faithful discharge" of his duties. There was evidence that, "for a considerable period," Jake Moore was a partner of and in debt to Dr. W. B. Hamby, the "largest lessee of convict labor" in the state, while at the same time, as "chief inspecting officer of the Prison Department," he had almost exclusive responsibility for ensuring that lessees obeyed rules and regulations governing leasing and that they "complied with the law . . . on pain of penalties and forfeitures."[47] Such an "intimate business relationship" between the state's chief officer of prisons and the chief lessee of the state could only make the grossest mockery of the idea that even an artificial or superficial distinction existed between those who upheld the law and those who broke it. In the Committee's words, and rather telling and most significant, is the reality that transferring lease contracts over which Moore presided "meant frequently the discontinuance of established camps, the establishment of new camps, the substitution of new lessees, the removal or transfer of deputy wardens, and like considerations of policy and interest to the State, and upon which the [Prison] Commission had a right to expect the disinterested opinion and advice of its chief officer before it approved such transfers."[48]

As the leading prison official, Moore could not protect the interests of the people of Georgia, much less those of the convicts, because he was in cahoots with the largest lessee and, *ergo*, a lessee himself. As long as the Jake Moores managed convict leasing, it was destined to remain susceptible to all of the calumnies for which it developed such a loathsome reputation.[49]

The myriad problems at the top worked their way down to

lower levels as well. "Practically all deputy wardens," the Investigating Committee reported, received compensation from lessees while on the state payroll, and "in one or more instances nearly twice as much as [they were] paid by the State."[50] Guards and physicians "received compensation and perquisites from lessees" too, and the Investigating Committee was "amazed at the indifference" displayed by all involved in this practice and the fact that it was "acquiesced in and sanctioned by" key prison officials and lessees. The Committee ultimately launched into a dissertation on the dereliction of duty by state officials with the responsibility for protecting the interests of the state and the welfare of convicts, "whose labor alone had been hired to lessees." They felt there was "no excuse which [could] palliate such conduct," even for "a money consideration at times from twenty-five to one hundred and fifty percent" above their salaries. "No mere man," they continued, "can serve two masters with conflicting interests."[51] The Investigating Committee's chagrin in criticizing leasing and the oppressive practices of lessees and state officials stands as a monument to their eloquence, but it came, in many ways, after the fact. By 1908, leasing was certain to end, with or without another investigation. The Committee's fusillade of criticism was merely one more straw on the back of the well-known camel.

Under categories two through eight of its charge, the Committee painstakingly outlined its findings. There were violations of the rules and regulations in working convicts at night and on Sundays. Sleeping and eating quarters in some camps were found to be "filthy and unsanitary"; the food had earlier been "severely condemned" and the requirement that "fresh meat" be provided was not met. Nepotism, "a curse to any government, institution or business," was a problem at the State Prison

Farms. Relatives of those in charge held various jobs, and Super-intendent A. B. Coombs at the State Prison Farm in Baldwin County employed his under-age "young sons and nephews" as guards. One son was eleven years old at the time of his appointment.[52] The superintendent also took great liberties in the procurement and use of state property, goods, and livestock. "Large quantities of groceries [were] bought, aggregating at times to as much as a thousand dollars a month" from a single supplier. Records of such transactions were poor when they were available at all and there was no public advertisement or competitive bidding. There is evidence that individuals who conspired in bidding for convicts double-crossed one another to obtain labor for themselves over their co-conspirators. John English, owner of the Chattahoochee Brick Company, was accused of bribing the porter who worked in the offices of the Prison Commission so that he could find out the "sealed bids of other lessees in order to prepare his company's bid." There were also complaints from prospective lessees that Jake Moore and members of the Prison Commission opened the bids in private rather than in public, as called for, and then pronounced the successful bids without revealing all other bids.[53]

Strong suggestion was made of misappropriation of funds in general expenditures and of questionable bookkeeping/accounting practices, as well. Payroll signatures were forged, which was found to be "quite a general practice," and journal and ledger entries contained "fresh writing," indicating that they were prepared long after the fact and after commencement of the legislative investigation. Convicts were illegally taken from the prison farm for day labor for private individuals, and there was "no proper record of the funds received. . . ."[54] Georgia convicts were even leased to private interests in the state of Florida.

Superintendent Coombs, or, as he was affectionately called, "Captain Coombs," rented convicts on his own to private local farmers for one dollar per day in complete violation of the law and total disregard for an absence of official supervision. Apparently he kept the money. The practice seemed well known because a prison guard told the Investigating Committee, "I have seen them passing through the city. It is a common thing for State convicts to be worked by farmers. . . ."[55]

Appearing before the Committee near the end of the deliberations, one Judge J. W. Awtry denied the accusation that he was "trafficking in convicts." However, there were some very revealing exchanges. The judge admitted that he had no authority to contract with private parties for convict labor. He reported that he had simply continued a custom that preceded his arrival on the bench. He justified his action with the argument that he did not "know of any law that prohibits it." In response to the question of the basis or legal authority for his decision to turn convicts over to private parties, Judge Awtry replied that questions of legality and propriety had existed for years, but that "the courts had never taken any steps in regards to it, and if the courts knock it out, I was ready to give in. It has been a mooted question for a long time." In the judge's view, it was more cost-effective to hire out the county convicts than to work them. Once county convicts were "sold" to another county, they became the responsibility of the buying county and fell under the supervision of the county working them. The proceeds from convict labor in such instances were supposed to go to "officers of the court"—for example, a "solicitor," Sheriff, or clerk. More likely it was the case that money disappeared without a trace.[56]

Many convicts disappeared, as well. Special attention was called, through the 1908 investigation, to the existence of "wildcat or misdemeanor camps," in which "the cruel and inhuman treatment of unfortunate convicts thus illegally sold into worse than slavery are [sic] a disgrace to a civilized people." That was the considered view of the Committee.[57]

Charges of cruelty pervaded the investigation and the Committee concluded that the charges were "well founded." At the Durham Coal Mines, the Lookout Mountain Mines, and the Chattahoochee Brick Company, especially, there were "unusually large" numbers of whippings. Whipping was the preferred method of punishment, and guards and wardens found innumerable ways to inflict maximum bearable pain on human beings—varying the size of the strap, administering blows on the sensitive parts of the body, putting notches in the strap or dragging it through the sand, and embedding "brass rivets" in the strap, to name a few.[58] A whipping, however, could be administered for reasons other than punishment. It was one way for prison officials to regularly demonstrate and reaffirm their place in the superior–subordinate relationship; therefore, convicts didn't even know why they were being whipped, at times, and so were unable to avoid it. Virtually anything could be a pretext for whipping.

The 1,750 pages of transcript from the 1908 investigation, however, show a range of "official" reasons why convicts were whipped, and the related circumstances. They were flogged "for shortages," for "failing to reach task and then for working overtime," for "noncompliance" with the rules, for "complaining of hunger," for "playing off" (trying to avoid work), for "attempting to escape" (in one case a prisoner was whipped and shot because a guard "thought" he was planning to escape), for "insubordination, idleness, carelessness," for "gambling, cursing, fighting, not working, laziness, impudence," and so on. Convicts were whipped until they could not stand or sit or walk, until they "messed all over" themselves, until "clothes stuck," until "bloody and fainted," until "testicles busted and kidneys ruptured" and "privates burst like they were an eggshell."[59]

Several further examples of heinous punishment were cited, including the case of a Black convict at the Flowers Farm at Jakin, whose name could not be remembered and who had "sweated" to death by being "wrapped head and body and feet in blankets and enclosed in a box."[60] Another case of a 16-year-old Black youth, serving a three-month sentence, was uncovered. It appears that the youngster attempted to escape, although that was not entirely clear. A guard shot "the left side of his face off" as the boy ran into the woods. The guards claimed that he had run "across the mountain" and that they could not find him, so tracking dogs were sent to locate him. After a week or so, a foul odor from the woods was "stinking so bad" that convicts working nearby "couldn't stand it hardly." A dog was soon noticed carrying the "torn-off arm" of the young fellow with the "fingers dragging the ground." The guard then got a couple of prisoners to make a pine box, retrieve the boy, and bury him.[61]

A third example of brutal treatment suffered by convicts, which was uncovered by the investigation, is the complicated homicide of a Black convict named Peter Harris, who was a prisoner at the Chattahoochee Brick Company. The company was notorious for its uncivilized conditions, for compelling convicts to work in inhumanely hot kilns, and for requiring convicts to trot while performing their tasks, on pain of being severely whipped, possibly fatally, for missing their "quota."[62] Harris was alternately alleged to have died from being whipped too severely, from congestion of the bowels, from congestion of the stomach, or from drinking too much water. The exact cause of his death was never resolved, as medical doctors, prison officials, and convicts gave conflicting testimony. The Peter Harris episode received more of the Committee's attention than any other single case and was one of a very few involving Black convicts that was investigated at all. Possibly one-half or more of the persons called before the Committee were questioned about Peter Harris and his mysterious death. There were no indictments in this case.[63]

An issue that was the subject of the Committee's dismay all through the long, hot summer of 1908 was the lackluster effort made by prison officials to strictly enforce racial segregation in situations where there were enough White convicts to generate interest in separating them from Blacks. One extreme to which the concern was carried was expressed by state Senator J. R. Stapleton, who, while reporting on a legislative subcommittee visit to the Spaulding County Road Camp, exclaimed in obvious exasperation that Blacks and Whites were "all breathing the same air."[64]

INCREASING PUBLIC DISAPPROVAL

For state legislators in Georgia, the summer of 1908, ordinarily a time of relaxation and recreation, was spent fine-tuning legislation to outlaw convict leasing. For ten weeks, through July, August, and early September, convict leasing dominated local and national news in Georgia. It even stole the thunder from the 1908 presidential campaign, during a season in which momentum was building behind the incumbent Theodore Roosevelt and the challenger and eventual victor, William Howard Taft. The exception to headline-capturing for Georgia leasing in a national context was the bloody August race riot in Springfield, Illinois.

In a Georgia context, it was the devastating Augusta flood as a local catastrophe.[65]

Abolition of leasing was on the minds of many Georgians even before publicity brought the convict lease legislative investigation to their attention. There had always been some opposition to leasing in Georgia from its inception. The voices of opposition simply had not been loud enough nor their clout substantial. Before the turn of the century, the issue had not resonated sufficiently with the citizenry. However, by 1908 several sister ex-Confederate states had already ended leasing. By the time Thomas S. Felder in the Senate and John Holder in the House of Representatives assumed the leadership in the legislative fight to end leasing in Georgia, they had the full weight of public opinion behind them and the reach of the *Atlanta Journal* and *The Georgian*, as well.

A mid-summer editorial in the *Journal* demonstrated its evolution to a position of opposition to convict leasing—a process representative of the changed attitudes of broad-based Georgia leadership on this burning issue of the day. The editorial mentioned its expanding opposition to leasing over the years and the building opposition of the community, "fresh from the hearts of the people [to] bitter denunciation of the infamies of the convict lease system and the imperative demands for its immediate abolishment." Despite its new disapproval, the *Journal* had earlier asserted that, in the interest "and actual necessities" of financial support for the public schools, given the "depleted condition of the State treasury," it was more prudent to urge conservatism or patience with regard to leasing's demise. The early view of many Georgians was that a period of adjustment was needed to prepare for the loss of income from convict labor. The anticipated crippling of the school system might have been premature because, as the editorial noted, Governor Hoke Smith indicated the public schools could function without revenue from the "obnoxious" lease system. At any rate, the question of state income aside, and even though the legislative Investigating Committee was only half-way through its work, disclosures to date had prompted the *Journal* to change its mind on the pace of abolition. The new position and the reasons for it were presented without equivocation:

> The conditions which have been shown to exist under the present convict lease system have shaken Georgia from one end of the state to the other. The testimony, which it is impossible to controvert, reveals a state of horror and cruelty scarcely surpassed. . . . The infamies and cruelties practiced upon the unfortunate criminals of the State, under the protection if not the absolute authority of the convict lease law as revealed by the sworn testimony of an army of witnesses, stamp this system as barbarous, inhuman, and disgraceful to a degree that its further existence is beyond the pale of justification, for any cause whatsoever.
>
> ¤ ¤ ¤
>
> Abolishment is justice pleading for mercy. It is humanity demanding recognition. The system must be destroyed, root and branch.[66]

Those in charge of leasing were now being considered almost bigger criminals than the victims of leasing. The people of Georgia were called to rally for the destruction of convict leasing whether it meant closing the schools or bankruptcy for the state treasury.[67]

The people of Georgia must have heard the call to organize

and mobilize, because the demand for abolition grew louder and more frequent. Some were inspired to protest leasing and appeal for its banishment before the editorial shift at the *Journal*. Various organizations and individuals, some with and some without portfolio, made known their disenchantment with leasing during this phase. Among them were labor and religious leaders and groups, politicians, and organization heads. The Georgia Farmers Union adopted a resolution at a meeting in Macon calling on the Georgia legislature to "take immediate action" to abolish leasing, which was vehemently condemned.[68] A protest rally in support of the abolition of leasing was endorsed by the International Association of Machinists—Atlanta Lodge No. 1.[69] The Atlanta Federation of Trades implored Georgia lawmakers to wipe out convict leasing, stating, ". . . we believe the administration of penal laws through the leasing of private parties is fundamentally wrong and is necessarily accompanied by abuses which should be eliminated. We respectfully suggest that the convicts of the state might be put upon the public roads without producing unfair competition with anyone."[70] Competition with non-prison labor was a long-standing theme in organized labor's revulsion against leasing. It was felt that free labor, union labor, was undermined as long as leasing existed.[71]

The citizens of Spaulding County, including the mayor and other officials of the town of Griffin, Georgia, joined the chorus for abolition and adopted a lengthy list of resolutions, which they forwarded to the legislature. They also resolved that "the present prison officials should be impeached and removed from office."[72] The City Council of Marietta, Georgia, in Cobb County, vigorously damned leasing and added to the calls for its immediate abolition.[73]

In a page-one story, the Sunday morning edition of the

August 2, 1908, *Atlanta Journal* announced a planned rally against the continuation of convict leasing, scheduled for that afternoon at 4 P.M. at the Grand Opera House, which had the largest auditorium in Atlanta. More than 10,000 people were expected and "ladies," especially, were "invited and expected." "PEOPLE TO DEMAND THAT SYSTEM GO" was the headline. "In nearly every pulpit of Atlanta," it was reported, there would be a "denunciation" of convict leasing. Two additional rallies were scheduled at the same time at the Central Congregational Church and the Wesley Memorial Tabernacle, to accommodate anticipated overflow crowds from the Grand. The occasion was billed as an "uprising of the people" and prominent Georgians were listed as speakers and invited guests; all were expected to rail against leasing. Governor Hoke Smith headed the list of confirmed guests (his letter of acceptance was printed by the *Journal*) and Representative and Judge W. A. Covington topped the list of scheduled orators. Memorials were sent from other towns and cities across Georgia, such as Mountrie, Webster, Baconton, and Jeffersonville, where rallies had already been held. "Practically the whole citizenry" in these places "turned out to condemn leasing," according to the *Journal* story.[74]

The eloquent outcry against convict leasing and demands for its burial met all advance expectations. Religious leaders, politicians, and others trotted out their most cherished vitriol for this special occasion. The huge crowd inspired them. Judge Covington added a bit of humor, generating laughter from the audience, when he offered, "I don't believe in taking a man who has stolen a ride on the railroad and putting him to work building a railroad for the men who have stolen it." He became serious again, touching an idea endemic in the late nineteenth and early twentieth centuries and encumbered with racism and paternalism: ". . . the white race," he said, "as lords of the earth, . . . by reason of their loftier position[,]" had responsibility than others. "In Georgia one of the white man's burden[s] is the welfare of the negro race that he dominates." Whites should not, he continued, go on "making money out of negroes crucified and destroyed. . . . The world expects us to do right." Therefore, he concluded, convict leasing must become extinct.[75]

The Prison Reform Association of Georgia was formed as a result of the Grand Opera House rally. Membership cards were distributed on-site and there were no fees and no dues. The organization was christened with more than one thousand members. The Association intended to help first offenders, and its stated objective was "cooperation with State officials in bringing about a better penal system."[76]

Anti-Leasing Legislation

The Georgia Prison Commission released its annual report in the third week of July, 1908. The report expressed alarm at the large number of misdemeanants being leased in disregard of the law prohibiting leasing. Since the five-year lease then in force was due to expire in early 1909, commissioners urged immediate action by the sitting legislature. From time to time since the termination of the old twenty-year lease, legislation had been introduced but not passed amending or modifying the law governing convict leasing. However, armed with the Prison Commission's recommendation for urgent action and faced with the reality that the convict issue could best be resolved before the next legislature convened, and, moreover spurred on by editorials in the *Atlanta Journal*, the *Atlanta Georgian*, and other newspapers, as well as by long-time critics of leasing, several legislators moved their attack on leasing into higher gear.[77]

On Monday morning, July 13, 1908, Thomas S. Felder introduced a measure in the Senate billed as "a solution to the convict lease problem which is now vexing the Legislature." Succinctly stated, the bill provided that:

1. Felony convicts would be available to work on public roads to each Georgia county desiring them. Remaining convicts could be leased for up to eighteen months. The state was to receive all earnings from subleasing and would pay expenses for land and housing. At the conclusion of the eighteen-month cycle, convict leasing in the State of Georgia would end.

2. All other convicts not disposed of in this way would be engaged in industrial work, the income from which was to be divided among counties not employing their full share of convicts and earmarked for the public schools or common schools.

3. A full accounting by the Prison Commission was required to be made to the governor's office. This legislation anticipated an end to leasing, and the eighteen-month lease was to allow time to raise money to operate a new prison system.

4. Similar proposals to the Felder Bill were promulgated in the House but no new legislation was adopted. In the meantime, a joint Senate–House resolution authorized the blockbusting investigation.[78]

More serious negotiations for consensus legislation to wipe out leasing began in mid-July. By July 16, several pieces of convict legislation were being considered. The House version sponsored by Representative Holder would allow each county to have a pro rata share of state convicts based on population.

Those counties desiring more than their allowable share could "purchase" them from counties where convicts were underutilized. The balance could be leased for up to five years to the highest bidder. The state reserved the right to cancel the lease after one year for just cause.

The Senate bill authored by Felder again called for the eighteen-month leases after county demands for convicts had been met. After a year and a half, prisoners would then work "forever on public roads . . . or other public works." There was to be no further convict leasing in Georgia.

The so-called substitute bill, which was crafted by six members of the House (Alexander, Covington, Candler, Wright, Burwell, and Perry), called for the immediate abolition of leasing. Convicts would be employed at public works or on public farms "forever."[79]

Most other legislation having to do with convict leasing introduced in the Georgia legislature (House or Senate) over the next two months, before leasing was outlawed in mid-September, was one variation or another on the aforementioned proposals. John Holder in the House and Thomas Felder in the Senate maintained their leadership in the effort, despite stiff challenges from colleagues with a range of motives but with the same objective.

The newspaper crusade, especially in the *Journal* and the *Georgian*, intensified, with sharper and more frequent editorials calling for an end to leasing. There were also more letters to the editor condemning leasing, and additional newspapers, such as the *Columbus Enquirer Sun* and the *Atlanta Constitution*, joined the fray. More church ministers used their pulpits in the attack on leasing, and it is entirely conceivable that discussions at the dinner tables of average citizens across the state were monopolized by the subject. That would be the case particularly after July 20, 1908, the date the Joint Legislative Investigation of Convict Leasing began. As disclosures of the iniquities of convict leasing became public, the public appetite for more information increased, and the inevitable collapse of the anachronistic system from the heavy weight of revulsion became merely a matter of time. The most difficult obstacle for legislators in their search for a solution to the leasing conundrum, "the albatross around Georgia's neck," was in accommodating the reality of having to surrender the revenue generated from convict labor. In addition to that loss, Georgia had to find new income to maintain a penitentiary system, an expense the state had not had for fifty years. For Georgia and other leasing states, this was a bitter pill.

Despite the formation of joint House and Senate committees to come up with a compromise convict bill and the appointment of Conference Committees to eliminate kinks, the legislature was unable to find common ground and agree on legislation that would bring down the curtain on convict leasing once and for all. A constitutional amendment supported by Governor Smith that would have abolished leasing when the clock struck midnight on New Year's Eve, 1910, was not passed. Late-August proposals that would have ended leasing on March 31, 1909, or April 1, 1909, were also not enacted. With the legislators stuck in the quagmire of stalemate, the governor promised to call them into Extraordinary Session to solve the problem, because public clamoring for a solution, with the Investigating Committee's report issued, and the manifold calamities of the system exposed, an intolerable situation was an eyelash away from reaching its limit.[80] It seemed the entire state was poised for Armageddon. Inaction was certain to be the Achilles' heel of any state chief executive who hoped to continue in office, much less one who had ambitions for higher office. Georgians held their breath and the governor kept his promise. To the dismay of some and the delight of many, an "Extraordinary Session" of the legislature was called.[81]

THE END OF CONVICT LEASING IN GEORGIA

There were some fits and starts in the new session, haggling over language, and massaging of egos—but few substantive differences. Between September 15 and 19, 1908, the swaddling clothes were finally removed from legislation that had negotiated minefields in both houses and disposed of convict leasing in Georgia. The sun would finally set on arguably the most notorious example of convict leasing in the New South.

The law is entitled "Employment of Convicts; System of Penology" and contains some twenty-four sections. It sought to leave no stone unturned in Georgia penology. With the ink on the stinging Investigating Committee report virtually still wet, and all of the criticism emblazoned on their consciences, and these legislators' deliberations under a Georgia microscope, and the people of the state in no mood for further excoriation, the lawmakers explicitly addressed the following: the disposition and disposal of felony and misdemeanor convicts, quotas, excesses, and county convicts in municipalities and on the farms. A separate section deals with "state farms, the central penitentiary and other farms." The duties, expectations, and liabilities of "officers and employees, superintendents and supervisors" and "court clerks" are spelled out in sections 11, 14, 19, 20, 21, and 22. The Prison Commission—sometimes the target of scathing criticism because of its failure to know about the fraud, corruption, and cruelty rampant in leasing, or worse, their inaction in the face of it—had their "powers and duties" outlined in sections 13, 15, and 23. The Commission was specifically instructed to have at least one of its members make unannounced site visits "to the various convict camps . . . every six months and to make a thorough inspection of every detail of management, plan of operation, and treatment of convicts." Sections 16, 17, and 18 treated the use of any "proceeds" from convict labor and the manner in which lands acquired for working convict labor would be managed and disposed of—including the state farm and central penitentiary. The "management, care and control" of convicts, as prescribed in an 1897 Act and as amended in 1903, "except as are [explicitly] changed by this Act [1908] would remain in force." The Georgia legislature saw fit to add a so-called Goodloe Yancy clause, regarding the Secretary of the Prison Commission. The salary for the position was fixed at $1,800 per year, and the secretary would be required to "give his entire time to the service of the Commission, and . . . to take an oath to faithfully discharge his duties, and give a bond in such amount as may be fixed by the Prison Commission payable to the Governor, conditioned for the faithful performance of his duties." Guards and wardens who had gotten fat collecting salaries for the state and "extras" from lessees had their salaries set at $50 and $100, respectively. A minimum age of twenty-one years was imposed for employment as a guard and "certificates of reference" were required for wardens, guards, or other employees. "Drinking intoxicating liquor to excess" was forbidden and no "warden or guard" could be hired who was not "a humane, sober and honest man."

The centerpiece of the 1908 Act was Section 7. Although counties and municipalities were authorized "to hire convicts from the Prison Commission . . . at . . . ($100) dollars, per capita, per annum" (Part 6), the previous section, reflecting the sentiments and echoing the language of many of the prior proposals, provided that all convicts not used by the state or by cities or counties could be deployed, for one-year periods after March 31, 1909, at the discretion of the Prison Commission and with the approval of the governor. In no event, however, was convict labor to:

> . . . be used in competition with skilled mechanical free labor, and under no contract by the terms of which the contractor is interested in the quantity of work a convict may be required to do per day; it being the fixed policy of this State that the control and management of its convicts, both felony and misdemeanor, shall never pass from it and its public officials into the control and management of any private corporation or person.[82]

Just in case anything was missed or in conflict, the final and catch-all section, Section 24, stated matter-of-factly: "Be it further enacted, That all laws and parts of laws in conflict with this Act, be and the same [*sic*] are hereby repealed."[83]

NOTES

1. Honorable W. A. Covington of Colquitt County, member of the Georgia House of Representatives, quoted in *Atlanta Journal*, July 16, 1908.

   In general, for surveys of convict leasing in Georgia, see A. J. McKelway, "The Convict Lease System of Georgia," *The Outlook* (September 12, 1908), 67–72; A. Elizabeth Taylor, "The Origin and Development of the Convict Lease System in Georgia," *The Georgia Historical Quarterly* 26 (March 1942), 113–28, and her much better, much more comprehensive, and more thorough 1940 U.S. history Master of Arts essay, written under Fletcher M. Green at the University of North Carolina, Chapel Hill, entitled, "The Convict Lease System in Georgia, 1866–1908."

2. There is a curious inconsistency in accounts of the burning of the penitentiary in sources on convict leasing. One source blames Sherman's army for destroying the penitentiary (Taylor, "The Convict Lease System in Georgia," 5.) Another source says it "appears likely" that convicts burned down the prison; James C. Bonner, "The Georgia Penitentiary at Milledgeville, 1817–1874," *The Georgia Historical Quarterly* 55, no. 3 (Fall 1971), 317. A third source, prepared by the Archives Institute of the Georgia Department of Archives and History, declares that "the cells, workshops and other buildings of the Penitentiary were destroyed by Sherman's army on the March to the Sea. . . ." *Records of the Georgia Prison Commission, 1871–1936* (Atlanta, Georgia, 1969), 2.

3. Bonner, "The Georgia Penitentiary," 318.

4. One contemporary writer states that the number of Black convicts increased because ". . . the enfranchised negroes began to manifest criminal tendencies to an alarming extent. . . ." McKelway, "The Convict Lease System of Georgia," 67.

5. For background on the early history of the Georgia penitentiary, see Bonner, "The Georgia Penitentiary," 303–28; Taylor, "The Convict Lease System in Georgia," chapter 1.

6. *Minutes of the Executive Department of the State of Georgia, 1866–1870*, 124. (Hereafter cited as *Executive Minutes*.)

7. Ibid., 131.

8. *Senate Journal, 1870*, 176.

9. Ibid.

10. "Georgia Laws, 1874," 26–27.

11. *Penitentiary Report, 1874*, 5–10; *Executive Minutes, 1874–1877*, 279–81, cited in Taylor, "The Convict Lease System in Georgia," 28–34.

12. *Georgia Laws, 1876*, 40–42; *Executive Minutes, 1874–1877*, 730–32; *Senate Journal, 1877*, 21–22.

13. All quotes from *Georgia Laws, 1876*, 43–44.

14. *Senate Journal, 1877*, 20–22.

15. *House Journal, 1897*, 52.

16. Ibid., 49–69.

17. Ibid., 67–69.

18. *Penitentiary Report, 1879*, 6, *passim*.

19. *House Journal, 1870*, 190–97; *Senate Journal, 1870*, 353–60. The *Senate Journal* also contains the full proceedings of the Investigating Committee, running for almost 200 pages (162–360), whereas that transcript is omitted from the *House Journal*.

20. *Senate Journal, 1870*, 282.

21. Ibid.

22. *Senate Journal, 1870*, 323; quote 345. In 1903 the Georgia legislature officially condemned "the practice of whipping women convicts and . . . recommend[ed] that the prison commission prescribe some more humane mode of punishment for violating the prison rules." *Georgia Laws, 1903*, 695.

23. Taylor, "The Convict Lease System in Georgia," 56.

24. Ibid., 59.

25. It should be noted that the twenty-year lease agreement was based on the prison population in 1876. One presumes that as more convicts became available with the growth of the prison, population adjustments were made in the lease contract. However, income for the state from convict labor did not appear to in-

crease. Irregular Treasurer's Reports show years when income for the "hire of convicts" was right at the $25,000 mark, but more years are shown when it was not at that level. Disbursements to the "Penitentiary Fund" also resemble "voodoo" and inconsistent accounting, with money going to "special accounts," "special funds," "general funds," and "penitentiary funds." See, for example, the Treasurer's Report for October 1, 1880 to October 7, 1881, in *Georgia Laws, 1880–1881*; Report for the Year Ending September 30, 1885, in *Georgia Laws, 1884–1885*; Receipts and Disbursements for the Year Ending September 30, 1887, in *Georgia Laws, 1886–1887*; Receipts and Disbursements for the Year Ending September 30, 1888, in *Georgia Laws, 1888*; Report for the Year Ending September 30, 1889, in *Georgia Laws, 1889*; Treasurer's Report for the Year Ending September 30, 1894, in *Georgia Laws, 1894*; Treasurer's Report for the Years Ending September 30, 1895, 1896, 1897, and 1898, in *Georgia Laws* (relevant years).

26. *Report of the Prison Commission, 1899–1901*, 7.

27. See Derrell Roberts, "Joseph E. Brown and the Convict Lease System," *Georgia Historical Quarterly* 44 (December 1960), 399–410.

28. Roberts, "Joseph E. Brown," 410.

29. None of the several full-length and limited biographies of Joseph E. Brown treats his convict leasing with rigor. Nevertheless, see Joseph Howard Parks, *Joseph E. Brown of Georgia* (Baton Rouge, 1977); Derrell C. Roberts, *Joseph E. Brown and the Politics of Reconstruction* (Tuscaloosa, 1973); and Louise Biles Hill, *Joseph E. Brown and the Confederacy* (Chapel Hill, 1939, repr. 1972).

30. *House Journal, 1895*, 829.

31. On the life and death of Robert Alston and this entire affair, see the following: Minnie Hite Moody, "Alston of DeKalb," *The Georgia Review*, No. 4 (Winter 1963); Derrell Roberts, "Duel in the Georgia State Capitol," *The Georgia Historical Quarterly*, No.

4 (December 1963); Taylor, "The Convict Lease System in Georgia," 49–53; *Senate Journal, 1878*, 246–48; *Atlanta Constitution* (December 17, 1878; December 12, 1882), and Rebecca L. Felton, *My Memoirs of Georgia Politics* (Atlanta, 1911), 438. Felton believed Alston was killed because of his opposition to convict leasing. Her view is shared by A. J. McKelway in "The Convict Lease System of Georgia," 67.

32. George Washington Cable, "The Convict Lease System in the Southern States," *Century Magazine* 5 (February 1884), 154.

33. *Enquirer Sun* (Columbus, Georgia), September 16, 1881.

34. *Enquirer Sun* (Columbus, Georgia), June 26, 1908. See also *Atlanta Journal*, June 26, 1908.

35. *Atlanta Georgian*, July 7, 1908.

36. Throughout the summer of 1908, there was not a single day in which some story on convict leasing was not printed in the *Atlanta Georgian* or the *Atlanta Journal*, and frequently stories were published in both.

37. This effort and the legislative investigation in Texas in 1910 were the most vigorous and far-reaching actions against convict leasing during its era, at least based on the length of their reports, both of which exceeded 1,000 typescript pages.

38. Charge to the "Joint Committee to Investigate Convict System" in *Acts and Resolutions of the General Assembly of the State of Georgia, 1908*, 1031–32. (Hereafter cited as *Georgia Laws, 1908*.)

39. "Proceedings of the Georgia Penitentiary Legislative Investigation Report, 1908," 1478–1516. (Hereafter cited as "Georgia Proceedings, 1908.") Some very interesting observations were made during Deadwyler's testimony, among them that slaves were better off than convicts, that Black convicts were injured more often than White ones because they were not as intelligent, and that Black convicts, "some of them," could not get along without a whipping.

40. See, for example, "Georgia Proceedings, 1908," 522, 548, 858, *passim*. At the Cherokee Brick Company and Cruger and Pace Brickyard, for instance, the superintendent and deputy warden (there was no warden on the premises) were the same person.

41. All quotes from "Message from the Governor," *Georgia Laws, 1908*, 1,049.

42. The leasing of misdemeanor convicts was against the law in Georgia. That did not stop the practice, however. During the 1908 legislative investigation, there were constant questions about it. See "Georgia Proceedings, 1908," *passim*. Daniel Long, a 14-year-old Black, was convicted in Cobb County for stealing a chain, was "sold" to a "wildcat camp" (an illegal camp of short duration, sometimes created for specific projects, which used free labor and subleased convicts illegally), and was later transferred to a misdemeanor camp in Albany, Georgia. The youngster testified that while he was illegally leased in the misdemeanor camp he was whipped twice a day, seventy-five licks each time, for several weeks because he did not reach his quota of "dipping turpentine." In the process he was maimed for life. He was probably saved from being killed in anonymity by his penniless but persistent mother, who traveled to southern Georgia and secured his release despite getting the run-around and being threatened with death by the "whipping boss," who told her he would kill her and throw her in a river as he had done "lots of other negroes," and that he did not "know anything about the Goddamned Black son of a bitch [her son]," although he "beat the hell out of him." For quotes, see "Georgia Proceedings, 1908," 509. For all of the testimony and the details, see "Georgia Proceedings, 1908," 501–09, 1270–71, 1609ff.

43. Ibid. For background on Hoke Smith and his racist proclivities, see Dewey W. Grantham, Jr., *Hoke Smith and the Politics of the New South* (Baton Rouge, 1967), 69–70, 139–52, *passim*.

44. *Georgia Laws, 1908*, 1029.

45. Moore was not alone in receiving a triple salary. One Goodloe Yancy, for example, received $100 a month as secretary of the Prison Commission, $30 a month as bookkeeper, and another $10 a month as bookkeeper for the state reformatory. The records of all were in a shambles. *Georgia Laws, 1908*, 1088.

46. Ibid., 1065.

47. Ibid., 1066–67. The Committee showed evidence that Dr. Hamby did not work his convicts but acquired them for speculative purposes and subleasing. An instance was noted in which Hamby contracted for fifty convicts and upon investigation had none on hand. It was also observed that he paid the state $221.25 per convict per year and subleased them for $630, giving him quite a windfall in this single instance. Ibid., 1089.

48. Ibid., 1064–65.

49. During his tenure as state warden, Jake Moore acquired personal property and possessions substantially exceeding what seemed possible on his salary—even the triple salary he was alleged to have received. Moore saw few improprieties in his irregular and illegal activities—for example, traveling at state expenses and conducting private business; serving as a middleman, go-between, or broker in buying, selling, and trading convict labor and collecting cash commissions from both buyers and sellers; permitting violations of the rules (work on Sunday and after hours, brutal treatment, poor diet, etc.) and permitting "emergency work" in violation of the law. Moore felt that "strict rules" could not be adhered to and some laws could not be obeyed. His underlying rationale was that he was always saving money for the state, which he claimed justified his unorthodox and illegal practices and style. On one occasion Moore bragged about making $25,000 in twelve months. An example of the handsome commissions he received in bartering convicts was one in which he got 60 percent of $1,340 for delivering fifty convicts. He testified to having land and real estate holdings aggregating in value to $35,000, declaring,

"[O]f course I borrowed all of that money. I have been a good borrower all of my life." That, it seems, was just the beginning. For Moore's boasting, see "Georgia Proceedings, 1908," 1671; for the 60 percent commission, 1670; and for the quotes, 1189. In general, for Moore's own incriminating testimony and that of others, see pages 1132–1208, 1665–75, *passim*.

50. "Georgia Proceedings, 1908," 1067.

51. Ibid., 1067–70.

52. Ibid., 1019–54.

53. Judson M. Strickland, who was a candidate for election to the Georgia Prison Commission in 1904, asserted that wardens were most likely to follow the orders of those who paid them the most money—that is, the lessees. When conflicts arose between the state's interest and private interest, private interest would prevail as the highest bidder. Mr. Strickland testified in part before the 1908 Georgia Legislative Investigating Committee: "[When] there were abuses on the part of the lessee . . . they [the wardens] would naturally decide with the people who paid them more money." "Georgia Proceedings, 1908," 1675, 1196, *passim*.

54. Ibid., 1070–77, 1093, 1096, 1099. Superintendent Coombs also hired his son-in-law as the bookkeeper. The prison farm at Baldwin was renowned for "voodoo" bookkeeping, when there were records at all, which was infrequent. Other relatives were hired in other capacities, sometimes making this entire penal operation almost a family affair. Moreover, Coombs acknowledges that he kept a separate bank account into which he deposited income from convict labor (sometimes cash), payments from the state (for various expenses), and other money. He paid cash for such things as the "transfer" of prisoners—which meant that he had no receipts and no records, and could answer no questions. On the appropriation and misappropriation of funds, see "Georgia Proceedings, 1908," 1087–96.

55. Ibid., 237ff. Misdemeanor convicts were also worked illegally by private parties. An official of the Southern Lumber Company testified before the Investigating Committee that he received his convicts from Tift County and Cobb County and that he was "just commencing to know" that it was against the law. Ibid., 684ff.

56. For all quotes and the testimony of Judge J. W. Awtry, see "Georgia Proceedings, 1908," 1609–20.

57. Ibid., 1086.

58. Ibid., 184–85.

59. Ibid., 171, 178, 180, 187, 305, 353, 205, 517, 616, 147, 382, 999, 817, 1337. (Page numbers correspond to the quotations.)

60. Ibid., 849, 948, 1078–82; *Atlanta Journal*, August 5, 1908.

61. "Georgia Proceedings, 1908," 189–90, 160ff., *passim*.

62. One Black convict testified that he "trotted" double-time for fifteen years at Chattahoochee without stopping. Ibid., 774.

63. Ibid., *passim*; *Atlanta Journal*, August 5–6, 1908.

64. Ibid., 370.

65. This conclusion is based on the daily headlines and news stories in two of Georgia's leading newspapers at the time, *Atlanta Journal* and *The Georgian*. The August 15–16, 1908, edition of the *Journal* printed all of the gory details of one of the major racial confrontations in United States history, a well-known episode among historians of the period. For particulars on the calamitous flood in Augusta, see *Atlanta Journal*, August 27–30, 1908.

66. *Atlanta Journal*, August 2, 1908.

67. Ibid.

68. *Atlanta Journal*, July 31, 1908; July 30, 1908.

69. *Atlanta Journal*, July 31, 1908.

70. *Atlanta Journal*, July 27, 1908. Alex Lichtenstein presents a compelling case, mainly discussing Georgia, for the substantial role of the labor movement and free labor in the abolition of convict leasing. See his Ph.D. dissertation, "The Political Economy of Convict Labor in the New South" (University of Pennsylvania, 1990), especially chapter 8. A condensed version of Lichtenstein's arguments can be found in his "Good Roads and Chain Gangs in the Progressive South: The Negro Convict Is a Slave," *Journal of Southern History* (February 1993), 85–110.

71. *Atlanta Journal*, June 2, 1908.

72. *Atlanta Journal*, August 1, 1908.

73. Ibid.

74. Ibid.

75. *Atlanta Journal*, August 3, 1908. The publicity attending the Grand Opera House rally was another interesting but not unusual irony of the period in that it was presented as a "representative gathering" at which "men from many walks of life" were present. No Blacks attended. In fact, Blacks held a parallel abolition meeting at the People's Tabernacle in Atlanta, and the uncompromising Bishop Henry McNeal Turner delivered the opening address.

76. Ibid.; see, also, August 5, 1908.

77. *Annual Report*, Georgia Prison Commission, 1908; *Atlanta Journal*, June 23, 1908. See the *Atlanta Journal* throughout the spring of 1908, especially the months of May and June, for examples of legislation being debated and some introduced for dealing with the question of Georgia convicts.

78. The full text of this Felder Bill, with 19 sections, was reprinted in the *Atlanta Journal*, July 13, 1908.

79. *Atlanta Journal*, July 16, 1908; July 19, 1908. *Columbus Enquirer Sun*, July 17, 1908.

80. At one point, Governor Smith also presented his own seven-point plan for "solving the convict problem." *Atlanta Journal*, August 25, 1908.

81. Governor Smith exaggerated his role in breaking the back of convict leasing in Georgia by claiming more credit than he deserves. See Grantham, *Hoke Smith*, chapter 10. On the governor's "Proclamation" announcing the Extraordinary Session, see the *Atlanta Journal*, August 20, 1908.

82. For all the details on this legislation and all of the quotes above, see *Acts and Resolutions of the General Assembly of the State of Georgia At Its Extraordinary Session* (convened August 25, 1908), also cited as *Georgia Laws, Extra Session* (1908), 1119—30.

83. Ibid.

CHAPTER FIVE

DESTRUCTION:
DECLINE AND ABOLITION

T HE BEGINNING AND END OF convict leasing were similar: the southern states adopted leasing in staggered fashion until, by the mid-1870s, all had done so. Abolition, too, grew unevenly, with each state legislature approving legislation that outlawed the convict lease system, one by one, until North Carolina, the last state to do so, ended the leasing nightmare in 1933. (See Figure 5.1.) The sociopolitical milieu in the United States in general, and in the South in particular, in the latter years of the nineteenth century and early decades of the twentieth century—a climate that accommodated the intensification of leasing as well as its overthrow—is at once confusing and contradictory. The realities of vicious race bigotry

Figure 5.1
YEARS CONVICT LEASING WAS OUTLAWED IN THE SOUTHERN STATES

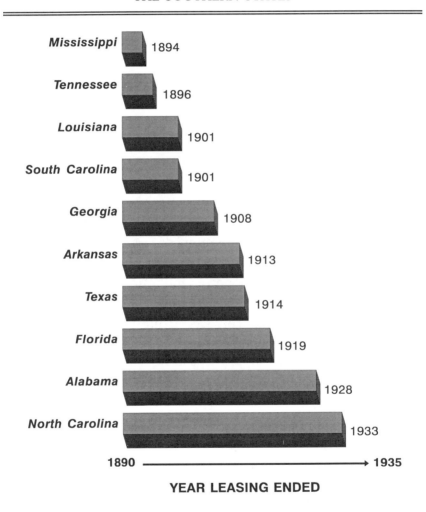

Mississippi 1894
Tennessee 1896
Louisiana 1901
South Carolina 1901
Georgia 1908
Arkansas 1913
Texas 1914
Florida 1919
Alabama 1928
North Carolina 1933

1890 ——————————————→ 1935

YEAR LEASING ENDED

NOTE: The state of Virginia never adopted a convict lease system comparable with those in the other former Confederate states.

that permeated the U.S. South for a generation after the end of the Civil War and the passing of World War I made it easy for leasing to flourish and especially for southern Blacks to be the primary victims. This development evolved notwithstanding the reformist tendencies and mood of progressivism that intruded on the country between 1890 and 1920. At the same time the heightened racism of the era did not forestall the collapse of leasing. Even the system's economic advantage could not prevent its demise once the evils of leasing were fully exposed. When leasing became more and more of an embarrassment for a particular state, the outlawing of the system became inevitable. As much as anything, the contradiction or inconsistency between race bigotry and the end of leasing in this instance demonstrates the enormous complexity of such a phenomenon, one that with equanimity tolerated leasing but did not impede its termination. One explanation, of course, is that the removal of convict leasing did not threaten or diminish the power and influence of racism. The various strains of race bigotry, inside and outside the South, were unaffected by an end to convict leasing. In addition, when southern state governments regained control of their convicts through the chain gangs and contract arrangements that succeeded leasing, the brutal treatment of convicts that had characterized leasing was virtually uninterrupted, but was now state-managed.[1] Blacks also remained the overwhelming majority of the southern prison population.

The extent to which the architects of abolitionism were influenced or inspired by progressivism is difficult to know. Those state legislators and others who took the lead in the crusade to end leasing appeared to be much more impressed with the reports of brutality at the various convict leasing locations in individual states, and with what sister states were doing about leasing, than with the ideas of enlightenment that informed the progressive movement. Progressivism has been thoroughly analyzed and found wanting for its failure to include African-Americans and their struggle against race bigotry and consequent oppression; therefore, there is no need to repeat that discussion here. It is peculiar, nevertheless, with the benefit of hindsight, how the iniquities and atrocities of convict leasing, even with Blacks as the main victims, could escape the agenda of the movers and shakers of progressivism. After all, the movement attacked and exposed, and drew the public's attention to, the need to act on many of the concerns of the day—taxes, woman and child labor reform, trust-busting, and preserving and protecting public lands. Progressivism, it is clear, never became leasing's "smoking gun."

The abolition of convict leasing in most southern states required action by the state legislature to outlaw the system, characterized in Tennessee by the *Knoxville Journal* as "speculation in blood and muscle."[2] Usually the system would end, according to the new legislation, at the expiration of the lease then in force. Sometimes the legislation adopted would lead to a phased climax for leasing, as was the case, for example, in Arkansas, where, prior to absolute abolition as of New Year's Eve, 1913, the "contract" or "state account" system replaced "pure leasing" in an 1893 law. As late as 1911, "surplus" convicts, those not employed on the state farm, were still being "hired out" to private entities in Arkansas in violation of the law.[3] Under the contract system, the said agreement was frequently with a private party.[4] In most states it was an increasingly impatient and expanding pro-abolition public, an aroused legislature, and a politically sensitive if cautious chief executive that collectively overturned leasing. In one state, Tennessee, it was primarily coal-miner militancy inspired by self-interest that best explained abolition.

TENNESSEE

The early years of the penultimate decade of the nineteenth century in Tennessee witnessed a series of coal miners' disruptions that culminated in the death blow for convict leasing in that state. Tennessee coal miners, as nonconvict labor, like wage labor elsewhere, had long been opposed to convict lease laborers being employed in the state's iron and coal mines.

Their motives were obviously to protect their jobs. Throughout 1891 tension was ongoing between coal miners and state officials, especially the governor, over the use of convicts in competition with free labor in Tennessee mines. Miners called for a discontinuation of convicts working in the mines altogether and even the termination of the hated convict lease system. State legislators, with an eye on the revenue-producing nature of leasing, were loath to end it. Public opinion, labor unions, and most newspapers initially supported the miners. Cost-conscious lessees preferred convict labor. Governor John B. Buchanan, who at first defended the lease system, reversed himself by the summer of 1891 and called for a repeal of leasing with caveats. Miners continued to reject the so-called iron-clad contract, relinquishing their right to strike, and grew restless at inaction in the state legislature on the abolition of leasing. When convicts were brought in by the Tennessee Coal Company to work in place of free miners who had lost their jobs and were threatened with the loss of their homes, and with "destitution and starvation" in the offing, the situation grew more tense. The miners retaliated on more than one occasion by forcibly removing and thereby freeing the convicts working in the mines. The crisis appeared to be resolved when state officials removed convicts from a Tennessee Coal Company mine, as the lessee had failed to adhere to the terms of the contract governing the use of leased convict labor. However, by the end of the summer of 1891, the convicts were back in the mines, to the chagrin of the coal miners, and contending factions were at loggerheads again.

During the fall and winter, as legislators analyzed and debated the pros and cons of convict leasing and wondered how to deal with increasing militancy among miners, the miners, for their part, continued to liberate convicts from the stockades of the state's coal mines. In October, 163 convicts were released from the Tennessee Coal Mine and 120 from the Knoxville Mine. In November, 200 of the "toughest of the tough" were freed from the Cumberland Mine. Miners, in some instances, were not content to simply free the convicts, but proceeded to raze the quarters that housed them and the facilities they used. Few of the revolting miners were ever jailed, and although many of the convicts were recaptured, quite a few others (some 150 in all) never were. In the process, with the state militia now stationed at the mines, and with convicts—most of them Black—on the loose, the miners lost the public's sympathy and support for their predicament, which they had once enjoyed. A law-and-order press that had earlier sided with the miners now criticized their "lawlessness." Meanwhile, the lessees complained about contract violations and the loss of convict labor, and demanded restitution. Governor Buchanan was repeatedly criticized for being unable to handle a situation that had gotten out of control. That was the state of affairs in Tennessee on the eve of what one analyst of the subject called "the volcanic uprising of August 1892."[5]

The summer months were ordinarily a slack period in Tennessee coal mining. The 1892 uprising was ignited in July by the layoff of half the miners (some three hundred nonconvict workers) employed by the Tennessee Coal, Iron and Railroad Company, the state's largest lessee, while all 360 convicts remained. The turbulent events of the next few months involved militant miners marching under arms to several mines demanding jobs (Tracy City and Inman mines, in particular,); miner-directed relocation of convicts to Nashville and elsewhere; destruction of stockades and blockhouses; several deaths; open warfare among miners, sheriffs' posses, and the state militia (one attack on Fort Anderson involved at least a thousand armed miners); widespread criticism of the governor's failure to manage the crises effectively; and Governor Buchanan blaming the legislature. Ultimately, hundreds of miners were arrested, as many as could be found. More than three hundred were indicted on a variety of charges, including conspiracy and murder. Some were fined and a few served short jail sentences. (Many could not be located, having retreated to the surrounding hills and countryside.) The leader of the insurrection, D. B. Monroe, was convicted in 1893 and sentenced to seven years in prison.

A direct result of this violent summer and fall of 1892 was the adoption of legislation outlawing convict leasing by the Tennessee General Assembly on April 4, 1893, and immediately signed by Governor Peter Turney. Turney had defeated Buchanan in the 1892 election, in part because of Buchanan's mishandling of the miners' revolt and in part for his failure to be more aggressive in ending leasing. This action by the General Assembly was preceded by a blistering joint legislative committee investigation of convict leasing in January, publicly airing atrocities that were by then well known in Tennessee. The new legislation abolished the lease system at the expiration of the existing lease, January 1, 1896, and provided for the construction of a new penitentiary and the purchase of state coal lands on which convicts would now be worked under state supervision.[6]

ARKANSAS

Several trends emerged as southern convict leasing declined in the late nineteenth and early twentieth centuries. These themes were discernible in several states, and Arkansas is a good example to use by way of illustration. Compared with the demise of Tennessee leasing, the end of the system in Arkansas and several other states was also eventful, but nonviolent. Second, state governors got much more involved in the movement for abolition than ever before.

By the turn of the twentieth century the major political parties and a long list of minor ones, varying from state to state, had taken unequivocal positions, incorporated into party platforms, in support of ending leasing. In addition, legislative investigating committees and commissions, now reporting almost annually in every state, made it virtually inevitable that leasing and its abolition would compete for the public's attention as one of the major social problems of the day. Labor unions in all states pushed abolition higher on their agenda, even though lease labor's competition with free and union labor had always been a central concern for them. Furthermore, it was around the close of the nineteenth century that quite a few southern penologists converted to the idea of using the penal plantation or prison farm in place of convict leasing, as a solution to the problem of what to do with state prisoners. After leasing's downfall, many convicts were worked inside the walls of the penitentiary, and many others began to be used on chain gangs for the construction of roads and other public works projects.

As the thinking in southern penology changed, the handling of prisoners differed from state to state, which makes it hazardous to generalize about common practices in all states . However, one way to speculate about what was beginning to happen is to suggest that, by the second decade or so of the new century, approximately 50 percent of the state's convicts were going to penal plantations and the other half were being deployed on chain gangs or employed in the penitentiaries, many of them newly constructed. In most cases, once the transition from leasing to whatever replaced it was complete, the state recaptured control over the labor and the lives of the convicts. At the same time, reports of brutality and mistreatment of prisoners continued and county convict leasing was often unaffected by changes in approach toward state convicts. Finally, the preoccupation with the need to treat Black and White convicts differently remained. Here, too, Arkansas was not atypical. When a 1907 legislative committee recommended that the lease system be abolished in Arkansas, it also proposed that Black convicts be worked on state prison farms at more demanding labor and that White prisoners be employed at easier tasks inside the penitentiary. The committee also proposed that Blacks should not be used to guard Whites. Some years earlier, then-governor James Eagle, without being explicit, had recommended in coded language that "intelligent" prisoners should work inside the prison and "ignorant" ones should be assigned outside work.[7]

Before George Donaghey was elected in 1908, several governors in Arkansas embraced the commitment to abolish convict leasing but were unable to carry it out. After three years of disappointment in his fight against leasing, and facing the prospect of forfeiting another chance if he were not re-elected, Donaghey decided on a bold and dramatic stroke to command attention for abolition. Influenced by his earlier attendance at a governors' conference in Virginia, where he first heard about the idea of mass pardons from Governor Cole Blease, a race demagogue from South Carolina, Governor Donaghey unconditionally pardoned 360 convicts in December 1912.[8] This act brought condemnation from critics and commendation from supporters, among them Eugene V. Debs, former labor leader and Socialist party candidate for president of the United States, and former President Theodore Roosevelt. His action got people's attention in Arkansas and beyond the state's borders. It did not, however, bring an immediate end to leasing in Arkansas. Governor Joseph Robinson, Donaghey's successor, would preside over the abolition of convict leasing in the state.

By 1890 all major and minor political parties in Arkansas were campaigning for an end to leasing. It was a dominant issue in state politics and in local and statewide elections. The Republican party took much of the heat for the existence of convict leasing because it controlled the state immediately after the Civil War, when leasing was established. The Democratic party was criticized, as well, because it replaced the Republicans as the controlling force in the state and maintained leasing. The Populist party, strong in Arkansas in the 1890s, led the attack against both major parties and leasing simultaneously. The Farmer's Alliance, the Knights of Labor, the Agricultural Wheel, and other minor parties echoed the denunciation of convict leasing and called for its eradication and for general change in prison policy. The Socialist party supported reform but did not advocate the abolition of convict leasing.

Under pressure from all political parties, the Arkansas

legislature finally acted to terminate convict leasing on February 5, 1913, to become effective on December 31, 1913.[9] Several other amendments were included in the legislation, such as the establishment of a new Board of Penitentiary Commissioners under the control of the governor, the acquisition of additional farmlands on which convicts would be worked, and the rehabilitation of existing stockades and provisions for new penitentiary construction. It was the case in Arkansas and elsewhere that the Louisiana plan and its Angola penitentiary farm became model replacements for convict leasing. The Angola idea emphasized the value of outdoor agricultural work. It was considered by one of the leading penologists in the United States at the time, Dr. Frederick Wines, to be "ideal . . . especially [for] Negro prisoners."[10]

LOUISIANA

It was, in some ways, a peculiar set of circumstances that led to the demise of convict leasing in Louisiana.[11] Little was unusual about the state's award of a twenty-one-year lease to Samuel Lawrence James and Company in 1870, because single individuals or companies were sole lessees for extended periods in other states, as well. As the state's only lessee from 1870 to 1891 and again from 1891 to 1901, James and Company gained complete control of the penitentiary and all convicts. James reportedly bribed his way into acquiring his first lease in 1869, said to have been "sold" by John M. Huger and Charles Jones, who had negotiated a five-year lease with Louisiana a year earlier.[12]

James was born in Tennessee and migrated to New Orleans, where he worked as a civil engineer. He rose to the rank of major in the Confederate army during the Civil War. By 1869

James had amassed sufficient wealth, although it is not clear how, to secure the Huger-Jones lease. After his death in 1894, James's estate was estimated to have grown to almost $2.5 million. Very little is out of the ordinary in the foregoing, unless one considers the fact that Louisiana was hard hit by the depression of the 1890s. Therefore, $2.5 million at the time could be considered extreme wealth. But then, Samuel James had no monopoly on Louisiana wealth. There were thirty-five millionaires in New Orleans alone by 1892.

A point of departure between Louisiana and several other leasing states begins with the role played by Black legislators during the life of convict leasing in the Bayou state.[13] Twenty-four of twenty-five voting Black legislators approved the 1870 lease with James and Company. The motive in post–Civil War Louisiana, like elsewhere, was economic necessity. The viciousness of convict leasing, with Blacks as the primary victims, had not yet become as well known as it would. At first there would appear to be some irony in the fact that Black legislators throughout the 1870s and 1880s more or less supported Samuel James and the James lease when efforts to abolish leasing surfaced in the legislature, and at a time when the more blatant horrors of leasing became public. James was adept at bribing both Black and White legislators and buying their votes and their support. This was especially significant in 1884 and 1886, when Black Republican legislators enjoyed a balance of power because White legislators in the Democratic and Republican parties were evenly divided between those in favor of leasing and those opposed to it. Black support for abolition could have ended the James lease. Black approval of leasing in the upper and lower houses of the legislature can also be seen several years later, in 1890, when a new ten-year lease was awarded to James and Company despite the fact that the brutality of leasing was, by that time, common knowledge in Louisiana. The four Black members of the Louisiana Senate and all but one of the ten members of the lower House voted to extend the lease for ten years.

Perhaps the stance of Black legislators is not so ironic, however, considering that they generally were rather conservative in both Louisiana and South Carolina, the two postbellum states in which Blacks enjoyed their greatest political influence in the nineteenth-century post–Civil War South, mainly by virtue of their large numerical percentages in the total state population. These Black legislators were influenced more by economic and class interests than by race. Therefore, even though most may have been aware of and repulsed by the evils of convict leasing, particularly the disproportionate number of Blacks who were victimized, they voted to establish, maintain, and extend convict leasing because they believed it would bring needed revenue, not to mention profits, to the state's coffers. Any humanitarian concerns they may have had, even for "kith and kin," were no doubt superseded by economic imperatives. In addition, it was the case that, frequently, Louisiana's Black legislators—many of whom were mulattos—did not identify with Blacks as Blacks. Consequently, many saw the victims of the convict lease system not as Blacks per se, but as criminals who were in prison and who wound up in leasing because of crimes they committed, and were therefore getting the punishment they deserved. They fell in line with the prevailing view that convict leasing was initially good, and still an asset overall for the state. Those legislators who were bribed did not care much about leasing or about much else except their payoffs, one way or another.[14]

It is worth noting that two years after a record-high death rate of 20 percent (216 deaths) was reported,[15] convict leasing in

Louisiana was weakened by an April 15, 1898, amendment to the Louisiana constitution. Prohibited was the leasing of convicts to private firms or to individuals after the expiration of the current lease in 1901.

The most intense struggle over the future of leasing in Louisiana took place in the last decade of the nineteenth century, a ten-year period that has been called the "worst" one for convicts, the "best" one for convict-furnished state revenue, and in some ways the "last" one for convict leasing.[16] A most interesting aspect in the story of abolition in Louisiana involved a campaigning "White supremacist" governor and former state senator, Murphy J. Foster, who was determined to bury convict leasing despite the fact that 90-plus percent of its victims were Black. Foster was stalled in his efforts, although not stopped, by a group of Black Republicans who wanted to retain the revenue from leasing and who held the balance of power in the General Assembly—thirteen years after "White supremacy" had supposedly been established.[17] The governor finally succeeded during his second administration, which began in 1896 with a campaign to end leasing. His abolition effort started in 1884 when he was a member of the state legislature. The system in Louisiana was effectively abolished in 1901, when Foster was a member of the U.S. Senate. It was a victory for which the governor, in later recollections of his thirty-two years of public service to Louisiana, never claimed credit.[18]

FLORIDA

The events leading up to the destruction of convict leasing in Florida lack the drama of the Tennessee miners' insurrection or the boldness of Governor Donaghey abruptly freeing 360

Arkansas convicts or the peculiar saga of a White supremacist Louisiana governor being forced to contend with a group of conservative Black legislators.[19] The road to abolition in Florida was relatively quiet, but sometimes fitful and contentious. The Florida press played a more significant role in leasing's overthrow than was the case in most other states, although the press campaign in several sister states should not be minimized.[20]

Because of the persistent role of the press, a few individual cases of brutality against Florida convicts got wider publicity than they would have. Some examples are Martin Tabert, George Campbell, Charles Dudley, and Oscar Anderson.[21] Abolitionist forces in Florida had to contend with nonsupportive governors throughout their campaign. During a high tide of low morality and many atrocities in Florida between 1906 and 1909, Floridians heard the impractical idea of sending convicts to work on the construction of the Panama Canal and the equally or more xenophobic notion of sending them to purposely established penal colonies in the newly acquired Philippine Islands. Neither of these possibilities, however, attracted much support. Meanwhile, Governor Albert Gilchrist vetoed legislation that would have abolished the system in 1911. A legislative override came up one vote short. Five years later, in the gubernatorial campaign of 1916, in which the disposition of state convicts was a major issue, not a single candidate called for the abolition of leasing. The inconsistency here was that public opinion, as reflected in the newspapers and in the legislature, favored an end to leasing. Nevertheless, the Florida legislature did not act decisively to wipe out leasing until the end of the second decade of the twentieth century, after labor unions, the clergy, and abolitionist organizations spoke with one forceful voice against the brutality, greed, and corruption of Florida leasing. County convict leasing was the first to fall, which laid the foundation, set the stage, and provided the momentum for a statewide anti-lease movement.

State political leaders in Florida and elsewhere were influenced by abolitionist developments in Georgia. They followed revelations of the 1908 legislative investigation there, which was widely publicized through the Georgia press and reprinted in Florida. Newspapers in the state that was Georgia's southern neighbor grumbled that "Georgia's convicts were given a new lease on life, [while] Florida's convicts were given a new lease in the phosphate mines and the turpentine farms."[22]

Park Trammell was elected governor in 1912. He spoke against leasing but did not call for outright or unconditional abolition. Instead, he proposed staggered or phased abolition over a two-year period between 1914 and 1916, which never became law. The legislature later adopted a 1915 measure by which, ultimately, only Black male convicts would be leased. Legislation in 1917, the Convict Lease Act, reinforced the earlier legislation and the situation grew progressively worse for leased convicts, by then all Black. By 1919 abolitionist sentiment was "stronger than ever," as possibly was brutality. In the spring in 1919, both houses of the Florida legislature passed legislation effectively outlawing state convict leasing, which was promptly signed by Governor Sidney Catts.

Essentially, the new law required convicts to be worked either on state farms or state roads and under state supervision.[23] Tragically, the abuses of convict leasing, which became a rallying point for abolition in Florida and in other states, outlived the system. Perpetrators of these abuses after abolition were officers of the state, under state supervision, rather than agents of private lessees. So the uniforms changed, and perhaps the bureaucracy was slightly different, but it was pretty much business as usual—

as studies and lore on the Florida and southern chain gangs attest. More often than not the only thing that changed was the law.

GEORGIA

The abolition effort in Georgia, already discussed in detail in chapter 4, brought together legislative leaders, journalists and newspapers, church ministers, outraged citizens, and the governor, who called the state legislature into extraordinary session for the *coup de grace* that would end leasing in the state. The compromise legislation that represented the passing order and fading flower for Georgia leasing was considered a "real victory" for opponents of the system and constituted a loss of "something over half a million dollars a year in net revenue" for the state.[24]

Several other states, most notably Florida, that had not yet outlawed leasing, watched developments in Georgia with a view toward the lessons to be learned. How much of a difference it made is difficult to discern, since none of the states that ended leasing after 1909 gave specific credit for their action to influence from Georgia. Nevertheless, it can be assumed—given the wide publicity that the day-to-day debates on leasing in the 1908 Georgia legislature received during the summer, and the far-ranging circulation of leaks from that year's convict lease investigation—that the few states in which leasing had not yet been legally abolished must have been considerably influenced, if not inspired or emboldened, by the Georgia example.

MISSISSIPPI

The background and details on Mississippi prior to the end of convict leasing are less well known than for other southern states. Mississippi, for its part, had (and still has) a reputation as one of the least developed southern states.[25] It was the last state in the nation to adopt a parole system.[26]

According to one contemporary observer of convict leasing, the Mississippi system had "an epidemic death rate without an epidemic," reaching as high as 17 percent in the 1880s and rarely falling below 10 percent.[27] It is reported that "no record" exists of the treatment of leased convicts during the early years of leasing and that an 1884 report "detailing the abuses inherent in the leasing system," after appearing in "a few newspapers," was either "lost or stolen" and did not appear in the *House Journal* of that year.[28] In an 1888 penitentiary report, "the names of all persons who are directly charged with cruelty to convicts . . . are suppressed." The explanation was that "the leasing system is dead, and so let the names of the brutes who helped to kill it die with it."[29]

One investigator of the Mississippi penal system concluded that there was no widespread opposition to leasing in the state because "inexpensive and reliable" labor was needed and the lease system saved the expense of "administering legal punishment" and "produced profits." The "driving force," this scholar found, however, "was probably the fact that the convict population of Mississippi was overwhelmingly black."[30] These factors prevailed in other states, too, even those with widespread penal reform movements.

To its credit, perhaps, Mississippi was the first state to outlaw convict leasing with a provision in its constitution, adopted at the infamous constitutional convention of 1890, which declared that "no penitentiary convict shall ever be leased or hired to any person or persons or corporation, private or public or quasi public, or board, after December 31st A.D., 1894. . . ."[31] It is doubtful that this provision was ever enforced, because

Governor James K. Vardaman is known to have undertaken a vigorous and ultimately successful campaign to put convict leasing behind the state of Mississippi during the first decade of the twentieth century. He admonished the 1906 legislature that the penitentiary and the convict lease system were still a "festering sore" in the state.[32] It was the 1908 legislature that finally abolished leasing in Mississippi at the behest of James K. Vardaman.[33]

Governor Vardaman's role in outlawing convict leasing in Mississippi, like that of his counterparts in Louisiana, Georgia, and South Carolina, is burdened with irony because he was an extreme White supremacist and race bigot (see chapter 1). As the chief executive and chief architect of abolitionism in Mississippi,[34] Vardaman's revulsion for wealth, greed, and the large plantation owners may have been almost as great as his hatred for Blacks. It should be remembered, however, that Blacks were not being set free. The lease system was ending and convict labor would no longer compete with wage labor and be "lady bountiful" for the unscrupulous lessees out to fleece the state and line their own pockets with as much gold as they could hold. The rich, to Vardaman, were getting richer, and that may have been intolerable to him.[35] It is worth repeating that even the notorious Ku Klux Klan opposed leasing, which should provide some perspective, if not clarity, for the anti-leasing disposition of Vardaman, Murphy Foster, Hoke Smith, Cole Blease, and others.

ALABAMA

Like Mississippi, details on Alabama prior to the end of convict leasing are sketchy. Over the decades of the nineteenth and twentieth centuries, Alabama—again like Mississippi—has enjoyed the dubious distinction of being conspicuous for its absence of enlightenment and progress in the broad area of social concern. As late as 1919, a time when Alabama was said to be determined to "rid itself" of convict leasing, it was called "one of the most backward States in prison conditions."[36] This latter view, despite the undue praise given to the Alabama prison system from time to time and notwithstanding the efforts of Julia Tutwiler, Alabama's most prominent late nineteenth-century social reformer, and her colleagues, who committed some energy to criticizing convict leasing in Alabama.[37] Moreover, the state of Alabama has been unique in many ways, not the least of which has been its history in race relations.

While an analysis of this enormous subject is certainly beyond the scope and purpose of this study, Alabama's reputation in this regard is fairly well known generally. (It is worth a passing reminder, all the same, that Alabama, "cradle of the Confederacy"—so-called because it was the first state home for the capitol of the Confederacy—was, more than any other southern state, the symbol of defiance during the civil rights movement in the United States during the 1950s and 1960s.) Not so unique was the reform-oriented but bigot-minded Anti-Convict League of the mid-1880s. This organization was dedicated to the eradication of convict leasing because of its inherent evils. It hoped to strengthen its case against leasing by suggesting that the large number of Black convicts in Alabama discouraged White immigration to the state.[38] Alabama's "unique convict lease" approach in the 1890s, not found in any other southern state, was displayed in its hiring practices, where convicts were employed "individually on the basis of their capacity to work. The wage scale [was] $18.50 per month for first class men, $13.50 for second, $9.00 for third and maintenance for fourth."[39]

Alabama's anti-lease movement was both similar to and different from that of other southern states. It was the next to last to outlaw leasing, in 1928. The press started out supportive of abolition, then changed its stance. There was the almost ritualistic "to-ing" and "fro-ing" in the legislature, which may have started in 1911.[40] Some governors favored the abolition of leasing; others opposed it; some about-faced on the subject. And one, William W. Brandon, in 1923, denied that Alabama had a lease system.[41] Convict leasing was a major issue in the 1926 gubernatorial campaign, with all candidates taking slightly different positions on the question. There was one huge lessee in the state, Pratt Mines, but other lessees existed as well at smaller mines, lumber companies, and turpentine operations, and as individuals. The state farm essentially replaced leasing during a 1928–38 transition period in Alabama penal history, and there was a good deal more county convict leasing both here and in Florida than in other states. Indeed, it is not clear that county leasing and state leasing were outlawed at the same time.

Mass meetings of aroused citizens were held after the revelation of particularly brutal incidents, and ministers were encouraged to call down fire and brimstone on lessees and state officials who continued such an ignominious system. There was also greater emphasis in Alabama, it seems, than in other states, on the value of the revenue for the state from convict leasing, not to mention the expense saved. This subject caused governors to waffle on the question of abolition and muted public pressure for an earlier obituary for leasing. The 1919 Alabama legislature made it unlawful to lease convicts after January 1, 1924.[42] In 1923 they acted again, making it illegal "for any person to lease or let for hire any State convict to any person, firm or corporation after March 31, 1927."[43] This extension resulted from the appeal for a change from Governor Thomas Kilby, who feared the fiscally damaging loss of income for the state. He believed that the Alabama treasury would be "drained of funds," estimated in 1923 to be $869,318.52 net from leasing, against net losses of $174,274.92 for Alabama, from nonlease convict labor.[44] The argument was compelling. It was repeated by other state officials; it caused individuals, organizations, and the press to rethink the issue of abolition, and prolonged the destruction of convict leasing in the Crimson State.[45] Later compromise legislation delayed the March 31, 1927, date to June 30, 1928, as the date on which the guillotine would fall on Alabama leasing. This delay was driven by the state's need for breathing space to better prepare for the impending loss of convict earnings. When the final group of eight hundred Black prisoners marched out of Alabama's coal mines on July 1, 1928, singing "Swing Low, Sweet Chariot," this chapter in Alabama's penal history came to an end.[46]

VIRGINIA

For most of the nineteenth century, management of the prison system in Virginia was provided for in a "Revised Code of 1819" in which the penitentiary was governed by a board of five "intelligent and discreet" citizens appointed by the governor, who also named the surgeon and "keeper of the penitentiary" or warden. By 1893-94, Virginia's penitentiary became so overcrowded that the legislature authorized the purchase of a farm that would house convicts unfit for service in the penitentiary. All prison officials were appointed by the governor or his designees, the superintendent of the penitentiary, or the manager of the farm. Overall governance remained in the hands of a "board of directors of the penitentiary," sometimes referred to after 1924 as the Prison Board. A State Convict Road Force was established in 1906 for felons and "jail prisoners." These convicts were to "build and maintain" Virginia's roads and streets and would be given "other public works" duties.[47]

The Virginia penal system has been called the "most peculiar one in the nation." The jails, facilities, and grounds were locally owned and managed by counties and cities, while the state paid for the maintenance of prisoners "whether convicted or awaiting trial [or] persons detained as witnesses." Prison officials such as sheriffs were elected locally and succeeded themselves indefinitely, leading to instances of tenure in excess of thirty years. The local officials were not accountable to state authority, even though most of their salary was paid by the state, with nominal salaries provided by the local government in the form of per-diem pay and with clear economic incentives based loosely on the number of convicts and the stage at which they were in the prison process, according to the following guidelines:[48]

For receiving a person in jail when first
committed . . . . $ .50

For keeping him and supporting him therein,
for each day $1.00

But when there are as many as three and less
than ten prisoners in jail, for each . . . . $ .75

Where there are ten or more prisoners in jail,
for each up to and including twenty-five . . . . $ .60

For each prisoner in excess of twenty-five, up
to and including fifty . . . . $ .50

For each prisoner in excess of fifty . . . . $ .25

The decentralized daily management of Virginia convicts seemed conducive to convict leasing and provided ample opportunity for corruption and brutality, with sheriffs and their deputies virtually taking the law into their own hands, doing what they pleased, and reporting to no one. It is not at all clear from the available record, however, that such was the case. The economic motive to develop a cost-free penitentiary was as strong in Virginia as in all the other southern states immediately after the Civil War. Virginia first tried railroad leases with unsatisfactory results, including financial losses and a convict death rate of over 20 percent by the 1880s. At that time, state officials experimented with a contract for convicts to make cheap shoes for a private manufacturer inside the prison. This effort eventually brought net earnings of more than $20,000, prompting both the adoption of a policy under which convicts worked on contracts inside the penitentiary, and the cancellation of railroad contracts.[49]

The literature on Virginia penal history, such as it is, makes little reference to convict leasing. Moreover, it appears as if the Virginia penitentiary, penal farms, and convict road gangs always remained under the control and general supervision of state officials. During the late nineteenth and early twentieth centuries, which marked the heyday for convict leasing throughout the South, Virginia—to its credit and despite its other shortcomings—never completely succumbed to the widespread practice of leasing its convicts outside the penitentiary.[50]

THE CAROLINAS

George Tindall, a prominent U.S. historian of the South, has suggested that South Carolina "muddled through" its arrival at a solution to its penal problems, including convict leasing.[51]

That description might fit North Carolina, too, since neither state seemed certain of where it wished to go with convict leasing and, once there, how to back away from the system. It cannot be gainsaid that many of the features found in leasing in other ex-Confederate states wound up in the two Carolinas. But there were aberrations also, especially in North Carolina, where leasing was abolished in 1917, subsequently revived, and outlawed again in 1933. In addition, unlike most other states, North Carolina officials remained in charge of the state's convicts throughout the era of leasing, surrendering control of the labor of convicts but not of their lives. Convicts worked mainly in "public account" activities that concentrated on internal improvements, especially roads and railroads—although sometimes illegally. Therefore, North Carolina resorted to the "modified" or "state-controlled" lease system and made limited use of the "general" or "pure lease" popular in the rest of the South. This "redeeming feature" distinguished North Carolina from its sister states and put a brake on the more inglorious aspects of leasing. A pioneer researcher of North Carolina leasing has cautioned, however, that "many of the state employees controlling convicts were just as brutal, irresponsible, and unworthy as any company boss. . . ."[52] It is also noted that general leases "were confined to no one or two of the standard types of labor . . . but included any type of work available. Occasional sub-leases indicate that State supervision . . . was exercised in these general leases less capably than in other projects."[53]

North Carolina leasing attracted little public notice and there was "no concentration of leasing nor any general law regarding the practice." There was little "into which the public could get its teeth. When some case of brutality or improvidence found its way to the light, the public quite naturally assumed that it was purely local, and refused, except in a few rare cases, to be aroused by isolated incidents."[54] To be sure, the economic incentive was present from the outset and throughout, even though it is reported that North Carolina did not enjoy the bonanza other states did. Lessees were "motivated by the spirit of enterprise and the temptation to exploit cheap labor; State officials were influenced by eagerness to put money in the treasury, and by a low estimate of public sentiment and intelligence."[55] Leadership in the state must have known about the bashing that convict leasing was taking from the public and the press in states situated to North Carolina's south and west. However, the state legislature very quietly banned leasing in the law of 1917 to "private or corporate interests."

The attention of the entire nation was diverted by the Great War and subsequent peace in 1918. Celebration and prosperity came in the 1920s, bringing with them high employment for free labor and a renewed demand for convict labor in North Carolina. The 1917 prohibition was simply ignored by prison authorities, and convict labor was again leased to private entities. Abolition the second time around came with an equal lack of hoopla, and was led by Governor Oliver M. Gardner, who canceled a lease contract with the Carolina Coal Company, costing the state $90,000 in annual convict earnings. Having been condemned as "hellish in principle and brutal in practice," by 1929 North Carolina leasing was swept up into a larger penal reform movement in the state; as a result, in 1933, the authority formerly held by a prison department and state highway commission was consolidated in the hands of a state highway and public works commission. The legislation passed by the General Assembly brought a range of reforms and uniformity to penitentiary affairs in a state where some one hundred different counties and prison units were doing their own respective and sometimes "worst conceivable" thing, with regard to convict management, and where the "road supervisor was a law unto himself." The North Carolina prison reform movement, enthusiastic and persistent as it was, moved into higher gear by the mid-1920s and contained most of the key aspects of movements elsewhere. Not to be ignored was the leadership of a Men's Club at the "Church by the Side-of-the-Road" in "hell and damnation" Greensboro.[56]

Almost everything about convict leasing in South Carolina was relatively "ordinary." It had an "ordinary" beginning in 1876–77, for "ordinary" economic reasons—to make the penitentiary self-supporting. Its passing in 1901 was "ordinary," following an "ordinary" tenure of more than two decades. Also "ordinary" were the reports of brutality and convict abuse, which rivaled those of convict leasing anywhere in the South. Yet the public reaction was no more than "ordinary," if measured by the impetus provided by some of the shocking accounts of convict slaughter for the dismantling of the system. For example, there was no public, press, or legislative outcry in South Carolina when it was revealed that the death rate for convicts leased to the Greenwood and Augusta Railroad in 1877, 1878, and 1879 could have been over 50 percent, and that ten of fifteen convicts received were reported on May 2, 1878, to have died (66 percent); of the rest, one had escaped, two were pardoned, one was unaccounted for, and one was on hand.[57] A study of Blacks in South Carolina sums up the reasons why convict leasing received scant attention, after observing that "early exposure of brutality" resulted in a degree of amelioration:

> White public opinion was never aroused to effective indignation over the system. In the first place, convict leasing was

almost altogether a system for the leasing of Negro prisoners. It was but one of many indignities suffered by Negroes, and few could become seriously aroused over it. Then, too, the stringent measure which was the only real solution—abolition of the system—seemed to involve expenses that the taxpayers of the State did not want to assume. It was also difficult for the public to become concerned over a problem with which it was not familiar, and convicts leased out on plantations, in phosphate mines, and in railroad camps did not frequently come to the public eye.[58]

The state constitution of 1895 started convict leasing in South Carolina down the path to a quiet and "ordinary" burial by providing that convicts would be supervised only by officers of the state. The final blow came when existing contracts ended on December 31, 1901.[59]

TEXAS

The end for leasing in Texas was perhaps more conspicuously quiet than in any other southern state. In March of 1871 the Texas legislature authorized, even required, "the governor to lease the state penitentiary together with the labor of the convicts. . . ."[60] Leasing the penitentiary was outlawed by the legislature in April 1883, although it was replaced by the "state account" and "contract labor system."[61] Essentially this meant that the state now sent convict labor directly to private entities on contract and the state was remunerated for the labor. Lessees were now excluded, and the state regained control of the penitentiary and the management of convicts, but private parties continued to employ them. It appears that the contract system, which faced opposition from the outset, was abolished in January 1914. Total responsibility for the Texas prison system was turned over to three full-time commissioners appointed by the governor.[62] However, at least as late as May 1923, the thirty-eighth legislature in Texas adopted a resolution opposing convict leasing.[63]

NOTES

1. A 1990 study declares that the difference between convict leasing and the chain gang was "negligible." Moreover, the suggestion is made that the treatment of convicts on chain gangs was as bad as or worse than that under leasing. See Alex Lichtenstein, "The Political Economy of Convict Labor in the New South," Ph.D. diss. (University of Pennsylvania, 1990), 378, chapter 8 and *passim*.

2. *Knoxville Journal*, August 24, 1892.

3. Jane Zimmerman, "The Convict Lease System in Arkansas and the Fight for Abolition," *The Arkansas Historical Quarterly* (Autumn 1949), 177–81ff.

4. An essential difference between the contract or state account system and leasing was that in the former, control of all convicts was to remain in the hands of state officials, and prisoners usually worked on state-owned property—for example, within penitentiary walls or on state farms.

5. A. C. Hutson, "The Overthrow of the Convict Lease System in Tennessee," *East Tennessee Historical Society Publications* 8 (1936), 91.

6. Accounts of the miners' insurrection in Tennessee between 1891 and 1893 and its role in getting convict leasing outlawed in the state can be found in contemporary Tennessee newspapers, most of which covered the story. Especially useful are the *Knoxville Journal*, the *Knoxville Tribune*, and the *Clinton Gazette*. Other valuable sources of information, with many details, are various issues of the *House Journal* and the *Senate Journal* (1891, 1892,

1893), which contain discussions in the Tennessee legislature, messages from the governor and the Penitentiary Commission, and other reports and pertinent information in appendices. On specific legislation, see *Acts of the State of Tennessee Passed by the Extraordinary Session of the Forty-Seventh General Assembly* for 1891. Joint legislative investigations for 1893 and 1895, especially, already cited in chapter 3, provide accounts of conditions in convict leasing in Tennessee. An important summary of the confrontation between the miners and state officials in Tennessee, as well as an overview of the prelude to the overthrow of leasing, is Hutson, "The Overthrow of the Convict Lease System in Tennessee."

7. Zimmerman, "The Convict Lease System in Arkansas," 176.

8. One account of the governor's frustration with his effort to get leasing abolished, which led him to take this dramatic action, can be found in the *Arkansas Democrat*, December 19, 1912.

9. *Acts and Resolutions of the General Assembly of the State of Arkansas* (1913), 210–25. Also useful on the decline of leasing in Arkansas are various issues of the *House Journal* and the *Senate Journal* from the early 1890s through 1919, which contain "Biennial Reports of the Arkansas State Penitentiary," and local newspapers, particularly the *Arkansas Gazette*.

10. For an examination of the ideas of Dr. Frederick Wines and his influence on the thinking of southern penologists, see his pamphlet publications, "The Prisons of Louisiana," in *Proceedings of the National Prison Association* (1906), and *Report Upon the Penal and Other State Institutions to the Reform Association of Louisiana* (1906).

11. A study of Louisiana penal history with attention devoted to convict leasing was done by Mark Carleton, entitled *Politics and Punishment: The History of the Louisiana State Penal System* (Baton Rouge: Louisiana State University Press, 1971). See also his "The Politics of the Convict Lease System in Louisiana: 1868–1901,"

Louisiana History 8, no. 1 (Winter 1967). Useful as well, especially for background, is Leon Stout, "Origins and Early History of the Louisiana Penitentiary," M.A. thesis (Department of History, Louisiana State University, 1934), and Elizabeth Wisner, *Public Welfare Administration in Louisiana* (Chicago, 1930). As is the case with other states, various issues of the *House Journal* and the *Senate Journal*, along with the collection of *Acts and Resolutions* for Louisiana, offer details on convict leasing, legislative debates, governors' messages, biennial penitentiary and related reports, and other information. For readers who desire a complete picture of the system of convict leasing from 1868 to 1901, local newspapers, especially those in New Orleans, complement all other sources on Louisiana leasing.

12.   Carleton, *Politics and Punishment*, chapter 1.

13.   A study of Black legislators in Louisiana during the last quarter of the nineteenth century was done by A. E. Perkins, "Some Negro Officers and Legislators in Louisiana," *Journal of Negro History* 14 (1929), 523–28.

14.   For insight into the attitudes of Louisiana's Black leadership during the post–Civil War era, see John W. Blassingame, *Black New Orleans, 1860–1880* (Chicago, 1973). For South Carolina and conclusions that may have been representative of the views of Black legislators in other states, see Thomas Holt's *Black Over White: Negro Political Leadership In South Carolina During Reconstruction* (Urbana, 1977). A valuable collection of biographies of Black legislators during the era of Reconstruction is Eric Foner, *Freedom's Lawmakers: A Directory of Black Officeholders During Reconstruction* (New York, 1993). For Black opposition to convict leasing in Georgia, see Clarence Bacote, "Negro Proscriptions, Protests and Proposed Solutions in Georgia, 1880–1908," in *The Negro in the South Since 1865: Selected Essays in American Negro History*, ed. Charles E. Wynes (Tuscaloosa, 1965).

15.   Carleton, *Politics and Punishment*, 77–78, and n. 34.

16. Carleton, *Politics and Punishment*, 70.

17. Ibid., 71. Further details on the opposition of Black legislators can be found in chapter 6.

18. On the life and career of Governor Foster, see Sidney J. Romero, Jr., "The Political Career of Murphy J. Foster," *Louisiana Historical Quarterly* 28 (1945), 1190–1230.

19. The details of anti-leasing and abolitionist developments in Florida are provided by Gordon Carper, "The Convict Lease System in Florida," Ph.D. diss. (Florida State University, 1964), chapters 8 and 9.

20. The best press coverage and editorials on leasing and abolitionism in Florida between 1900 and 1919 are found in the *Tampa Morning Tribune*, the *Tallahassee Weekly True Democrat*, and the *Times-Union* (Jacksonville, Florida).

21. For details on these cases, see chapter 3.

22. Carper, "The Convict Lease System in Florida," 256, citing the *Tampa Tribune*, April 8, 1909, and the *Live Oak Suwannee Democrat*, April 10, 1910.

23. *Acts and Resolutions of the State of Florida* (1919), 65–66. In general, this is a rich source of information, along with various issues of the *Senate Journal* and the *House Journal*, on the role of the legislature and other state officials throughout the era of convict leasing in Florida.

24. *The Outlook*, October 3, 1908, 238–39.

25. Hilda Jane Zimmerman, "Penal Systems and Penal Reform in the South Since the Civil War," Ph.D. diss. (University of North Carolina, Chapel Hill, 1947), 442–45.

26. Ibid.

27. J. H. Jones, "Penitentiary Reform in Mississippi," *Publications of the Mississippi Historical Society* 2 (1902), 112, 119.

28. Ibid. See also Ruby E. Cooley, "A History of the Mississippi Penal Farm System, 1890–1935: Punishment, Politics and Profit in Penal Affairs," M.A. thesis (University of Southern Mississippi, 1981), 18. Three other, older Masters' theses shed some light on convict leasing in Mississippi and therefore are worth seeing: Lyda G. Shivers, "A History of the Mississippi Penitentiary," M.A. thesis (University of Mississippi, 1930); Marvin Lee Hutson, "Mississippi's State Penal System," M.A. thesis (University of Mississippi, 1939); and Thomas Buford Rowland, "The Legal Status of the Negro in Mississippi from 1832–1860," M.A. thesis (University of Wisconsin, 1933).

29. Jones, "Penitentiary Reform in Mississippi," 117.

30. Cooley, "A History of the Mississippi Penal Farm System," 15.

31. For the full text, see Article 10, Section 223 of the 1890 Constitution. See also Fletcher M. Green, "Some Aspects of the Convict Lease System in the Southern States," in *Essays in Southern History Presented to Joseph Gregoire de Roulhac Hamilton . . .*, ed. Fletcher M. Green (Chapel Hill, 1949), 121, and Jones, "Penitentiary Reform In Mississippi," 118.

32. *Mississippi House Journal* (1906), 18–19.

33. Paul B. Foreman and Julien R. Tatum, "The Short History of Mississippi's State Penal Systems," *Mississippi Law Journal* 10 (April 1938), 267–68.

34. The valiant efforts of Frank Johnson and Messrs. John Martin and Roderick Gambrell (the latter losing his life) in the 1880s should not be overlooked. However, the legislature did not outlaw leasing until 1908. On the "crusade of Frank Johnson," especially, see Cooley, "A History of the Mississippi Penal Farm System," 24–25.

35. For a consideration of Vardaman's anti-leasing stance, see William Holmes, *The White Chief: James Kimble Vardaman* (Baton Rouge, 1970), chapters 2, 6, and 8.

36. See Zimmerman, "Penal Systems and Penal Reform," 391–92, on Alabama's desire to "rid itself" of convict leasing, and Albert Burton Moore, *History of Alabama and Her People*, vol. 1 (New York: American Historical Society, 1927), 981, on Alabama as "one of the most backward states in prison conditions."

37. One example of undeserved praise, at a time when local newspapers and others were reporting continuing and, in some cases, increasing atrocities at Pratt Mine and elsewhere in Alabama, is found in an article by Ogden Chisholm in *Prison World* 1 (April 15, 1924). This kind of defense and praise, not uncommon during the era of leasing, amounts to the well-known "whitewash" of the evils of the system by apologists for it. Useful, although brief, on Julia Tutwiler's efforts with leasing, is Clara Pitts, "Julia Strudwich Tutwiler," Ed.D. thesis (George Washington University, 1942).

38. *Montgomery Advertiser*, August 4, 1995.

39. Malcolm Moos, *State Penal Administration in Alabama* (Tuscaloosa: University of Alabama, 1942), 14–15.

40. Zimmerman, "Penal Systems and Penal Reform," 391. Zimmerman notes that a vigorous movement to stop leasing began in 1917 and later observes (p. 407) that the fight to abolish leasing began with the 1911 legislative session.

41. Ibid., 398.

42. Zimmerman, "Penal Systems and Penal Reform," 393.

43. Moos, *State Penal Administration in Alabama*, 20.

44. Zimmerman, "Penal Systems and Penal Reform," 395–98.

45. Ibid., 400–01.

46. *New York Times*, July 1, 1928. For a general survey of the movement to end leasing in Alabama, perhaps the only one, see Zimmerman, "Penal Systems and Penal Reform," 391–409; also consult Moos, *State Penal Administration in Alabama*, chapter 1.

Worth seeing as a history of the treatment of convicts in Alabama is Gladys King, "History of the Alabama Convict Department," M.A. thesis (Alabama Polytechnic Institute, 1937); R. H. Dawson, "The Convict System of Alabama—As It Was and As It Is," in *Handbook of Alabama*, ed. Saffold Berney (Spartenburg: The Reprint Company Publishers, 1975), 254–66. From the vantage point of a contemporary with a vested interest as a prison official, see John Milner, "A Review of the Convict Situation in Alabama." The publication date of Milner's review and the correct title of the newspaper or journal in which it appears are confusing. It was originally published as a supplement to the *Iron Age* in Birmingham and reprinted as a supplement to the *Montgomery Daily Advertiser* and/or the *Montgomery Advertiser* (weekly); the dates are difficult to pin down but are likely to have been sometime in the 1880s.

47.   Virginia Advisory Legislative Council, *Report to the Governor: Jails, Prison Farms, Probation and Parole* (Richmond, 1939).

48.   For all quotes and the guidelines, see the report of the Legislative Jail Commission to the General Assembly of Virginia, entitled *The Virginia Jail System Past and Present with a Program for the Future* (Richmond, 1937), 9–10.

49.   Dan Carter, "Prisons, Politics and Business: The Convict Lease System in the Post–Civil War South," M.A. thesis (University of Wisconsin, 1964), 93.

50.   There appears to be no modern study of Virginia's penal past. Nevertheless, see Frank William Hoffer et al., *The Jails of Virginia: A Study of the Local Penal System* (New York, 1933).

      Information on convict leasing in the state is indeed scarce. Hilda Jane Zimmerman's magnum opus, "Penal Systems and Penal Reform," surprisingly contains no discussion of convict leasing in Virginia in its 535 pages of narrative, although there is a brief discussion (440–42) of Virginia's post-WWI "social awakening" and general penal reform movement. None of the other works cited in this study discusses Virginia leasing either.

51. George Tindall, *South Carolina Negroes, 1877–1900* (Columbia, 1952), 276.

52. Herbert Stacy McKay, "Convict Leasing in North Carolina, 1870–1934," M.A. thesis (University of North Carolina, Chapel Hill, 1942), 60–61, *passim.*

53. Ibid., 91–92.

54. Ibid., 9.

55. Ibid.

56. In general, for the outlawing of leasing in North Carolina, see Zimmerman, "Penal Systems and Penal Reform," 409–24, and McKay, "Convict Leasing in North Carolina," chapters 1–4.

57. *Reports and Resolutions of the General Assembly of the State of South Carolina* (1880), 433.

58. Tindall, *South Carolina Negroes*, 273.

59. Albert D. Oliphant, *The Evolution of the Penal System of South Carolina from 1866 to 1916* (Columbia: The State Company, 1916), 11. This fourteen-page pamphlet is one of a very few early studies of the penal system in South Carolina.

60. *House Journal*, 12th legislature (1871), 534.

61. Herman Lee Crow, "A Political History of the Texas Penal System, 1829–1951," 139–40.

62. Ibid., 180–81.

63. *General Laws, Texas Legislature*, 1923, first, second, and third called sessions, 141–42.

CHAPTER SIX

EPILOGUE:
THE REACTION OF
BLACK LEADERSHIP

T HE SIXTY-EIGHT YEARS FROM the end of the Civil War to the outlawing of the lease system in 1933 by North Carolina—the era of convict leasing—was devastating for African-Americans in the U.S. South. Those years brought hard times all around, and they were primarily about survival for most Blacks. National Black leadership concentrated its attention on the dominant challenges that cried out for redress: lynching, segregation, disenfranchisement, and general and pervasive racial discrimination, with all of its far-reaching manifestations and consequences. Among highly visible national Black

228

leaders and organizations, convict leasing and the disproportionately high victimization of Blacks was relatively, but not totally, unknown. This was the case at least insofar as a knowledge of leasing and its carnage resulted in concrete action against it, or reaction to it, in the form of criticism, condemnation, protest, or efforts to get it abolished. Leasing never generated the kind of national groundswell of opposition as did, for example, the crusade against lynching, the efforts to get the Fifteenth Amendment upheld, or attempts to stall the malignancy of Jim Crow. There were limits on the extent to which the small cadre of Black leaders could address the many issues facing them, and therefore choices had to be made and priorities established. The comparative silence on convict leasing is best explained by the limited knowledge Black leaders had of its atrocities and the demands of what were considered more pressing realities. In addition, Black leaders fell victim to the notion that "criminals" were getting what they deserved and, despite the cruelty of convict leasing, a crusade on behalf of prisoners was not seen as more important than fighting the lynching bee, opposing voting restrictions, or protesting the acts of racial bigotry that abounded. Those who accepted this analysis failed to fully appreciate how many of the convicts victimized by leasing were kidnapped, held beyond their sentences, or actually innocent of the crimes for which they were incarcerated, the total number of which will never be known.

There were some Black individuals and organizations of national prominence and many others, locally based, to whom convict leasing was very familiar, who were outraged by it, and who let that be known without reservation or qualification.

BLACK LEADERS RESPOND

We know precious little about the views on leasing of Frederick Douglass, Martin Delaney, Harriet Tubman, P. B. S. Pinchback, Robert Smalls, Hiram Revels, Blanche K. Bruce, and other Civil War–Reconstruction era Black leaders whose organizations enjoyed some degree of visibility, since they were preoccupied with the new demands that freedom required of four million ex-slaves. These former prisoners of bondage were now forced to adapt to survive in a changing South and United States of America that would never again be what it once was. Furthermore, convict leasing did not begin to mature in the South until a decade or so after the Civil War ended, so that the second generation of Black leaders in the post–Civil War period offers a better window on Black leadership's priorities and attitudes and their reaction to the southern system of convict leasing.

Emigration

The overall situation got so bad for Blacks in some places in the South by the late 1870s and 1880s that a few local Black leaders decided anyplace was better than the former slave states. Benjamin "Pap" Singleton, for example, was anxious to get his flock out of the South and into Kansas or Oklahoma or anywhere, including Liberia or Greece, in order to escape the persecutions that Blacks faced in the states of the Old Confederacy. Later, Alfred Charles "Chief" Sam adopted a similar view that Blacks would not enjoy their rights as free citizens in the United States in general and in the southern states in particular, and therefore opted to head, with his minions, for the Gold Coast, West Africa, with tragic consequences.[1] These individuals and others, including some who were influenced by the position of the

American Colonization Society, hardly knew or cared much about convict leasing. Their sense of an answer to the troubles faced by African-Americans was different. It did not include reform or changes in penology. A solution for them to the injustice Blacks faced in the South might be found in exodus.[2] Bishop Henry McNeal Turner, among the better-known late nineteenth-century advocates of Black emigration, also vigorously protested discrimination and inequality for Blacks throughout the United States. He was a lifelong critic of the United States' failure to meet its obligation and maintain its commitment to its Black citizens. Turner also took occasion to criticize the convict lease system in Georgia. He was instrumental in organizing the parallel anti-lease meeting in Atlanta in the summer of 1908 at the People's Tabernacle, called by Blacks because they could not participate in the effort organized by Whites.[3]

Mary Church Terrell

Mary Church Terrell did not enjoy name recognition as great as Frederick Douglass, Booker T. Washington, or W. E .B. DuBois. However, she was no voice in the wilderness on issues of human rights and equality for African-Americans. She also found time early in the twentieth century to mount an attack in a contemporary journal on convict leasing that suited her style and influenced many others, both Black and White. Her analysis considered leasing a "modern regime of slavery" in which Blacks were jailed on "trumped up" charges and relegated to "gaol . . . in dark, damp, disease-breeding cells . . . overworked, underfed, and only partially covered with vermin-infested rags." She called the convict lease system "less humane" than slavery because slave owners had an economic stake in keeping slaves healthy and at maximum productive capacity, while no such consideration existed among lessees, who obtained their convict labor by virtue of being the highest bidder at auction. There was little difference to her between peonage, the chain gang, and convict leasing, and she cites cases of Blacks being kidnapped, "torn from their homes," and forced to work when labor was needed. "This practice," she writes, prevailed for a long time in largely Black Madison County, Texas. Men were captured during a particular planting season, "released with empty pockets," and recaptured when they were needed again. Large-plantation owners and others who ran southern convict leasing, Terrell felt, were much more sophisticated and less likely to face trouble than the kidnappers. Her general description of the fate that befell the mostly Black victims of convict leasing is worth noting at length:

> Colored men are convicted in magistrates' courts of trivial offenses, such as alleged violation of contract or something of the kind, and are given purposely heavy sentences with alternate fines. Plantation owners and others in search of labour, who have already given their orders to the officers of the law, are promptly notified that some available labourers are theirs to command and immediately appear to pay the fine and release the convict from gaol only to make him a slave. If the negro dares to leave the premises of his employer, the same magistrate who convicted him originally is ready to pounce down upon him and send him back to gaol. Invariably poor and ignorant, he is unable to employ counsel or to assert his rights (it is treason to presume he has any) and he finds all the machinery of the law, so far as he can understand, against him. There is no doubt whatever that there are scores, hundreds perhaps, of coloured men in the South today who are vainly trying to repay fines and sentences imposed upon them five, six or even ten years ago.

The horror of ball and chain is ever before them, and their future is bright with no hope.[4]

Despite the efforts of some in the state to improve conditions, Terrell believed that Georgia had the worst record of violence under convict leasing—although no southern state was spared from her scorn for embracing such a barbaric system. But Georgia was especially bad, and more of her assessment concentrated on Georgia than on all the other southern states combined. She was powerfully impressed by Colonel Alton Byrd's investigation of Georgia's convict camps, as much for what it uncovered as for the fact that the Colonel was a southerner and a Georgian and, therefore, it was presumed, less likely to exaggerate the realities of convict leasing. Terrell quoted the Byrd report repeatedly and in detail as part of her larger effort to discredit leasing and stimulate support for the recognition of the crime it represented. One chain gang case to which she refers contains a graphic example of penitentiary officials' vested interest in maintaining the system:

> A colored man was convicted of larceny and sentenced to twelve months on the chain gang. The county solicitor personally took charge of him, carried him to a private camp, where the contractor gave him 100 dollars in cash for this prisoner. A few months later it was discovered that the man was innocent of the crime. Both the judge and the jury before whom he was convicted signed a petition to the Governor praying for the prisoner's release. The county solicitor refused to sign it, however, because he had received his 100 dollars in advance and distributed it among the other court officials and did not want to pay it back.[5]

Booker T. Washington

Booker Taliferro Washington, leading Black educator and guru of Tuskegee, favorite of White wealth and influence, champion of self-help, inspiration to Marcus Garvey, sometime adversary of W. E. B. DuBois, and quiet supporter of various Black causes—including a Black press that criticized his philosophy—has his name embroidered on the era that paralleled the years of leasing. His voice was loud and persistent on most of the issues that affected the lives and future of African-Americans during his stewardship as "foremost" black leader of his time, and as one of the most influential Black individuals in United States history.

As much as, or more than, anything, Booker T. Washington was controversial. The debate over his tactics and style, his leadership, his strategy, and his philosophy persists, even continues to grow, among scholars and nonscholars alike, producing in the process a good deal more heat than light. Washington's demanding list of priorities made room for concerns about peonage, noted above.[6] He also devoted some attention explicitly to the evils of convict leasing. Operating from his Alabama Black-belt perch in Tuskegee from 1881 until his death in 1915, and traversing the South and the United States regularly on one crusade or another, Washington often had a close-up view of leasing. He also heard from others on the subject, no doubt feeling that his voice of criticism or opposition to leasing would command much greater attention than their own.

Julia Strudwick Tutwiler, well-known educator and prison reformer in Alabama, "who opposed leasing but found it too entrenched to abolish," contacted Booker T. Washington in early March 1891 on behalf of two hundred Black youngsters under seventeen years of age who were "in training for the lives of a professional criminal." She indicated that these boys were now "hired out" to lessees along with adult convicts and proposed that Booker T. Washington hire them instead as part of his mission to "uplift the colored race." She also recommended that he establish an Industrial Reform School for them. Ms. Tutwiler further proposed that Washington pay the youngsters the going rate of the day, erect new buildings (including one for women), and call this new arrangement a "Children's Prison." Washington was assured that such a "Christ-like" effort would attract support and advice from northern friends and indicated that the principal of Tuskegee could use her letter "in any way you please, but not my name." Apparently, she preferred to be in direct touch with anyone to whom appeals would be made. Booker T. Washington, who was not so well known outside the South in 1891, seems to have been selected on the basis of his potential and position and because this prison reform crusader "believed that if these people can be helped it is by their own race, who understand them, who sympathize with them, and who are willing to make sacrifices for them."[7]

Professor Washington also heard from D. E. Tobias, the son of illiterate former slaves from South Carolina and a self-proclaimed authority on penitentiaries in the South, throughout the United States, and abroad. Mr. Tobias explained, in response to Washington's speeches, which he received and read at his own request, that the reasons for the large number of Black convicts in the South could be reduced to one, the convict lease system. In comparing the length of sentences in Rhode Island and Mississippi, Tobias reported averages of two years and 356 days, and twelve years and 116 days, respectively. The reason for the disparity, asserted Tobias, was that "Rhode Island has no convict lease system: by means of which, prisoners are manufactured for the market. . . ." The lease system was "so prevalent" in ex-slave states, Tobias went on, that it was "responsible for such a large number of coloured prisoners being found in the United States." Tobias's appeal to Booker T. Washington was to do what he could to have "this huge evil" abolished and "the mischief . . . abated."[8]

Writing to Booker T. Washington on another matter, Blanche K. Bruce, one of two Blacks who represented Mississippi in the United States Senate some years after the Civil War, made reference to the activities of their wives, which included the annual conventions of the National Association of Colored Women, of which both Mrs. Washington and Mrs. Bruce were officers. At their 1897 annual meeting in Nashville, a resolution was adopted that called for the "humanization of the convict lease system."[9] Another correspondent with Booker T. Washington, Charles B. Spahr, a member of the editorial staff of *Outlook* from 1886 to 1904, wrote to Washington on behalf of Lyman Abbott to thank him for a congratulatory letter from the "Wizard of Tuskegee" to Joseph F. Johnson, then governor of Alabama. Johnson, a Democrat, former Confederate Army officer wounded four times in the Civil War, businessman, and lawyer before becoming a two-term governor (1896–1904), had senatorial aspirations. He initially supported the disenfranchisement of Blacks in Alabama by constitutional amendment in convention, but changed his mind and led the opposition to such a move when he realized that many of his key poor White constituents could also lose a chance to vote.

At any rate, Booker T. Washington seems to have told Abbott about Governor Johnson's message to the Alabama legislature calling for convict parole for good behavior, speedy trials for serious crimes, and an end to the convict-lease system.[10]

Booker T. Washington's own offensive against convict leasing, such as it was, may have begun with a letter to the editor of the *Southern Workman* in 1886. "With few exceptions," Washington opened, southern convicts were hired to private contractors for a certain amount of money. There was "terrible suffering" as a result, and convicts were not reformed but rather were worse off when released. Washington thought that "some Christian reformer" ought to dedicate his life to the uplift and reformation of criminal elements. Washington's assessment of the state of affairs in southern prisons was illustrated in his letter with the gruesome story of a young Black convict whose feet "rotted off" and the "pitiful" tale of a Black convict named Alex Crews, "unlawfully forced into prison in the first place and while there was so inhumanely treated that he dropped dead before he could reach his home after being released." The *Montgomery Daily Dispatch* asked Crews, as he was dying, "Are there other convicts as bad off as you are?" "Oh, yes, boss," he was reported to have answered, "some of them are a heap worse." In closing, Washington called for general condemnation of the miserable treatment of convicts in southern prisons.[11]

It is not clear that Booker T. Washington, like many of his contemporaries, made a significant distinction between peonage and convict leasing. His efforts, especially his behind-the-scenes private ones, on behalf of poor southern Blacks victimized by debt slavery or peonage, are better known than his involvement with convict leasing. Washington was very helpful, though quietly so, with the Pink Franklin case in South Carolina and the Alonzo Bailey case in Alabama.[12] He told Oswald Garrison Villard in 1903 that a local Alabama judge, Thomas G. Jones, was to be congratulated for his work in exposing peonage. The state's attorney also kept him informed of efforts being made to bring those guilty of peonage practices to justice but was "baffled . . . until the Federal authorities took hold."[13] A few years later he told Villard how much he and others rejoiced over the U.S. Supreme Court decision declaring peonage unconstitutional, but lamented the fact that more money was being paid for leased Black convicts in Alabama than for teachers, "about $46 per month" for first-class convicts and $36 and $26, respectively, for second- and third-class ones, compared with some "Black belt counties" where teachers were paid $15 to $17 per month.[14]

Washington formulated no special strategy for the destruction of convict leasing, but encouraged others to expose its evils. He thought, at least on one occasion, that rather than producing "a lot of discouraging figures showing the bad side of the Convict Lease System . . . ," a better approach might be to demonstrate how leasing was supporting state and local governments. "A careful investigation would show," he declared, that 90 percent of the $400,000 net turned into the Alabama State treasury in 1907 was earned by Black convicts. Such information would "off-set" the "oft repeated cry" that Blacks did not bear their fair share of the tax burden. Washington felt that this was a "strong and interesting point," but that such a revelation did not necessarily harm convict leasing. Indeed, it might have worked to strengthen the resolve of leasing's supporters, bolstering the argument of economic necessity.[15] On the other hand, it is possible that Washington believed this information would demonstrate to potential opponents how Blacks were being used as virtual slaves of the state.

W. E. B. DuBois

William Edward Burghart DuBois, Washington's sometime nemesis—although not his "equal" as a "Black leader"—was not as eloquent in attacking the human destructiveness of convict leasing as he was on so many other issues of his day, a "day" that spanned a life of ninety-five years. DuBois was arguably the most prolific African-American scholar and writer ever. However, although isolated notes on convict leasing penned by DuBois can be found, there is no coherent or systematic analysis of or commentary on leasing in his thousands of letters, newspaper columns, editorials, and scholarly publications, or in the pages of *Crisis* magazine and other journals during the many years he presided over their publication. The phenomenal DuBois was, after all, human and, despite much evidence to the contrary, he could not do everything—no matter how hard he tried. His strongest analysis of leasing appears in a fairly obscure church publication in 1901. Here we find glimpses of the DuBois brilliance and persuasive mastery, strength of analysis, and literary skill that make him the legend that he rightly is among people of letters. The essay on leasing is not a classic, however, in the tradition of, say, "The Propaganda of History," "Of Mr. Booker T. Washington and Others," or "The African Roots of War," all of which followed it.

Like countless other observers and analysts, DuBois likened leasing to slavery, calling it "the direct child of slavery." Characteristically, his opening volley was historical. In the pre–Civil War South, he pointed out, as did many others, slaves rarely came into contact with the criminal justice system because crime and punishment for them was the purview of slavemasters. Therefore, the system of "criminal jurisprudence" dealt "almost exclusively" with the White population. "The law," DuBois observed, "was lenient in theory and lax in execution." He traced the growth of the convict population and explained how Black convicts came to predominate in the system, stating, "the small peccadilloes of a careless, untrained class [of Blacks] were made the excuse for severe sentences."[16]

DuBois then synthesized the manifold abuses of southern convict leasing that were presented by many others, but he maintained continuity in the argument that leasing "had the worst aspects of slavery without any of its redeeming features" (whatever those were). He jumped on Georgia for brutality, citing the case of a young girl outraged by her captors before dying in childbirth in a convict camp. Mississippi and Louisiana were not spared by DuBois as he proceeded to criticize the double standard of justice for Blacks and Whites in the South, and as he made a case for the economic windfall that prisons represented.

Convict leasing had a "deplorable" effect on Blacks, according to DuBois. "It linked crime and slavery indissolubly in their minds," he continued, "as simply forms of the White man's oppression." Punishment became ineffective as a deterrent and becoming a criminal generated "pity" rather than "disdain." The courts and juries lost respect and all appearance of integrity among Blacks and, "worse than all, the chain gangs [which he considered synonymous with leasing] became schools of crime which hastened the appearance of the confirmed Negro criminal upon the scene." It was injustice in the courts in the South, DuBois felt, that explains the "enormous increase in crime and vagabondage" in the Black community. Despite all of that, DuBois lamented the rise in the South, since the Civil War, of "a class of Black criminals, loafers, and ne'er-do-wells who [were] a menace to their fellows, both black and white."[17]

Additional themes that DuBois pursued in this treatise had to do with the "correct theory" of imprisonment, preferably for the "correction"—the rehabilitation—of the criminal, not employment for profit. He also argued against convict labor being in competition with "free labor." Here he felt that consideration was given only if the "free labor" was White and voting. Free Black laborers displaced in brick-making, mining, road-building, grading, and quarrying mattered little. Before resting his case, DuBois took a swipe at the "mischievous idea" of mixing adult and juvenile criminals, concluding that this integration "manufactured" criminals too fast for reform efforts to reduce them.

Crime among southern Blacks, DuBois proposed, was "a symptom of wrong social conditions." Blacks did not possess natural criminal tendencies. Rather, Blacks were usually law-abiding. The explanation for their large numbers in the penitentiary was "socio-historical." DuBois ended his position as follows:

> If slavery, the convict-lease system, the traffic in criminal labor, the lack of juvenile reformatories, together with the unfortunate discrimination and prejudice in other walks of life, have led to that sort of social protest and revolt which we call crime, then we must look for remedy in the same reform of these wrong social conditions, and not in intimidation, savagery, or the legalized slavery of men.[18]

THE BLACK ELITE AND THE RANK-AND-FILE

We generally know most about the past through the views of leadership and the literati—those who are most literate and most likely to have their perspective and thinking recorded on the leading issues of the day. This is history from the top down and raises serious questions about reliability, not to mention accuracy, in an attempt to get a representative view of *most* people's attitudes at a fixed point in time. The alternative to "elitist history" is to depend on other data and sources left by the nonliterate, such as oral histories from both the remote and not-too-distant past. Such an approach may ultimately be even less reliable, accurate, and illustrative than the record left by leaders. Getting a correct and representative moving picture or snapshot of the past is a real challenge for the professional historian, and the Black reaction to convict leasing is no exception. Much more is known about the opinions of highly visible Black leaders and how elites felt about the system than did rank-and-file Blacks—although even the former data base is limited. At the opposite end of the spectrum from the Booker T. Washingtons and W.E.B. DuBois' were the convicts, ex-convicts, and their families, who, to be sure, had a different vantage point from the "talented tenth."

Sandwiched between these extremes are some perspectives that may offer a bit of balance. The Black response to leasing included the views of obscure, "common" types, who were nonetheless more "intellectual" than "average" and who had definite opinions on the subject. One such view comes from D. E. Tobias , mentioned earlier, who appears to have committed a good portion of his life to studying prison systems—especially convict leasing—in the United States and abroad.[19] Not much is known about Tobias except that his parents were illiterate former slaves and that he was born in South Carolina around 1870. He described himself as "a member of the effete African race" and indicated that he was educated in the South and North, an education he financed by working with his hands. In 1899 Tobias published an essay entitled, "A Negro on the Position of the

Negro in America," in which he analyzed the condition of African-Americans at the end of the nineteenth century, and in which he considered "the infamous convict lease system . . . the main question of the Negro race in the South." Tobias characterized leasing as "worse than the old system of slavery," of which it was "a relic and direct consequence." The "sole purpose" of the South going to war, noted Tobias, was to keep Blacks enslaved. After the Civil War, the White South ignored 1866 civil rights legislation, Tobias continued, and concocted "an ingenious scheme" to imprison Blacks on "any sort of flimsy charges" and then "farmed [them] out to the highest bidders for human flesh." There were in the South, observed Tobias, "hundreds and thousands" of Blacks who never knew emancipation because of this "new form of slavery."

Tobias was very astute in chronicling the circumstances that often resulted in Black incarceration as the mere allegation of a crime being tantamount to guilt; "officers are sent out to bring in the culprit" and if the person could not be found, they would "bring in any negro," was the way Tobias put it. Standing the principle of presumption of innocence on its head, Tobias asserted that the burden of proof was in this case on the innocent Black. The failure to prove innocence, "which is absolutely impossible [for a Black person] in a Southern Court," means being sent to prison and providing profit for the state and the lessee. Tobias's analysis showed that leasing was, by 1899, a "thirty-three-year-old" experiment adopted immediately after the Civil War because freedom produced "so many negro criminals" and now Blacks were being "manufactured annually for the prison market." Tobias was thorough in describing the types of work done by leased convicts, where they worked, and the work conditions, all of which were consistent with other accounts of convict camps where "immorality" abounded and the "death rate [was] simply enormous." Like so many others, Tobias identified Georgia as a state where convicts were "as badly treated . . . as ever they were." A point he made, not readily found elsewhere, was that Whites conspired to deprive Blacks of the right to vote by jailing them; once a Black voter was imprisoned, Tobias said, "he [was] forever thereafter disenfranchised."[20]

ORGANIZED PROTEST

The major Black organizations of the period were fledgling and virtually silent on the subject of convict leasing. What little noise they made came through the voices of their leaders, although resolutions denouncing leasing were sometimes adopted at annual meetings.[21] There were fewer planned protests aimed at White local or national business and legislative leaders, governors, or presidents. This subdued activity, of course, is understandable given the political climate of the times. It could have been dangerous for Blacks in the South or elsewhere to engage in peaceful protest, and in some instances it was fatal. In addition, as mentioned earlier, the key organizations such as the Afro-American Council, the American Negro Academy and the National Negro Business League had other priorities. The Niagara Movement, of the first decade of the twentieth century, which evolved into the National Association for the Advancement of Colored People (NAACP), was, in 1910, essentially White-founded and led. W. E. B. DuBois was the lone Black in its leadership hierarchy. By the time the NAACP matured, many southern states had outlawed leasing and others were poised to do so. Even so, the NAACP, through its organ *Crisis*, under DuBois's editorship, has a spotty record, although *Crisis* fared better than the organization's annual reports and annual convention proceedings, even lashing out against the system of convict leasing at times. Most convict-related stories in *Crisis* had to do with peonage. For so many people, it is worth reiterating, the lines between leasing, peonage, and the chain gang were so thin as almost to be nonexistent.[22]

The Black press, lacking the staff, the resources, and the interest, mounted no crusade comparable with that of some of the White press. They reprinted some stories from White newspapers, but more newsworthy for southern Black newspapers were problems of housing or education, bigotry and race relations, and the achievements of individual Blacks and the race in general. These latter episodes were intended to serve as a counterweight to the massive anti-Black literature and propaganda of the era.

The Black church, too, placed survival and advancement of the race at the top of its agenda. In addition, the National Baptist Convention (Southern Black Baptists) and the African Methodist Episcopal (AME) and African Methodist Episcopal Zion (AME Zion) churches, which had more Black members and followers than the Presbyterians, Catholics, and others, were experiencing growing and reorganizing pains, which, along with their social activities and missionary and proselytizing work, left little time and energy for convict leasing. Individual churches, like the Baptist Tabernacle in Georgia, joined a chorus of criticism or anti-leasing exercises from time to time, but these were occasional and episodic and not coordinated with other, similar Black efforts critical of or opposed to convict leasing.

Black Legislators

Also uncommon was the call by an 1883 Black convention in South Carolina for the legislature to repeal the law that permitted convict leasing.[23] Exceptional as well was the uprising to administer "convict justice" by a group of Black convicts against an episode of excessive cruelty in Mississippi.[24] Another special case of Black reaction to convict leasing was that of Louisiana legislators who, albeit with some exceptions, supported lessees and the continuation of leases, and who blocked abolition.

Contrasted somewhat with the position that Black lawmakers held in Louisiana is that of Georgia's legislators. Soon after Georgia formally adopted convict leasing in the early 1870s, one Black legislator, James Blue of Glynn County, appealed to his Georgia House of Representatives colleagues to adopt an 1876 "Prison Reform Bill." Blue opposed the leasing system and was drawn to the subject out of concern for "his people [who] composed three fourths of the convicts." He advocated reforms that would reduce or remove the inhuman treatment of convicts so that prisoners "would not go back into the world cripples and invalids in health or outlaws in morals." Blue's entreaty was well received and the 1876 legislation passed, but conditions for convicts did not improve.[25] At the next major debate in the Georgia legislature on the subject of convict leasing, the voices of Black legislators were again heard in opposition to leasing. In 1881, two of the five Black members in the House, Ishmael Lonnon and John McIntosh, spoke publicly against the system. Lonnon was not opposed "to leases but to the system," which he felt should be abolished "forever." McIntosh sought "justice for his people" in favoring the abolition of leasing, which he doubted would happen. His plea, then, was for reform. One of his anti-leasing speeches provided insight on more than just his views on prison reform. It offers a preview of the "Tuskegee philosophy" contained in Booker T. Washington's often-quoted Atlanta Compromise speech of 1895. McIntosh states, in part:

> Men . . . smile when we ask them to talk about the system of punishing criminals. . . . The colored people of the South will be as true to you in freedom as they were in slavery. . . They were true to you then at home and often on the field of battle, and they will be true to you yet if you will protect them. . . . The colored people come to you and in the name of pity ask you to do something to improve the system [of convict leasing].[26]

Despite its Black legislators and others opposed to the system of leasing convicts, Georgia went on to become the most infamous of southern leasing states.

℘

What all of this means is that the rise, tenure, and fall of southern convict leasing had little to do with African-Americans in the southern United States, except as its victims. When state legislatures, chief executives, businesspeople, planters, and others decided to adopt the system of hiring out convicts to private parties, Blacks on the whole had little to do with it. Throughout the seven decades during which convict leasing existed in the ex-slave states, Blacks could do little about it. And when leasing gave way entirely to other methods of convict management, Blacks—who had almost single-handedly borne the brunt of the convict lease system—made little difference in the debates and decisions about its passing one way or the other.

NOTES

1. On Pap Singleton, see Nell I. Painter, *Exodusters: Black Migration to Kansas After Reconstruction* (New York, 1979). For Chief Sam, see William E. Bittle and Gilbert Geis, *The Longest Way Home: Chief Alfred Sam's Back-To-Africa Movement* (Detroit, 1964), and Milfred C. Fierce, "Chief Sam's Back-To-Africa Movement," in his *The Pan-African Idea in the United States, 1900–1919* (New York, 1993), chapter 5.

2. Although published in 1961, the most thorough study of the American Colonization Society remains P. J. Staudenraus's *The African Colonization Movement* (New York, 1961).

3. *Atlanta Journal*, August 3, 1908. See chapter 4, above. The reason why Bishop Turner has not attracted a full-length biographer continues to baffle this writer. Nevertheless, for starters, see Edwin Redkey, *Black Exodus: Black Nationalist* (New Haven, 1969), Edwin Redkey, *Back-to-Africa Movements, 1890–1910* (New Haven, 1969), and Edwin Redkey (ed.), *Respect Black: The Writings and Speeches of Henry McNeal Turner* (New York, 1971).

4. Mary Church Terrell, "Peonage in the United States: The Convict Lease System and the Chain Gangs," *The Nineteenth Century* 62 (1907), 308.

5. See Terrell, "Peonage in the United States," 310.

6. See chapter 4.

7. Julia Strudwick Tutwiler, to Booker T. Washington, March 7, 1891, in *Booker T. Washington Papers*, vol. 3, *1889–1895*, ed. Stuart B. Kaufman and Raymond W. Smock (Urbana: University of Illinois Press, 1974), 135–36. (Hereafter cited as *BTW Papers*, various volumes.)

8. D. E. Tobias to Booker T. Washington, July 17, 1899, *BTW Papers, 1899–1900*, vol. 5: 159–63.

9. Blanche K. Bruce to Booker T. Washington, September 8, 1897, in *BTW Papers, 1895–1898*, vol. 4: 327.

10. Charles B. Spahr to Booker T. Washington, *BTW Papers, 1895–1898*, vol. 4: 245–46.

11. Booker T. Washington, letter to the editor of the *Southern Workman*, February 18, 1886, cited in *BTW Papers, 1860–1889*, vol. 2: 296–97.

12. Pink Franklin was an illiterate, Black South Carolina farmer who killed two White men attempting to arrest him in 1910 for violation of state peonage laws that had already been declared unconstitutional. Booker T. Washington was instrumental in getting the governor of South Carolina to commute Franklin's death sentence to life imprisonment. The Alonzo Bailey case, discussed in chapter 1, was the one that resulted in the U.S. Supreme Court's finding in 1911 that peonage anywhere in the nation was unconstitutional. Booker T. Washington played a leading role in this court decision. See Louis R. Harlan, *Booker T. Washington: The Wizard of Tuskegee, 1901–1915* (New York, 1983), 249–51.

13. Booker T. Washington to Oswald Garrison Villard, June 16, 1903, *BTW Papers, 1903–1904*, vol. 7: 178–79.

14. Booker T. Washington to Oswald Garrison Villard, January 10, 1911, *BTW Papers, 1909–1911*, vol. 10: 540–44.

15. Booker T. Washington to Ray Stannard Baker, July 23, 1907, and to Hugh Mason Browne, July 23, 1907, *BTW Papers, 1906–1908*, vol. 9: 302–03, 552–53.

16. W. E. B. DuBois, "The Spawn of Slavery: The Convict Lease System in the South," *Missionary Review of the World* 24 (October 1901), 738–40.

17. Ibid., 744–45.

18. Ibid., 737–45.

19. Another was Wilford T. Smith, a Black lawyer who, in "The Negro and the Law," very briefly discusses peonage and leasing in the context of prevailing law. See *The Negro Problem: A Series of Articles by Representative American Negroes of Today* (New York: James Pott and Company, 1903).

20. See D. E. Tobias, "A Negro on the Position of the Negro in America," *The Nineteenth Century* 46, no. 274 (December 1899), 957–73.

21. Clarence Bacote, "Negro Proscriptions, Protests and Proposed Solutions in Georgia, 1880–1908," in *The Negro in the South Since 1865: Selected Essays in American Negro History*, ed. Charles E. Wynes (Tuscaloosa, 1965), 164, n. 50.

22. See for examples the following issues of *Crisis*: vol. 2, no. 4 (May 8, 1911); vol. 6, no. 5 (1913); vol. 9, no. 3 (1915); vol. 11, no. 6 (Winter 1915); vol. 22, no. 2 (1921); vol. 32, no. 6 (1926); vol. 33, no. 2 (1926); vol. 34, no. 9 (1927); vol. 35, no. 2 (1927).

23. George B. Tindall, *South Carolina Negroes, 1877–1900* (Columbia, 1952), 273.

24. Paul B. Foreman and Julien R. Tatum, "The Short History of Mississippi's State Penal Systems," *Mississippi Law Journal* (April 1938), 263, n. 21.

25. Bacote, "Negro Proscriptions," 163.

26. Ibid., 163–64.

Conclusion

W RITING IN 1904, A PRISON OFFICIAL named James Abbott, disgusted by what he found as he traveled the South observing the condition of convicts, summed up perhaps the most telling aspect of Blacks and convict leasing with this very apt thought: "The Negro Convict Is A Slave."[1] Some former slaves—jailed for failure to pay small fines for petty theft or vagrancy, or for something similar, and sometimes even kidnapped—were snagged by leasing so soon after the adoption of the Thirteenth Amendment that they never knew freedom. For them convict leasing was not a revisit to slavery because they had never left it: freedom's interlude completely passed them by. For countless others the torment they endured at the hand of the lessees, or state and county officials in the service of lessees, or managers of chain gangs, was so reminiscent of their pre–Civil War bondage that it indeed constituted a revisit to slavery.

In the middle of the sixth decade of the nineteenth century, when the principals of policymaking and the founders and architects of southern leasing (for example, governors, state and local legislators, law enforcement officials, and others) began searching for an expedient method to finance a penitentiary system in the post–Civil War South, the priority was to save money for the state, and then, if possible, to make money. They did not necessarily have Black victimization uppermost in their minds. Herein was a useful analog with slavery in which the initial rationale, as much as anything else, was economic. As increasing numbers of Blacks fell prey to the well-documented injustices of the contemporary legal system, they overwhelmingly came to dominate the prison population. As race bigotry intensified with the passing years, and the number of Black convicts began to grow even more, and the lease system matured, race and race control became factors in the widespread brutality that prevailed, and in the perpetuation of southern convict leasing. That is, as the depredations of leasing became better known among government and prison officials, among the local population, and even among some lessees (especially those who did not have a "hands-on" relationship with the farms, mines, or prison camps that they owned), the fact that the victims of leasing were overwhelmingly Black helped to stem any early outrage that convict brutalization might have otherwise pro- voked. Further, the pace of decline and the eventual abolition of convict leasing in the various southern states, while stymied by the states' reluctance to lose leasing revenue, was perhaps as much impeded by the reality that convict leasing was indivisible with Blackness.

To the extent that the courts and other aspects of legal administration either fed the system with Black convicts or obstructed their release out of concern about a would-be "Black menace" in their midst, and therefore were preoccupied with the matter of race control, another analog with slavery is provided. In early nineteenth-century southern states like Virginia and others, Whites became increasingly fearful of the growing number of free Blacks among them resulting from instances of owner, especially "deathbed," emancipation. In the interest of race control, restrictions were imposed on the process of Black freedom. Emancipation frequently became conditional on Blacks leaving the state. So the idea of race control was a factor in slavery and a factor in the revisit to slavery—convict leasing.

Not unlike other periods and other injustices African-Americans have faced throughout United States history, those Black leaders who knew about leasing, and felt provoked to do or say something about it, wanted to help stop the savagery of the system. Their influence was limited, and the weapons in their arsenal (petitioning, letter-writing, personal contacts) were few. Despite the limitations, their efforts, from the "big name" leaders like Booker T. Washington to the unknown, were valiant, but finally, they were ineffective in modifying or ending leasing. Bishop Henry McNeal Turner is an example of a dedicated leader among Blacks with little clout among leasing's power brokers. Bishop Turner was a militant Black nationalist and African Methodist Episcopal Church cleric who, during the Civil War, was appointed the first Black chaplain in the U.S. military by President Abraham Lincoln. Turner was also a Georgia legislator during Reconstruction and may have been the era's most persistent and uncompromising critic of the failure of the United States government to protect its citizens who were Black. He was the primary advocate of Black emigration to Africa in the 1890s until his death in 1915. Through church-based periodicals and newspapers such as *The Voice of Missions* and *The Voice of the People*, and possibly a dozen others, Turner was well known in the southern and national Black communities. When he addressed issues of convict labor and prison reform, as he invariably did, individuals who were in positions of influence and connected with convict leasing knew nothing about it, and it probably would not have affected their decisionmaking if they had.[2]

When the "other shoe fell" for southern convict leasing, when governors and state legislatures could no longer avoid destruction of such an abomination, despite possible revenue losses, responsibility for state convicts returned to public officials. Sadly, in many and probably most cases, the treatment of southern convicts—still overwhelmingly Black—did not change significantly for the better under chain gangs, contract systems, or whatever method of convict control eventually replaced leasing.

NOTES

1. Alexander Lichtenstein, "The Political Economy of Convict Labor in the New South," Ph.D. diss. (University of Pennsylvania, 1990), 383.

2. See Carol A. Page, "Henry McNeal Turner and the Ethiopian Movement in South Africa, 1896–1904," M.A. thesis (Roosevelt University, 1973), 11, 14.

Appendix I

To Lessees of the Georgia Penitentiary:

EXECUTIVE DEPARTMENT, ATLANTA, GA., July 1, 1885.

The following Circular Order to Lessees of the Penitentiary, having been prepared and submitted by the Principal Keeper, was approved by the Governor and ordered to be issued, to-wit:

OFFICE PRINCIPAL KEEPER GEORGIA PENITENTIARY,
ATLANTA, GA., July 1, 1885.

General Notice to Lessees Georgia Penitentiary:

RULE 1. From and after this date no lessee, or any of his employees, shall allow convicts to guard convicts, or in any manner whatever have control of convicts, or permit convicts to go beyond prison bounds, unless accompanied by a sufficient guard. And all convicts must wear the striped clothing at all times.

RULE 2. All cases of escapes or deaths must be reported to this office on the day they occur, with all the facts attending the same, as each escape must be settled for at the end of sixty days from the time of said escape.

RULE 3. Within the stockade convicts shall be released from the chain on the Sabbath day, and allowed to attend divine worship. The Sabbath shall be strictly observed as a day of rest, and no convicts will be allowed to work on the Sabbath day by their own consent or for wages.

RULE 4. Lessees and their superintendents are required to keep the male convicts separate from the females, providing them with separate buildings at night, and in assigning them to work due regard must be had to their sex and physical condition. Each convict must be assigned to such duty only as he or she may be able to perform without injury; and in no case shall a convict be required to resume work after a spell of sickness until restored to health and discharged by the attending physician, and the shackles must be taken off convicts during severe sickness while in the hospital.

RULE 5.   The hours of labor shall be from sunrise to sunset, with one hour for rest and meal at noon, during the months of November, December, January and February, one hour and one-half for the months of March, April, September and October, and two hours' rest for the months of May, June, July and August.

RULE 6.   Convicts shall be furnished with a sufficient quantity of striped woolen clothing in the winter, and striped cotton clothing in the summer, so that each convict shall have a clean shifting suit, and be required to cleanse their person and change their clothing once a week. Shoes and hats must be furnished when needed.

RULE 7.   In all cases of sudden death of a convict, without previous illness, there must be a coroner's inquest over the body before interment, and the finding, or a certified copy thereof, forwarded to this office.

RULE 8.   The monthly reports must be made with great care, showing the exact number of convicts under the charge of the superintendent, giving condition as to health, their conduct; and the casualties occurring each month. Said report *must be made under oath* and forwarded promptly at the end of each month (three days being allowed to transmit by mail). Lessees are required to notify the Principal Keeper in writing of any bad conduct on the part of convicts, specifying the nature of the offense and the date of its commission. Lessees must deliver to convicts promptly any papers ordering the discharge of the latter, received from this office, signed by the Principal Keeper. Should there be found any mistake has been made in the date or name, it is their duty to notify the Principal Keeper of such mistake before releasing such convict from prison. And convicts must be allowed to receive and write letters to their relations at least once a month, subject to the inspection of the superintendent of the camp.

RULE 9.   Each lessee is required to appoint, subject to the approval of the Governor, some discreet and responsible person charged with the duty of inflicting corporal punishment when absolutely necessary to enforce discipline. There shall not be more than one of said whipping bosses at each camp, and no other persons shall directly or indirectly inflict corporal punishment upon convicts. Such punishment shall in no case be excessive. The person of females shall not be exposed while undergoing punishment. Whipping bosses must report under oath once a month through this office to the Governor.

RULE 10. Lessees are required by law to furnish each convict with a suit of citizens' clothes, not to cost less than six dollars, and transportation back to the county from which he or she was sentenced, to all discharged and pardoned convicts, if desired by said convict. In order to show that the requirement has been complied with, the lessee will forward to this office a receipt for the amount so furnished to said discharged or pardoned convict.

RULE 11. The superintendent of camps must see to it that the chaplain, appointed by the county in which the camp is located, has opportunity of preaching and holding such religious service as he desires, and that good order be kept during such service among the convicts.

RULE 12. The prison buildings shall be of sufficient dimensions to give each convict therein confined five hundred cubic feet of air or breathing space. If, however, the excrement or night-soil is deposited through funnels with covers into vessels beneath the floors, and the floors of the buildings are sufficiently tight and sufficiently high from the ground to prevent the ascent of the gases emanating from the night-soil entering the prison building, four hundred cubic feet of air or breathing space shall be deemed sufficient.

RULE 13. Each prison shall be provided with two bed-ticks, made of bedticking, or other stout material, for each convict therein confined. The bed-ticks shall be six and a half feet long and three feet wide, and filled with hay or soft straw in sufficient quantities to make a comfortable bed. The bed-sacks shall be emptied, thoroughly washed in boiled water and re-filled with fresh, soft straw or hay once every four weeks.

The blankets shall be washed once every four weeks. The blankets and bedding shall be thoroughly aired and sunned twice each week when the weather will permit.

RULE 14. The prison building shall be cleansed by sweeping, or if soiled by any offensive droppings, scrubbed every day.

Once every two weeks the prisons shall be emptied of all the bunks, and a thorough cleansing shall be made of the floors by washing and scrubbing; and every second scrubbing, or once a month, the walls shall be thoroughly whitewashed with lime.

The floors of prisons shall not be covered with lime to hide the filth that may accumulate, which must be removed by washing and scrubbing.

Those in charge of camps will see to it that there are no vermin, as lice, bedbugs, etc., permitted to infest the prison beddings, or clothing of convicts, to interfere with their rest at night.

Preparations shall be made within the stockade by the construction of bath tubs, and the means of having water the proper temperature, for all the convicts to bathe each Sunday. It shall be the duty of those in charge of the camps to see that each convict is thoroughly cleansed on that day with soap and water from head to feet.

At each prison preparation shall be made to give the convicts an opportunity to wash their hands and face when they return from the day's labor.

RULE 15. Each camp shall have a hospital building of sufficient dimensions to give each sick convict therein confined six hundred cubic feet of air or breathing space. The building shall be of sufficient size to give accommodation to ten per cent of the number of convicts in camp. The hospital shall be comfortable, well ventilated, well warmed in winter, and well lighted all the time.

Each bed in the hospital shall be provided with a mattress and pillow, and one-third the number of beds with extra mattresses and pillows for emergencies. Each bunk or bed shall be comfortable, of sufficient length, width and height, and so constructed that they may be readily moved.

Each bed shall be provided with two pairs of sheets and an oil cloth or rubber cloth to protect the mattress. Each pillow must have two pillow cases. The sheets must be sufficiently wide and long to serve the purposes for which they are intended. Each bed shall be provided with two suits of hospital clothes, to be worn only in the hospital or while convalescing. No convict shall be an inmate of the hospital with his working clothes.

A bath-tub shall be provided for the hospital, in which those entering the hospital may be bathed when they enter, if practicable, or in which to take a bath at any time during their stay by direction of the physician in charge.

RULE 16. Each hospital shall be supplied with a hospital steward and as many nurses as the physician in charge may think necessary. The physician in charge shall be the judge of the competency of the steward and nurses. Such diet shall be furnished the sick as the physician may prescribe. The physician in charge will see to it that he has on hand all the time such articles of diet for the sick as may be demanded. He will, above all, see to it that the steward and nurses keep the hospital and bedding scrupulously clean, and in all particulars do their duty.

RULE 17. Owing to the fact that scurvy with its ravages has appeared from time to time in many of the camps, it is regarded as essential that all lessees and their officials in charge of camps should be familiar with the causes producing this disease.

There are only two causes proper: 1st. The absence of fresh meat as a ration, or its introduction in insufficient quantities, or not sufficiently often. 2d. The absence of fresh or succulent vegetables as a part of the diet, or their introduction in quantities insufficient or not sufficiently often. With a sufficiency of the above two mentioned articles of food, scurvy never makes its appearance.

Dried beans, peas, rice, wheat and such like cereals are not vegetables, in an anti-scorbutic sense, having no more effect in preventing scurvy than the bread made from the different grains, as wheat, corn, rye, oats, etc. Physicians differ as to which is the best anti-scorbutic, fresh meats or fresh vegetables; but all, however, agree that the two combined, fresh meat and succulent vegetables, make the very best anti-scorbutic diet and when served to the human being in sufficient quantities and sufficiently often make scurvy impossible.

Fresh meats, as beef, mutton or pork, shall be served two different days each week, at least, and fresh succulent vegetables at least three days each week in sufficient quantities. On the days that fresh vegetables are not served dried fruits, such as peaches or apples well-cooked, or sauerkraut, may be served one meal a day. Molasses of good quality may be served two meals each week. Vinegar of good quality, with salt and pepper, shall be served without stint.

The rations for each convict, when fresh beef or mutton is issued, shall be two pounds per day. When side bacon is issued, three-fourths of one pound per day shall be the ration. If fresh pork is allowed, one pound shall be issued per day for each convict. Wheat bread shall be given the convicts twice each week and corn bread five days in the week. Bread of both varieties shall be issued without stint.

It shall be the duty of the lessees, or those in charge of camp, to see that the ration is properly prepared, properly cooked and properly served. No bread made from the meal of musty, or corn that has been over-heated, will be allowed served to convicts.

The health and well-being of the convicts in camp will to a great extent depend upon the preparation of their food, and it is urged that the lessees give special attention to the detail of the culinary department of their camps.

RULE 18. Superintendents are required to frame with glass front and hang these rules in some open, conspicuous place within the stockade and office of the superintendent of camp.

JOHN R. TOWERS,
Principal Keeper Penitentiary

Source: Georgia Department of Archives and History, Atlanta, Georgia.

APPENDIX II

ENABLING LEGISLATION, GEORGIA, 1874.

No. XXIV. (No. 415.)

An Act to authorize the Governor to farm or lease out the Convicts of the Penitentiary of the State of Georgia, and for other purposes.

§1. SECTION 1. *Be it enacted, etc:*, That the Governor is hereby authorized and directed to farm or lease out the convicts of the Penitentiary for a term of years, not less than one nor more than five years, and in such numbers as in his discretion he may deem proper, to any person or persons, or company of persons, as shall take the said convicts at a consideration to be agreed upon with the Governor, and give sufficient bond and security, as the Governor in his discretion may require, for the faithful and full compliance with their contract with the State, and which contract shall require the humane treatment of the convicts, their security and management, in accordance with the rules and regulations now in force for the control of the convicts, in so far as the same may be consistent with the working of the convicts on any public or private works in the State of Georgia, and the Governor is hereby authorized and directed to turn over to the lessee or lessees hereafter contracting under this Act, such convicts as may hereafter be sentenced to the Penitentiary, having due regard to the rights of contractors, and the priority of date of their contracts: *Provided*, no contract shall be made which shall not relieve the State from all expenses, except the salary of the Principal Keeper;

[Marginal notes:]
Governor authorized to farm out convicts.

Term.

Consideration. Bond, etc.

Conditions.

Convicts hereafter sentenced.

State relieved of expenses.

and provided, the lease here in provided for shall not go into effect and operation until the present lease of the convicts shall expire.

Takes effect when.

§2. SEC. II.   That all the officers and employees now required by law in and about said Penitentiary shall be discharged, except the Principal Keeper thereof, after such contract or contracts as hereinbefore named shall have been made, and the convicts turned over to the contractors. The Principal Keeper shall continue in office as inspector of convicts, and shall report to the Governor any and all violations of the contracts by the persons to whom the convicts shall have been farmed or leased, and discharge all the duties now required of him by law, as well as those of Inspector of the Penitentiary, so far as such discharge shall be consistent with the carrying out of the contract or contracts hereinbefore authorized.

Officers, etc. of Penitentiary discharged.

Principal keeper excepted.

His duty.

§3. SEC. III.   That the lessee or lessees of said convicts shall not be permitted to work the convicts outside of the limits of the State, nor more than ten hours each day; nor shall the convicts be permitted to work on the Sabbath day; nor shall corporeal punishment be inflicted upon any of said convicts, unless the same shall be absolutely necessary to secure discipline; and, at the expiration of the lease, the said lessee or lessees shall deliver possession of the machinery, buildings, fixtures, and other property received by them, in as good repair as the same is when received by them.

Convicts— When and how worked.

Corporeal p'nishment.

Buildings, etc., returned at expiration of lease.

§4. SEC. IV.   That upon the failure of the lessee or lessees to faithfully comply with their contract with the State, in regard to the humane treatment, security and management of said convicts, in accordance with the rules and regulations now in force for the control of the convicts; that the Governor be, and he is hereby, empowered, in his discretion, to annul and cancel the contract or

Governor may annul contract— when.

contracts of the lessee or lessees so violating, and to farm out the convicts so leased by him, or them, for the unexpired term remaining after said breach of contract as aforesaid.

§5. SEC. V. That his Excellency, the Governor, be authorized and required to nominate, in the contract, or contracts, which may be made, all items of public property which may be turned over by the Principal Keeper of the Penitentiary to the contractor or contractors under this Act, and it shall be the duty of the lessee, or lessees, faithfully to return and account for the same at the expiration or termination of their contract, or contracts, from any cause.

§6. SEC VI. That it shall be the duty of all lessees of the Penitentiary, and all persons having charge or control of any convicts, to discharge such convicts immediately upon the expiration of the term for which he or she may have been convicted and sentenced, or when such convict or convicts shall have been pardoned, and any lessee or other person having the custody, charge or control of such convicts, who shall willfully violate any of the provisions of this section, shall be deemed guilty of a misdemeanor, and, upon conviction, shall be punished as prescribed in section 4310 of the new Code.

§7. SEC. VII. That in the event of the convicts being farmed or leased out to more than one party, in separate squads, then the disabled and feeble shall be proportioned in proportion to the number that each of said parties may have.

§8. SEC. VIII. That the Governor be, and he is hereby authorized and directed, so far as is practicable, in the distribution of the convicts, to make a classification thereof, so as to keep separate such convicts as are or may

Governor may make new contract.

Governor required to itemize public property.

Lessee's duty.

Expiration of convict's term, pardon, etc.

Violation of any section.

Penalty.

More than one party leasing— feeble to be proportioned.

Classification of convicts.

be convicted of crimes involving no great moral turpi-
tude, and to provide, so far as possible, for their humane
and kind treatment.

§9. SEC. IX.   If any of said convicts shall escape
from the custody of said lessee or lessees, and be thereafter re-taken, such convicts shall be indicted for an escape,
and, on conviction, shall be punished by imprisonment
and labor in the Penitentiary for the term of four years.

§10. SEC. X.   That it shall be the duty of the Principal Keeper to make reports to the Governor, of the
names of all convicts whose uniform good conduct show
them to be proper subjects for Executive clemency, and
the Governor is hereby authorized to make such com-
mutation of time for such convicts, as in his discretion
shall seem proper.

§11. SEC. XI.   That if any lessee, or lessees, their
agents or employees, or overseers of said convicts, shall
violate any of the criminal laws of this State in the treatment or management of said convicts, said person or persons so offending shall be indicted or presented in any
county of this State where such offense may have been

committed, and upon conviction, shall be punished as prescribed by law for such offense.

§12. SEC. XII.   That in case the Governor cannot
let or hire out said convicts as provided for in this Act,
then he is hereby authorized and directed to return said
convicts, or such of their number as he may not have
hired out, to the Penitentiary at Milledgeville, in this

State, and have them confined in the prison walls of said
Penitentiary, to labor as provided by law, and shall also

appoint such officers as may be necessary in and about
said Penitentiary, and the Principal Keeper shall appoint
such employees as may be required in and about said

Penitentiary, and the Governor is hereby authorized to draw his warrant on the State Treasurer for a sufficient amount of money to put said Penitentiary in a good, safe condition, if such a contingency as is provided for in this section should happen.

Contingent appropria-tion.

§13. SEC. XIII. Repeals conflicting laws.

Approved March 3, 1874.

Source: Georgia Laws, 1874.

APPENDIX III

LEASE OF 100 CONVICTS FROM FRENCH AND JOBES TO E. RICHARDSON

October 8, 1875

The State of Mississippi, Hinds County

This Indenture made and entered into this 8th day of October 1875, between O. C. French and C. S. Jobes of the first part, and Edmund Richardson of the second part, Witnesseth That whereas under and by virtue of an act of the Legislature, of the State of Mississippi, approved the 26th day of February 1875, entitled an act to amend an act for the regulation, control and support of the Penitentiary approved – March 28th, 1872, the said parties of the first part have made a contract with the Board of Inspectors of the Mississippi State Penitentiary in the words and figures following to wit.

Art 1st   That the party of the first part hereby agrees to lease to the parties of the second part two hundred and fifty able bodied male convicts with such additional numbers as may hereafter be spared from the prison on such terms as may there be agreed upon to be worked outside the walls within the limits of the State in accordance with the provisions of an act to amend an act for the regulation, control, and support of the Penitentiary approved February 26th, 1875 which lease shall extend until January 1st 1880, unless declared annulled or violated under the provisions of the law.

Art 2nd   That the parties of the second part agree to pay all expenses for the maintenance of said convicts during the time they are employed by them as follows to wit, transportation for the prisoners and guards to and from the prison at Jackson to the place where worked, good substantial food for Officers, Guards, and Convicts, subject to inspection by the Superintendent, Board of Inspectors, Sergeant of the Guard or such person, as may be designated by the Governor, furnish ammunition for use of Guards and Officers, Tobacco for Convicts, disinfectants, soap, writing material and stamps for one letter per month for each convict and pay Sergeants and Guards, and Physicians, furnish necessary medicine for the sick, substantial clothing, shoes, hats, blankets and socks, and shall allow the convicts the time every Saturday afternoon under the rules of the prison, and furnish each convict at time of discharge with one suit of clothes and ten dollars in currency.

Art 3rd   The parties of the second part agree to give bond in the sum of ten thousand dollars to secure the payment of the guards and employees, the maintenance, support and kind treatment of the convicts and the faithful performance of the terms of the contract in accordance with law.

Art 4th   The parties of the first part agree – to furnish proper arms for the Guards, and the parties of the second part are to return same number to the prison in as good condition as received whenever this contract shall terminate.

Art 5th   The lessees shall have the privilege of selecting and hiring all necessary guards and employees (subject however to the approval of the Superintendent), said guards and employees to be governed in all respects by the rules and regulations in force for the government of the Penitentiary, and said rules and regulations shall apply to the government and treatment of all convicts leased or hired under this contract.

Art 6th   And it is further provided and agreed by the parties to these presents that the said French and Jobes may sublet the whole or any number of the convicts leased by them, but such subletting or leasing shall be submitted to the Board of

Inspectors for their approval before the same shall take effect and the party or parties subleasing such convicts shall in all respects take the place of the original lessees and shall in his or their contract or lease assume all the obligations of the original lessees in respect of the management and treatment of such convicts and shall enter into bond for the faithful performance thereof payable to the said Board of Inspectors and such sub lessee or lessees shall transact all business pertaining to said convicts and the carrying out of such sublease directly with the said Board of Inspectors and Superintendent and shall have the same legal relations to the said Board and Superintendent which the original lessees sustain to the same and said original lessees on the approval of such sublease and the due execution by such sub lessee or lessees of the proper bond to the said Board of Inspectors shall be discharged from their obligations to the extent of the convicts so subleased, but nothing in this section shall be so construed as to effect or work a forfeiture of the Bond of the said French and Jobes.

Art 7th   That this contract shall take effect from and after the 1st day of March 1875 and whereas on the 13th day of May 1875 the parties of the first part made an additional contract with the Board of Inspectors of the Mississippi State Penitentiary under, and by virtue, of an act to amend an act for the regulation, control, and support of the Penitentiary Approved March 28th 1872 which act was approved February 26th 1875 to lease two hundred more able bodied male convicts, in which it is agreed that the number of convicts therein leased, as well as those leased by the contract dated February 27th 1875, shall be kept up to the full number of two hundred for each contract when reduced below that number by death or discharge, and whereas the said parties of the first part for valuable consideration to them paid and in consideration of the covenants and stipulations herein contained on the part of the party of the second part have this day leased and assigned to the party of the second part and by these presents do hereby lease and assign to the party of the second part one hundred able bodied male convicts in addition to one hundred heretofore leased and assigned by contract dated February 27th 1875, for the period mentioned in the first article of the above recited contract "viz," from this date until the 1st day of January 1880 on the terms and conditions expressed in the above recited contract and second article there of to wit – that the party of the second part agrees to pay all expenses for the maintenance of said convicts during the time they are employed by him, as follows, to wit – transportation for prisoners and guards to and from the prison at Jackson to the place where worked, good substantial food for officers and guards and convicts subject to inspection by the Superintendent, Board of Inspectors, Sergeant of the Guard or such person as may be designated by the Governor, furnish ammunition for use of Guards, and Officer's tobacco for convicts, disinfectants, soap and writing material, and stamps for one letter per month for each convict, pay Sergeants, and Guards, and Physicians, furnish necessary medicine for the sick, substantial clothing shoes, and hats, blankets, and socks, and shall allow the convicts the time on every Saturday afternoon under the rules of the prison and furnish each convict at time of discharge with one suit of clothes and ten dollars in currency. And the said party of the second part agrees to give bond in the sum of ten thousand dollars to secure the payment of the Guards and Employees, the maintenance, support and kind treatment of the convicts and faithful carrying out of the provisions of this contract in accordance with law. And the said parties of the first part agree to deliver to the said party of the second part the due and proper proportion of the arms supplied to them under the 4th Article of the above recited contract, and the party of the second part agrees to return the same as in 4th Article is provided. And it is further agreed that the said party of the second part shall have the privilege of selecting and hiring all necessary guards and employees subject to the approval however of the Superintendent of the Penitentiary or Sergeant in the absence of the Superintendent, said Guards and Employees to be governed in all respects by the rules and the regulations in force for the government of the Penitentiary and said rules and regulations shall apply to the treatment and government of all leased or hired under this contract.

And it is further agreed that this lease and assignment aforesaid of said convicts is made upon the terms and conditions contained and set forth in article 6 of the before mentioned and recited contract and that upon the approval of this contract by the Board of Inspectors in said 6th article of the contract aforesaid and upon the execution of the bond by the party of the second part as in said article provided, payable to the said Board of Inspectors of the Penitentiary in the sum of ten thousand dollars with good and sufficient security to be approved by the said Board of Inspectors then and from that time the said party of the second part takes upon himself and assumes all the obligations and duties respecting said convicts hereby leased and assigned which devolved upon the said parties of the first part by their contract aforesaid and hereby binds himself to fulfill said obligations.

And it is further agreed that the convicts herein leased and assigned shall be kept up to the full number of one hundred as well as the one hundred leased by contract dated February 27th 1875, whenever they fall below that number from death or discharge as provided in contract of the parties of the first part above mentioned and dated May 13th 1875 by the Superintendent delivering to said party of the second part in installments of ten or more without any reference to the said parties of the first part and that they the said parties of the first part will not interfere with or in any ways attempt to control the party of the second part in his arrangements respecting the treatment and management of the said convicts, but that in all matters pertaining to the carrying out of this contract the party of the second part is to deal with and be responsible only to the said Board of Inspectors and Superintendents.

In witness whereof we have here unto set our hands this the 9th day of October 1875.

O. C. FRENCH
C. S. JOBES
E. RICHARDSON

Approved by:
Board of Inspectors
ADELBERT AMES, Governor

Jackson, Mississippi
January 5, 1876

I herewith certify that the foregoing is a true and correct copy of the original contract.

T.E. STRAIPPAILMANN
Clerk

Source: "Contracts for Leasing Convicts 1875 and 1880"
"Penitentiary Records"
Mississippi Department of Archives and History
Jackson, Mississippi

APPENDIX IV

GEORGIA, FULTON COUNTY:

WHEREAS, On the fifth day of November, A.D. 1868, a contract was entered into by his Excellency Rufus B. Bullock, as Governor of the State of Georgia, and Overton H. Walton, Principal Keeper of the Georgia State Penitentiary, and Grant, Alexander & Co., by which said Governor and Principal Keeper contracted to furnish to said Grant, Alexander & Co. from one hundred to five hundred able-bodied convicts from the State Penitentiary, if there should be that number therein, which said contract is now in force, and said Grant, Alexander & Co. have in their possession, in pursuance of the terms, certain convicts;

AND WHEREAS, An act was passed by the Legislature of Georgia, at its session in 1868, entitled "an act to provide for farming out the Penitentiary, and for other purposes," therefore, we, Rufus B. Bullock, Governor of the State of Georgia, and Grant, Alexander & Co., agree as follows:

The said Rufus B. Bullock, as such Governor, and for, and in behalf of the State of Georgia, hereby transfers into the hands of Grant, Alexander & Co., for the term of two years from this date, the Penitentiary of the State of Georgia, together with all the appurtenances, fixtures and property thereto belonging, to be held, used and controlled by them for their own use and benefit, subject to the provisions of this contract. And the said Governor, for and in behalf of the State of Georgia, guaranteed unto said Grant, Alexander & Co. the quiet and undisturbed enjoyment of said property the term aforesaid. And the said Grant, Alexander & Co. agree, and bind themselves, to receive all convicts as may now be in the Penitentiary, or may hereafter be sentenced to the same, including all such as are now hired out, and to humanely treat each one of said convicts, and to securely keep and manage them in accordance with the rules and regulations now of force for their control, so far as the same may be consistent with the working of the convicts on any public works in the State of Georgia. And they further agree to pay all expenses incident to the receiving, control and management and discharge of said convicts, except the salary of the Principal Keeper. And they further agree that the Principal Keeper shall have such reasonable and easy access to said Penitentiary and said convicts as the duties of his office may require. And in case of dispute or difference between said Principal Keeper and Grant, Alexander & Co., in order to settle the matter of difference, his Excellency the Governor shall select one arbitrator, said Grant, Alexander & Co. another, the two to select an umpire if it be necessary, and the award of any two of them, in writing, shall be binding between and upon the parties. And they further agree not to work said convicts more than twelve hours per diem, from April to November, and not more than ten hours from November to April, and not to work them, or either of them, outside the limits of this State; and at the expiration of said term of two years, to deliver to the State of Georgia possession of the said Penitentiary, its machinery, building and fixtures, in as good repair as when received by them. And they further agree to account, at the expiration of this contract, for all the buildings, stock and materials of any kind, provisions, tools and machinery, and manufactured articles, embraced in the inventory, made under the oath of his Excellency the Governor by the persons appointed in said act for that purpose. In consideration of the making of this agreement, said contract, dated November 8, 1868, is hereby rescinded. This agreement embraces the convicts heretofore hired to William A. Fort, but Grant, Alexander & Co. are not to pay the expense of their delivery at the Penitentiary. They are to be delivered at the Penitentiary, free of expense, to Grant, Alexander & Co. within a reasonable time after the expiration of said Fort's contract; that is, such time as may be necessary for their delivery.

This June 28, 1869.

For the State of Georgia:

RUFUS B. BULLOCK,
Governor.

By the Governor:

EUGENE DAVIS, [SEAL]
Secretary Executive Department

Witness: JOHN HARRIS.

GRANT, ALEXANDER & CO.

EXECUTIVE DEPARTMENT,
ATLANTA, June 28, 1869.

I, Eugene Davis, Secretary Executive Department, do hereby certify that the foregoing and within is a true copy of the original on file in this office.

(Signed) EUGENE DAVIS,
Secretary Executive Department.

Source: *Senate Journal*, Georgia (1870).

SELECT BIBLIOGRAPHY

Appearing in this select bibliography are only those sources explicitly cited in the text. Much more material consulted but not cited had to be omitted because of space limitations.

STATE ARCHIVES

Most of the official records cited were located in the respective state archives, such as, for example, "Georgia Laws." Notable exceptions were the states of Florida, Louisiana, South Carolina, and Texas, where university libraries yielded good official records and generally more useful information. Listed below are the locations of the state archives in the twelve southern states covered in this study and the four university libraries.

I would refer readers to the comments of Edward Ayers in the Appendix of his book *Vengeance and Justice*, especially those on the elusive and uneven nature of penitentiary records of southern states throughout the nineteenth century, which I enthusiastically underscore.

ALABAMA
Alabama Department of Archives and History
Montgomery, Alabama

ARKANSAS
Arkansas History Commission
Little Rock, Arkansas

FLORIDA
Bureau of Archives and Records Management
Division of Archives, History and Records Management
Department of State
Tallahassee, Florida

Florida State University Library
Special Collections (especially Samuel D. McCoy papers)
Tallahassee, Florida

GEORGIA
Department of Archives and History
Atlanta, Georgia

KENTUCKY
Division of Archives and Records
Department of Library and Archives
Frankfort, Kentucky

LOUISIANA
State Archives and Records
Baton Rouge, Louisiana

Louisiana State University Library
Special Collections
Baton Rouge, Louisiana

MISSISSIPPI
Archives and Library Division
Mississippi Department of Archives and History
Jackson, Mississippi

NORTH CAROLINA
Archives and Records Section
Division of Archives and History
Raleigh, North Carolina

SOUTH CAROLINA
South Carolina Department of Archives and History
Columbia, South Carolina

South Caroliniana Library
University of South Carolina
Columbia, South Carolina

TENNESSEE
Tennessee State Library and Archives
Nashville, Tennessee

TEXAS
Archives Division
Texas State Library
Austin, Texas

Barker Texas History Center
University of Texas
Austin, Texas

VIRGINIA
Archives Division
Virginia State Library
Richmond, Virginia

NEWSPAPERS AND PERIODICALS

1. *Arkansas Democrat*
2. *Arkansas Gazette*
3. *Atlanta Georgian*
4. *Atlanta Journal*
5. *AME Church Review*
6. *Clinton Gazette* (Tennessee)
7. *The Crisis*
8. *Daily Advertiser* (Montgomery, Alabama)
9. *Enquirer Sun* (Columbus, Georgia)
10. *Iron Age* (Alabama)

11. *Jackson Weekly Clarion* (Mississippi)
12. *Knoxville Journal*
13. *Knoxville Tribune*
14. *Live Oak Suwannee Democrat* (Florida)
15. *New Mississippian*
16. *New York Age*
17. *New York Times*
18. *Prison World* (Alabama)
19. *Tallahassee Weekly True Democrat*
20. *Tampa Tribune*
21. *Times-Union* (Jacksonville, Florida)

DISSERTATIONS, THESES, AND MANUSCRIPTS

Carper, N. Gordon. "The Convict Lease System in Florida, 1866–1923." Ph.D., Florida State University, 1964.

Carter, Dan. "Prisons, Politics and Business: The Convict Lease System in the Post–Civil War South." M.A., University of Wisconsin, 1964.

Cooley, Ruby E. "A History of the Mississippi Penal Farm System, 1890–1935: Punishment, Politics and Profit in Penal Affairs." M.A., University of Southern Mississippi, 1981.

Crawford, Robert G. "A History of the Kentucky Penitentiary System, 1865–1937." Ph.D., University of Kentucky, 1955.

Crow, Henry Lee. "A Political History of the Texas Penal System, 1829–1951." Ph.D., University of Texas, 1963.

Crowell, John W. "The Challenge of the Disenfranchised." Occasional Paper No. 22. Washington, D.C.: American Negro Academy, 1924.

Curtin, Mary Ellen. "Legacies of the Struggle: Black Prisoners in the

Making of Post–Bellum Alabama, 1865–1895." Ph.D., Duke University, 1992.

Gilmore, Harry Williams. "The Convict Lease System in Arkansas." M.A., George Peabody College for Teachers, 1930.

King, Gladys. "History of the Alabama Convict Department." M.A., Alabama Polytechnic Institute, 1937.

Lichtenstein, Alex. "The Political Economy of Convict Labor in the New South." Ph.D., University of Pennsylvania, 1990.

Page, Carol A. "Henry McNeal Turner and the Ethiopian Movement in South Africa, 1896–1904." M.A., Roosevelt University, 1973.

Pitts, Clara. "Julia Strudwick Tutwiler." Ph.D., George Washington University, 1942.

McKay, Herbert Stacy. "Convict Leasing in North Carolina, 1870–1934." M.A., University of North Carolina, Chapel Hill, 1942.

Rowland, Thomas Buford. "The Legal Status of the Negro in Mississippi from 1832–1860." M.A., University of Wisconsin, 1933.

Shivers, Lydia G. "A History of the Mississippi Penitentiary." M.A., University of Mississippi, 1939.

Stout, Leon. "Origins and Early History of the Louisiana Penitentiary." M.A., Louisiana State University, 1934.

Taylor, A. Elizabeth. "The Convict Lease System in Georgia." M.A., University of North Carolina, Chapel Hill, 1940.

Thompson, George. "The History of Penal Institutions in the Rocky Mountain West, 1846–1900." Ph.D., University of Colorado, 1965.

Wallenstein, Peter. "From Slave South to New South: Taxes and Spending in Georgia from 1850 through Reconstruction." Ph.D., Johns Hopkins University, 1973.

Zimmerman, Hilda Jane. "Penal Systems and Penal Reform in the South Since the Civil War." Ph.D., University of North Carolina, Chapel Hill, 1947.

BOOKS AND PAMPHLETS

Archives Institute, Georgia Department of Archives and History. *Records of the Georgia Prison Commission, 1871–1936.* Atlanta: Georgia Department of Archives and History, 1969.

Ayers, Edward L. *Vengeance and Justice: Crime and Punishment in the 19th-Century American South.* New York: Oxford University Press, 1984.

Barnes, Harry E. *The Evolution of Penology in Pennsylvania.* Indianapolis, 1927.

Bennet, Lerone. *Before the Mayflower: A History of the Negro in America, 1619–1964.* New York: Viking Penguin, 1993.

Bergman, Peter. *The Chronological History of the Negro in America.* New York: Harper and Row, 1969.

Berney, Saffold. *Handbook of Alabama.* Spartanburg: The Reprint Company Publishers, 1975.

Berry, Mary F. and John W. Blassingame. *Long Memory: The Black Experience in America.* New York: Oxford University Press, 1982.

Bittle, William and Gilbert Geis. *The Longest Way Home: Chief Albert C. Sam's Back-to-Africa Movement.* Detroit: Wayne State University Press, 1964.

Blassingame, John W. *Black New Orleans, 1860–1880.* Chicago: University of Chicago Press, 1973.

Blesser, Carol R. *The Promised Land: The History of the South Carolina*

Land Commission, 1869–1890. Columbia: University of South Carolina Press, 1969.

Carleton, Mark T. *Politics and Punishment: The History of the Louisiana State Penal System*. Baton Rouge: Louisiana State University Press, 1971.

Cash, Wilbur. *The Mind of the South*. New York: Random House, 1991.

Cohen, William. *At Freedom's Edge: Black Mobility and the Southern White Quest for Racial Control, 1861–1915*. Baton Rouge: Louisiana State University Press, 1991.

Cooper, William J. and Tomas E. Terrill. *The American South: A History*. Volume 2. New York: McGraw Hill, 1991.

Daniel, Peter. *The Shadow of Slavery: Peonage in the South, 1901–1969*. Urbana: University of Illinois Press, 1972.

Daniel, Peter et al. (eds.). *The Booker T. Washington Papers*. Volume 2, *1860–1889*. Urbana: University of Illinois Press, 1972.

Drago, Edmund L. *Black Politicians and Reconstruction in Georgia: A Splendid Failure*. Baton Rouge: Louisiana State University Press, 1982.

Drake, St. Clair. *Black Folk Here and There: An Essay in History and Anthropology*. Volume 2. Los Angeles: Center for Afro-American Studies, University of California at Los Angeles, 1990.

Felton, Rebecca L. *My Memoirs of Georgia Politics*. Atlanta, 1911.

Fierce, Milfred C. *The Pan-African Idea in the United States: African-American Interest in Africa and Interaction with West Africa, 1900–1919*. New York: Garland Publishing Company, 1993.

Foner, Eric. *Freedom's Lawmakers: A Directory of Black Officeholders During Reconstruction*. New York: Oxford University Press, 1993.

———. *Reconstruction: America's Unfinished Revolution, 1863–1877*.

New York: Harper and Row, 1988.

Franklin, John Hope. *From Slavery to Freedom*. New York: Alfred Knopf, 1987.

———. *Reconstruction After the Civil War*. Chicago: University of Chicago Press, 1961.

Frederickson, George M. *The Black Image in the White Mind: The Debate on Afro-American Character and Destiny, 1817–1914*. New York: Harper and Row, 1971.

Ginzburg, Ralph (ed.). *One Hundred Years of Lynchings: A Shocking Documentary of Race Violations in America*. New York: Black Classic Press, 1962.

Going, Allen Johnston. *Bourbon Democracy in Alabama, 1874–1890*. Westport: Greenwood Press, 1972.

Grantham, Dewey W., Jr. *Hoke Smith and The Politics of the New South*. Baton Rouge: Louisiana State University Press, 1967.

Hall, K. L. *Police, Prison, and Punishment: Major Historical Interpretations*. New York: Garland Publishing Company, 1987.

Harlan, Louis R. (ed.). *The Booker T. Washington Papers*. 14 volumes. Urbana: University of Illinois Press, 1972–89.

———. *Booker T. Washington: The Wizard of Tuskegee, 1901–1915*. New York: Oxford University Press, 1983.

Harris, Robert L., Darlene Hine, and Nellie McKay. *Three Essays: Black Studies in the United States*. New York: Ford Foundation, 1990.

Hill, Louise Biles. *Joseph E. Brown and the Confederacy*. Chapel Hill: University of North Carolina Press, 1939.

Hoffer, Frank et al. *The Jails of Virginia: A Study of the Local Penal System*. New York: Appleton-Century Company, n.d.

Holmes, William F. *The White Chief: James Kimble Vardaman*. Baton

Rouge: Louisiana State University Press, 1970.

Holt, Thomas. *Black Over White: Negro Political Leadership in South Carolina During Reconstruction*. Urbana: University of Illinois Press, 1977.

Kaufman, Stuart B. and Raymond W. Smock (eds.). *The Booker T. Washington Papers*. Volume 3, *1889–1895*. Urbana: University of Illinois Press, 1974.

Kaufman, Stuart B. et al. (eds.). *The Booker T. Washington Papers*. Volume 4, *1895–1898*. Urbana: University of Illinois Press, 1975.

Kraft, Barbara S. (ed.). *The Booker T. Washington Papers*. Volume 5, *1899–1900*. Urbana: University of Illinois Press, 1976.

——— . *The Booker T. Washington Papers*. Volume 7, *1903–1904*. Urbana: University of Illinois Press, 1977.

Legislative Jail Commission. *The Virginia Jail System Past and Present with a Program for the Future*. Richmond, 1937.

Lehmann, Nicholas. *The Promised Land: The Great Black Migration and How It Changed America*. New York: Alfred Knopf, 1991.

McKelvey, Blake. *American Prisons: A Study in American Social History Prior to 1915*. Chicago: University of Chicago Press, 1936.

McPherson, James. *Battle Cry of Freedom: The Civil War Era*. New York: Oxford University Press, 1988.

McTigue, Geraldine and Nan E. Woodruff (eds.). *The Booker T. Washington Papers*. Volume 10, *1909–1911*. Urbana: University of Illinois Press, 1981.

Martin, Tony. *Race First: The Ideological and Organizational Struggles of Marcus Garvey and the Universal Negro Improvement Association*. Westport: Greenwood Press, 1976.

Meier, August. *Negro Thought in America, 1880–1915: Racial Ideologies in the Age of Booker T. Washington.* Ann Arbor: University of Michigan Press, 1969.

Meier, August and Elliot Rudwick. *From Plantation to Ghetto: An Interpretive History of American Negroes.* New York: Hill and Wang, 1966.

Moore, Albert Burton. *History of Alabama and Her People.* Volume 1. New York: American Historical Society, 1927.

Moos, Malcolm. *State Penal Administration in Alabama.* Tuscaloosa: University of Alabama, 1942.

Newby, I. A. *Jim Crow's Defense: Anti-Negro Thought in America, 1900–1930.* Baton Rouge: Louisiana State University Press, 1965.

Novak, Daniel A. *The Wheel of Servitude: Black Forced Labor After Slavery.* Lexington: University of Kentucky Press, 1978.

Oliphant, Albert D. *The Evolution of the Penal System of South Carolina from 1866 to 1916.* Columbia: The State Company, 1916.

Oubre, Claude F. *Forty Acres and a Mule: The Freedmen's Bureau and Black Land Ownership.* Baton Rouge: Louisiana State University Press, 1978.

Painter, Nell Irvin. *Exodusters: Black Migration to Kansas After Reconstruction.* New York: W. W. Norton and Company, 1979.

——— . *Standing at Armageddon: The United States, 1877–1919.* New York: W. W. Norton and Company, 1987.

Parks, Joseph Howard. *Joseph E. Brown of Georgia.* Baton Rouge: Louisiana State University Press, 1977.

Powell, J. C. *The American Siberia, or Fourteen Years' Experience in a Southern Convict Camp.* Montclair: Patterson Smith Reprint Series, 1970.

Proceedings of the Annual Congress of the American Prison Association,

September 13–19, 1923, Boston, Massachusetts. New York: American Prison Association, 1923.

Quarles, Benjamin. *The Negro in the Making of America.* New York: MacMillan, 1987.

Redkey, Edwin S. *Black Exodus: Black Nationalist and Back-To-Africa Movements, 1890–1910.* New Haven: Yale University Press, 1969.

—— (ed.). *Respect Black: The Writings and Speeches of Henry McNeal Turner.* New York: Arno Press, 1971.

Report of the Legislative Jail Commission to the General Assembly of Virginia. *The Virginia Jail System: Past and Present With a Program for the Future.* Richmond, 1939.

Rice, Lawrence D. *The Negro in Texas, 1874–1900.* Baton Rouge: Louisiana State University Press, 1971.

Roberts, Derrell C. *Joseph E. Brown and the Politics of Reconstruction.* Tuscaloosa: University of Alabama Press, 1973.

Rule, Lucien V. *The City of Dead Souls and How It Was Made Alive Again: A Hundred Years Within the Walls.* Louisville: Kentucky Printshop, 1920.

Smith, John David (ed.). *Anti-Black Thought, 1863–1925: The Negro Problem.* Eleven volumes. New York: Garland Publishing Company, 1993.

Sneed, William C. *A Report on the History and Mode of Management of the Kentucky Penitentiary From Its Origin in 1798 to March 1, 1860.* Frankfort: Yeonam Office, Senate of Kentucky, 1860.

Spear, Alan H. *Black Chicago: The Making of a Negro Ghetto, 1890–1920.* Chicago: University of Chicago Press, 1967.

Stampp, Kenneth. *The Era of Reconstruction, 1865–1877.* New York: Random House, 1967.

Staudenraus, P. J. *The African Colonization Movement.* New York: Columbia University Press, 1961.

Tindall, George B. *South Carolina Negroes, 1877–1900.* Columbia: University of South Carolina Press, 1952.

Trelease, Alan. *White Terror: The Ku Klux Klan Conspiracy and Southern Reconstruction.* Westport: Greenwood Press, 1979.

Virginia Advisory Legislative Council. *Report to the Governor; Jails, Prison Farms, Probation and Parole.* Richmond, 1939.

Wharton, Vernon Lane. *The Negro in Mississippi, 1865–1890.* Chapel Hill: University of North Carolina Press, 1947.

Wines, Frederick. *Report Upon the Penal and Other State Institutions to the Reform Association of Louisiana.* 1906.

Wisner, Elizabeth. *Public Welfare Administration in Louisiana.* Chicago: University of Chicago Press, 1930.

Wolters, Raymond. *Negroes and the Great Depression: The Problem of Economic Recovery.* Westport: Greenwood Press, 1970.

Woodruff, Nan E. (ed.). *The Booker T. Washington Papers.* Volume 9, *1906–1908.* Urbana: University of Illinois Press, 1980.

Woodward, C. Vann. *Origins of the New South, 1877–1913.* Baton Rouge: Louisiana State University Press, 1951.

——— . *The Strange Career of Jim Crow.* New York: Oxford University Press, 1966.

ARTICLES AND ESSAYS

Bacote, Clarence. "Negro Proscriptions, Protests and Proposed Solutions in Georgia, 1880–1908." In *The Negro in the South Since 1865: Selected Essays in American Negro History.* Ed. Charles E. Wynes. Tuscaloosa: University of Alabama Press, 1965.

Baker, Ray Stannard. "A Pawn in the Struggle for Freedom." *American Magazine* (September 1911).

Bayliss, Garland. "The Arkansas State Penitentiary Under Democratic Control, 1874–1896." *Arkansas Historical Quarterly* (1975).

Bonner, James C. "The Georgia Penitentiary at Milledgeville, 1817–1874." *Georgia Historical Quarterly* (Fall 1971).

Cable, George Washington. "The Convict Lease System in the Southern States." *Century Magazine* (February 1884).

Carleton, Mark. "The Politics of the Convict Lease System in Louisiana: 1868–1901." *Louisiana History* (Winter 1967).

Carper, N. Gordon. "Martin Tabert, Martyr of an Era." *Florida Historical Quarterly* (October 1973).

Cox, LaWanda. "The Promise of Land for the Freedmen." *Mississippi Valley Historical Review* (1958).

Crowe, Jesse Crawford. "The Origin and Development of Tennessee's Prison Problem, 1831–1871." *Tennessee Historical Quarterly* (June 1956).

Curtin, Mary Ellen. "The Daily Struggles of Black Prisoners in Alabama: A Gender Analysis." Paper presented at the meeting of the Southern Historical Association, Atlanta, Georgia, November 7, 1992.

Daniel, Peter. "Up From Slavery and Down to Peonage: The Alonzo Bailey Case." *Journal of American History* (December 1970).

———. "The Tennessee Convict War." *Tennessee Historical Quarterly* (1975).

Dawson, R. H. "The Convict System of Alabama—As It Was and As It Is." In *Handbook of Alabama*. Ed. Saffold Berney. Spartanburg: The Reprint Company Publishers, 1975.

DuBois, W. E. B. "The Spawn of Slavery: The Convict Lease System of the South." *Missionary Review of The World* (October 1901).

Felton, Rebecca L. "The Convict Lease System of Georgia." *Forum 2* (1886–1887).

Fierce, Milfred C. "The Black Struggle for Land During Reconstruction." *The Black Scholar* (February 1974).

Fleming, Walter. "Pap Singleton, The Moses of the Colored Exodus." *Journal of Negro History* (January 1948).

Foreman, Paul B. and Julien R. Tatum. "The Short History of Mississippi's State Penal System." *Mississippi Law Journal* (April 1938).

Garvin, Roy. "Benjamin or 'Pap' Singleton and His Followers." *Journal of Negro History* (January 1948).

Green, Fletcher M. "Some Aspects of the Convict Lease System in the Southern States." In *Essays in Southern History Presented to Joseph Gregoire De Roulhac Hamilton. . . .* Ed. Fletcher M. Green. Chapel Hill, 1949.

Henderson, John N. "The Lease System in Texas." *National Prison Association Proceedings for 1897.* Pamphlet published by the National Prison Association.

Hutson, A. C., Jr. "The Overthrow of the Convict Lease System in Tennessee." *East Tennessee Historical Society Publications* (1936).

Jones, J. H. "Penitentiary Reform in Mississippi." *Publications of the Mississippi Historical Society* (1902).

Lee, W. D. "The Lease System of Alabama." *National Prison Association Proceedings 1890.* Pamphlet published by the National Prison Association.

Lichtenstein, Alex. "Good Roads and Chain Gangs in the Progressive

South: The Negro Convict is a Slave." *Journal of Southern History* (February 1993).

McKelway, A. J. "The Convict Lease System in Georgia." *The Outlook* (1908).

Miller, Thomas E. "A Plea Against the Disenfranchisement of the Negro." In *The Voice of Black America: Major Speeches by Negroes in the United States, 1797–1971.* Ed. Phillip Foner. New York: Simon and Schuster, 1972.

Moody, Minnie Hite. "Alston of De Kalb." *The Georgia Review* (Winter 1963).

Moulder, Rebecca Hunt. "Convicts as Capital." *East Tennessee Historical Society Publications* (1976).

Nieman, Donald G. "Black Political Power and Criminal Justice: Washington County, Texas, 1868–1884." *Journal of Southern History* (August 1989).

Perkins, A. E. "Some Negro Officers and Legislators in Louisiana." *Journal of Negro History* (January 1929).

Roberts, Derrell. "Duel in the Georgia State Capitol." *The Georgia Historical Quarterly* (December 1963).

———. "Joseph E. Brown and the Convict Lease System." *The Georgia Historical Quarterly* (December 1960).

Romero, Sidney J., Jr. "The Political Career of Murphy J. Foster." *Louisiana Historical Quarterly* (1945).

Smith, Wilford T. "The Negro and the Law." *The Negro Problem: A Series of Articles by Representative American Negroes of Today.* New York: James Pott and Company, 1903.

Stevens, Lester D. "A Former Slave and The Georgia Convict Lease System." *Negro History Bulletin* (1976).

Taylor, A. Elizabeth. "The Origin and Development of the Convict Lease System in Georgia." *Georgia Historical Quarterly* (April 1942).

Terrell, Mary Church. "Peonage in the United States: The Convict Lease System and the Chain Gangs." *The Nineteenth Century* (1907).

Tobias, D. E. "A Negro on the Position of the Negro in America." *The Nineteenth Century* (December 1899).

Wines, Frederick. "The Prisons of Louisiana." *Proceedings of the National Prison Association* (1906).

Zangrando, Robert L. "The NAACP and a Federal Antilynching Bill, 1934–1940." *Journal of Negro History* (April 1965).

Zimmerman, Jane. "The Convict Lease System in Arkansas and the Fight for Abolition." *Arkansas Historical Quarterly* (Autumn 1949).

——— . "The Prison Reform Movement in the South During the Progressive Era, 1890–1917." *Journal of Southern History* (1951).

INDEX

Abbott, James, 251
Abbot, Lyman, 236
Abbot, Robert S., 48
"Abraham Lincoln and Blacks:
   Some Notes on a Continuing
   Controversy" (Fierce), ix
Adams, Henry, 49
Africa, 230
*Africana Studies Outside the United
   States: Africa, the Caribbean
   and Brazil* (Fierce), ix
African-Americans
   disenfranchisement of, 5
   economic destitution of, 6–8
   education of, 29–30
   and the Great Migration, 48–50
   leadership of, 228–47
   legislators, 203–4
   resistance, 46–53, 105, 118,
      130–31n42
   response to racism, 46–53,
      228–47
   victimization of, vii–viii, 2, 27,
      229, 252
African Methodist Episcopal
   Church, 245, 253
African Methodist Episcopal Zion
   Church, 245
Afro-American (Baltimore), 48
Afro-American Council, 47, 244
Afro-American League, 47
Agricultural Wheel, 201
Alabama, 12, 38, 42
   corruption in, 124
   end of leasing in, 210–13
   income from leasing, 238
   leasing conditions in, 86, 88,

90–91, 109–10, 112–16,
   127–28n8
penitentiary system in, 69
treatment of children in, 108
Alexander, Thomas, 144
Allen, Thomas, 92–93
Alston, Robert Augustus, 155–57
American Colonization Society, 49,
   231
American Economic Association,
   45
American Negro Academy, 52
American Prison Association, 90
Ames, Adelbert, 271
Ammon, Otto, 44
An American Siberia (Powell), 117
Anderson, Oscar, 109, 206
Anderson County, Tenn., 120–21
Angola penitentiary farm system,
   202
Anti-Convict League, 211–12
Arkansas, 12, 38, 67–69
   corruption in, 121
   earnings from leasing in, 124–25
   end of leasing in, 199–202
   subleasing in, 119–20
Association for the Study of Negro
   Life and History, 52
Atkinson, W. Y., 144–46
"Atlanta Compromise"
   (Washington), 48–49
Atlanta Constitution, 177
Atlanta Federation of Trades, 173
Atlanta Georgian, 151, 158, 171,
   175, 177, 185n36
Atlanta Journal, 36, 110–11, 158,
   171–75, 177, 185n36

291

"Convict Lease System in the
    Southern States" (Cable), 157
Convict leasing, 1–2
    beginnings of, 8–11, 65
    black leadership responses to,
        228–47
    of children, 108–9
    conditions of, 10–11, 86–87,
        90–99
    corruption in, 121–25
    economics of, 77–78, 124–25,
        151–55
    end of, 192–94
    reform of, 11–13, 155–59,
        170–75
    sample lease for, 272–74
    of whites, 84–85, 87–90
    of women, 28–29, 105–8
    See also Subleasing
Coombs, A. B., 166–67, 188n54
Corruption in leasing, 121–25,
    165–67
Covington, W. A., 112, 174
Cox, Minnie, 28
Cox, William, 156–57
Crews, Alex, 237
Crime, 7, 64, 128–29n16, 146–47,
    186n42, 241
    See also Punishment
Crisis (NAACP), 239, 244–45
Crop lieners, 42
    See also Sharecropping system
Cropping, 64
Cumberland Mine, 197
Cureton, Hubbard, 150

Dade Coal Company, 143, 154–55
Daniel, Peter, 1, 42
Darwin, Charles, 44
Darwinism, social, 5, 44–45
Davis, Eugene, 274

Deadwyler, C. E., 161, 185n39
Death rates, convict, 218, 255, 256
Debs, Eugene V., 201
Delaney, Martin, 230
Democratic party, 40–41, 201, 203
Detroit, 49
The Descent of Man (Darwin), 45
Diet, convict, 259–60
Disenfranchisement, 35–41
Disenfranchisement Amendment
    (Miss.), 38
Dixon, Thomas, 32
Donaghey, George, 200–201, 205–6
Dotson, Andy, 38
Douglass, Frederick, 230, 231
Douglass, Harman, 97–99
Driscoll, T. J., 100
DuBois, W. E. B., 23, 53
    and the Great Migration, 48
    and the NAACP, 244–45
    reaction to convict leasing
        system, 231, 234, 239–41
Dudley, Charles, 104–5, 206
Duke, David, 31
Durham Coal and Coke Company,
    102, 103
Durham Coal Mines, 168

Eagle, James, 200
Eastern Stars, 51
Eastland, James, 31
Economics of leasing, 77–78,
    124–25, 151–55, 183–84n25
Education, 29–30, 52–53
Eight Box Law, 40
Emancipation, 3, 75–78
England, 64
English, John, 166
Entrepreneurs, Black, 50–51
Escapes, 255

About the Author

Milfred C. Fierce is a professor in the Department of Africana Studies at Brooklyn College of the City University of New York (CUNY) and a senior consultant on South Africa and Southern Africa at the Ford Foundation in New York. Dr. Fierce's previous publications include *The Pan-African Idea in the United States* (Garland Publishing Company, 1993) and *Africana Studies Outside the United States* (Africana Studies and Research Center, Cornell University, 1991). Dr. Fierce received his Ph.D. from Columbia University.